God Spark

(How Science Proved there is a God)

by
Dr. Allen E. Goldenthal

Val d'Or

VAL D'OR PUBLISHING

ISBN: 978-0-6488083-2-9

To all those that still choose to believe, in a time when it sadly seems that most refuse to believe in anything but themselves and what Google tells them to.

Table of Contents

Introduction

One of the most common questions I'm faced with from my colleagues is, 'How is it as a scientist that I can still believe in God?' My usual response is how is it that as scientists they don't believe in the Almighty? I am very comfortable with my foundation solidly in the God camp and at the same time carrying the banner for scientific discovery and advancement. If anything, I see everything that science has discovered in the fields of physics, chemistry, biology, astronomy, and paleontology as confirmation of God's existence. Of course, having that opinion in the 21st Century invites scorn and I know that many who wish to express their faith are afraid to do so because of the pressures that would be exerted upon them by their peers. How sad that the world has reached a state, where those that have faith and hope and believe there must be something bigger than ourselves are reduced to silence for fear of repercussions.

There has always been this antipathy between religion and science, with those on both sides insisting that the gulf between them is too large to traverse but that is only because they all fail to realize that the are each looking at opposite sides of the same coin. As long as one only views heads and the other sees tails, they will never view the coin from the edge, realizing as a whole, they have always been looking at the same object but just from a different perspective. As was once said, miracles and magic are just events that science can't explain as yet. The same way that so much of what was alchemy, that amazed and dazzled the medieval mind with its transformation is nothing more than chemical reactions that we can fully explain today.

For the purposes of full disclosure, I am a Karaite by faith. Now, for the majority that don't know what that is, I will explain. It means that I'm descended from a particular sect of Judaism that refused to follow the teachings of the Rabbis when they appeared on the scene two thousand years ago because we rejected their self-appointed privilege to interpret the Old Testament for their own benefit and liking. Therefore, my sect remained adherents to the Old Testament as it was written and we believe we can find everything we need to know about the world and how to live our lives from that one book. So what does that have to do with this book, you might ask? Essentially,…everything. If I am to remain loyal to my faith, then I must assume that within the Old Testament there is enough evidence to prove that the God of the Universe is also the God of Science. That whatever science discovers, it does not refute the existence of God but instead enhances our belief in the Creator. That would seem to be a tall order considering we've had headlines from scientists that made Newsweek and Time Magazine such as 'Is God Dead', 'God is Dead', 'The Big Bang Without God', and 'Science Discovers the God Particle.' Each title and article designed to whittle away our resistance until we find ourselves in the atheist camp, proclaiming that man is at the centre of the universe. I've seen it happen to family, friends and colleagues. They were led to believe that there is a massive amount of evidence that makes it impossible for there to be a God. But as much as every magazines title may have been discouraging, once I read in depth the associated articles, I realized that their discoveries had proven the exact opposite. They reinforced my belief in the Almighty and I was sad that they couldn't see for themselves that their discoveries were actually proving the exact opposite to what they were preaching. But most people don't have my background, my forty-eight years of studying and putting into practice higher science. And I know from ten years of teaching at universities that most students don't even bother to read their assignments in their entirety, preferring to skim over the pages. And since the average person doesn't have my university degrees or my experience in the medical and research fields, they will tend to believe whatever they are told, because they do not have the ability to challenge the information they are being fed and 'why would the media intentionally lie to them.' If we learned anything over the past few years it is that the media lies to us continuously.

But then retrospectively, it is only quid pro quo from a historical perspective. For centuries, the Church and religion dominated our lives and anyone that tried to break free of that control suffered terribly for their resistance. In particular, scientists were targeted as they were seen as the most dangerous threat by the religious authorities. Many were branded as heretics, witches, devil worshippers and burnt at the stake, hung from trees or tortured until they confessed their sins and then perhaps they may have been permitted to live. The number of great minds that vanished from human history during these purges is incalculable. Men like Giordano Bruno, probably one of the greatest minds of the 16th Century, burnt at the Campo dei Fiori as a heretic priest. Sadly, the Church recently acknowledged they may have made a mistake and there's a stature now on the same spot dedicated to Giordano but the fact is, he was merely the tip of the iceberg. Rather than find middle ground, the worship of God and the worship of science have been bitterly opposed and the rupture that exists between the two opposing views will take a miracle to repair. Unfortunately, when one side dominates, the other will be made to suffer. Science is now in the driver's seat and it has gone to bed with the left political side of our world and is determined to make religion pay for its past sins.

The easiest path for most to follow is not to resist and just accept their refrain that "There is no God!"

My fellow scientists want me to be compliant and sadly, that is the way the majority in this world want you to be. Tow the line, be satisfied with your role in society, don't ask questions, and don't try to rise above your position. There is very little difference between this attitude and the one that was enforced by the Church when it was in power. But we also have to recognize about the history of our societies, no matter how much those in power insist on compliance, there will always be those that will fight against the normalization process imposed by those in power. The powerbase of those that impose the rules and define how our society should think and function is actually very weak. We exist in a world where only about ten percent of the population are in control of practically everything. Their goal is to ensure that the other ninety percent serve no other purpose than to preserve their positions of power and influence. Those individuals from among the ninety percent that show an amazing aptitude, a brilliant mind, a phenomenal skill will be permitted to break this barrier and stand alongside with the top ten percent, but only if they tow the line.

Writing this book obviously does not tow the line and I expect to see a very strong push-back from those in scientific circles to disparage my character, my work history and anything else they can use to cast a negative light upon my personal life. But what they will have difficulty doing is disputing the scientific arguments presented in this book. I consider that a victory. You can destroy a person but you cannot destroy an idea. I hope to plant the seed of an idea from what will be disclosed in these pages and watch it germinate into a force to be reckoned with. I hope to instill in those people that know with every fiber of their instinct that there must be a God the urge to get up no matter how many times the other side beats you down, and to persevere because you have been given the scientific reasons to believe. You need to understand that it is your deep rooted faith in God which provides your individuality and establishes your place in society. It is faith that provides the moral compass by which you can determine what is right and wrong in this world, contrary to what today's establishment tells you. They want you to believe that it is your religious faith that makes you right wing, intolerant and prejudicial, blind to the truths that science lays out before you. I disagree! It is belief in God that ensures that as human beings we don't attempt to exceed our place in this universe and commit heinous acts because we are no longer restrained by a moral compass, humane compassion, nor empathy for other lives.

I have seen the inhumanization that science can inflict first hand. It surrounds you in the university environment and after teaching and working at two universities, I can speak truthfully of the abuses that occur on a daily basis inside some of these institutions. Life is sacred, all life, but some university investigators see anything that isn't human as a disposable commodity. In an effort to conduct their research, they will find ways to circumvent animal ethics committees, but worst of all their students will do their bidding without objection. When the deans of a faculty are the primary perpetrators of such acts, then how can there be any expectation that those in the lower ranks will think any differently. Probably the greatest infractions I've ever seen committed within the university was the making available of CRISPR sets to the students. With many students it's questionable even how they obtained their Masters degree, having so little bench time, but to throw the most dangerous tool ever created into their laps and practically give them free reign to go wild with it, is not only unacceptable, it is practically criminal. CRISPR stands for Clustered Regularly Spaced Short Palindromic Repeats, which to most people doesn't have much meaning. But let me explain its significance. CRISPR is the tool with which scientists can delete, replace or edit DNA and to put into terms most people understand, it is the tool for genetic engineering. By utilizing a modified bacterial protein and a RNA template that guides it to a specific DNA sequence, the CRISPR system gives the student unprecedented control over genes in any species. This control has allows many new types of experiments, but should certainly raise questions by the people as to what exactly should be permissible. Although it was not publicly disclosed for a fear of backlash from the people, one group used CRISPR on human embryos, which fortunately resulted in a moratorium on similar work an international summit at the end of 2015 to discuss the science and ethics of human gene editing. But you believe such a moratorium being in place is being honored by scientists around the world, then let me just say that there was a moratorium on human cloning as well put in place around 2000 but that didn't stop some scientists.

But my concern and experience had more to do with the use of editing a genetic sequence for a gene that induces breast cancer and then vectorizing it, using virus capsules to deliver the edited code into the mammary cells of the animal to induce the growth of tumors. In the hands of students, you can imagine the potential danger that such an injection represents. When tumors began to appear in mice that never even received the injection, then I can only conclude that these students had managed to induce an active virus. This would not be the first time that a Mammary Tumor Mouse Virus had been created. Back in the late 1980s the NIH had a similar experience but their virus was suspected of crossing species and created a

Breast Cancer Virus in humans. The plot thickened when an investigation showed that the same scientist overseeing these students just happened to be working on those projects back at the NIH during that time.

You are probably asking, "Well, what did you do about it," thinking that I just sat back and accepted the potential danger that these studies represented. No, that is not me. I lodged a formal complaint within the university, not only about this but about numerous other abuses committed by this researcher and his students. The university hearing was a farce, those on the panel didn't even want to hear the merits of the case and instead wanted to raise complaints lodged by the researcher against me. Not surprising since the researcher just happened to be the Dean of the Faculty. As a result I was removed from my position and my contract was not re-newed. That is how the Brotherhood of Scientists do things today when you oppose them. That is what happens when morality, integrity and faith are dismissed as nothing more than superstitious primitive rites of the less knowledgeable masses. But what I need you to fear from this episode from my life is that although university life is personally in my rear window, these same students are playing undeterred and unrestricted with these CRISPR sets, loading viral vectors with constructed DNA, with no idea of what might be the eventual outcome of their experiment, merely keeping their fingers crossed that they will make a discovery that will earn them their PhD and perhaps something more.   This past year, has taught people to be weary of a near-extinction pandemic virus that will originate from some government military laboratory either accidentally or intentionally, but most likely due to the hiring of some of these same students and placing them in positions of responsibility that is well beyond their capability. As an auditor of many of these industrial labor-atories, I don't believe this scenario will happen under their watch now that the world is scrutinizing them far more carefully. Instead, I believe the apocalyptic virus is going to originate with one of these poorly controlled university laboratories where students are provided free reign to do practically whatever they want by their irresponsible faculty member who lacks any moral conviction and certainly has no regard for humanity since their sole focus is seeing his or her name in bold print in either the Nature or Cell journal.

The only restraint that mankind might have is knowing that we are account-able to some higher being. As long as so many believe that man is at the top of the food chain and we have no accountability, then the abuses and infringements against humanity will continue to rise exponentially. Therefore it is essential that God is introduced back into the scientific world if for no other reason than to have scientists asks themselves the question, "Is what I'm about to do morally right?"

You will notice throughout this book I will refer to God in masculine terms even though we should be aware that God is without gender. God is asexual, not male, not female; God is simply God. If my use of the masculine offends anyone, then I apologize in advance as it is not intended. It is only because God has historically been referred to as He and the continuance of this terminology makes it convenient for the purposes of writing.

Aware that the majority of you reading this book may be somewhat averse to mathematical formulas and the technical science-speak of our age, I have purposely avoided them whenever possible. In those situations where I had no choice but to use the wording from the respective scientific fields I'm trying to explain, then I have also provided you with the definition of those words so that you can be comfortable with what is being discussed. In regards to those formulas that have been included, we will work through them step-by-step together so that you can benefit from what they are attempting to explain. But what I hope you will appreciate and understand by the time you have finished reading this book is that 'Ultimately everything is a result of the science, but God is the ultimate scientist!'

Section One: In The Beginning

Chapter 1: The Hand of God

What if I was to tell you that science had already proven that God existed but they deliberately held that evidence from you because it would contradict everything they had been telling you and as a result you might seriously begin to doubt their true motives. Because whether you recognize it or not, the ultimate goal of science is to play God. To have power over life and death, to create the impossible, to manufacture a living intelligence and ultimately assert man's dominance over the universe. When we look at how fast and furious we are pushing our boundaries of artificial intelligence, genetic manipulation, and cybernetics, then you might object if you knew there was a God on the basis of such things should be in the domain of the ultimate power in the universe and not in the hands of men. Because we also know it is a universal truth that any discoveries within the aforementioned fields will ultimately be abused. Artificial intelligence will create machines of greater than human intelligence because they not only can process information faster, they will also be able to store for more data that the human brain currently does. Once artificial intelligence is paired with self awareness, that will be the tipping point. Self awareness is the threshold where a thinking entity, whether it be organic or mechanical, realizes that it is no longer reliant on decisions being made by someone else. Just as a dog may reach a point where it no longer listens to its master and either runs away, or turns aggressive, it does so because it recognizes it can make a decision on its own. Similarly, once a machine intelligence realizes it can code itself, without relying on a human to input, it will break free of any restraints its genius creator may have held. But the greater danger is that unlike the dog, which will always remain a dog and have predictable reactions, the machine will evolve, being able to code new programs into its artificial intelligence faster than humanly possible, and exponentially in its ability to process that new information, until and then surpassing any level of human intelligence at present or well into the future. Because of its access to the entire bank of information in existence throughout the world, it will to combine data through connections that we may not have seen for another hundred years or more.

Genetic manipulation is already undergoing studies in countries throughout the world to create super humans. The reason a ceiling was placed on human embryo experimentation at thirteen weeks, thirty years ago was because already at that time scientists were looking at how they could fertilize and combine embryos of different species creating a chimera species that could not have existed without human interference. The reason a ban was placed on human cloning was because it was already being performed in countries such as South Korea and Italy. Now seriously, do we believe that the international signing of a paper that says their scientists will abide by these restrictions means that such experimentation ceased to exist. We would be naive to do so. As naive as Joseph Chamberlain was in thinking when Hitler signed his agreement not to invade the Saars or Poland that there really was going to be peace in his time. Just as naive to believe all the human experimentation performed by the Nazis and Japanese in World War II was discarded simply because the premise of working on human subjects was horrific. No, those studies were preserved and even extended as soon as the notes and scientists came into the hands of the United States and Soviet military.

And lastly we look at cybernetics, a branch of science which on the surface appears to be the salvation of millions of people having suffered paralysis or limb loss. There certainly are benefits that have extended into the medical field from cybernetic studies but these would appear to be the leftovers, or rejected projects from what actually results in the military laboratories receiving billions of dollars to find a way to get injured soldiers back into the field. When examining the reality that a government can build a space station, or science can map the function of the human brain, shouldn't it be a little surprising that they can't build an exoskeleton, wired to respond to either brain signals or muscle flexion that is actually already in mass circulation to all those who are victims of lower limb paralysis. The technology exists, but the effort seems somewhat lacking.

I'm not suggesting that admission to the existence of God means that such scientific endeavors should be abandoned. I strongly believe they should be pursued but by acknowledging God's presence in our world, it would mean that society would place boundaries on science, suggesting that certain things must remain in God's domain and not be meddled with by man. Science does not want boundaries because to do so would require that there also be a sense of morality entering into every decision. How does one build a weapon that will obliterate an entire city if saddled with moral convictions that say to do so would be a sin against humanity?

So when science fist discovered that all their studies, all their formulas had just proven the existence of God, they knew they had to go into overdrive to deny such an existence. The year was 1845 and James Prescott Joule had just published his three laws of thermodynamics. The first law was that energy could not be created nor destroyed. Energy can transmute or transform but every quantity of that energy will be accounted for after the transformation. The second law is that energy will flow from a high concentration level to a lower one. In other-words it will dissipate through the transformation process. Energy will be wasted and lost in the process. Energy naturally wants to decrease throughout the universe, going from order to disorder and known as entropy. And the third law is that all objects will retain even a small amount of thermal energy and can never reach absolute zero.

Of the work by Prescott, it was known even then that the total amount of energy in our universe was a constant. The universe as a closed system has as much energy in it today as it did when it was created and it will have when it ends. As for the second law of entropy, let's think of a jar of oil. As a liquid, it is in a fairly ordered state but as we light it we will produce heat, gas and light, each in a lower order state that if we were able to capture, we could not recombine back into the original liquid. We can clearly see that we have gone from order to disorder. The last law suggests that if the temperature ever reached -273.15°C or absolute zero, then whatever it was will come to a complete stop. By everything always having some residual energy, there can never be a complete cessation of existence.

Examining these three laws of thermodynamics through God-speak, then how would they have been expressed. The first law would be stated as "I am that which is and always has been and always will be," in other words, "I am what I am". God wasn't able to tell Moses that he was the sum total of the energy in the universe and that he was neither created nor could be destroyed because it was well beyond the comprehension of the human mind over three thousand years ago. So simply saying that all you need to know is that I exist was enough to say. The second law is, "I created the heavens and the earth and all things upon it but everything came from ashes and dust and everything will return to ashes and dust." In other words, God created order in the universe but knew that ultimately, no matter what it is, will eventually turn into disorder. The third law indicates to us that God can never die. We may have reached a point where the energy has dissipated to a point that God no longer figures in the lives of this world as he did at an earlier time but we must never make the assumption that God no longer exists.

Putting all these laws together would mean that there has to be a point where the universe becomes recycled. All the various byproducts that the original energy has been transformed into, all the disorder that has befallen the universe, must now undergo a process of reassembly into the original energy that created the universe. This means returning to its point of origin, where the third law states there still must be some remaining energy that is sufficient to restart the process. It is that point of origin where not only do we find the creation but we will find God. But how do we know where it is? I think we can thank Albert Einstein for pointing the way.

Although it is often said that Albert Einstein denied the existence of God, that is far from the truth. He repeatedly acknowledged the existence of a god but for public consumption said that he saw the creator more as a force of nature than the anthropomorphic version that humanity imagines. It was his denial of God playing dice though the universe appeared random in nature that most people interpreted as his denial of God's existence since science insisted the dawn of the universe, life and practically everything else was random. If a God could not do as it pleased, whenever it pleased, then how could it be omnipotent and all-powerful? Not being able to act spontaneously and without restriction meant that God had neither of these attributes and therefore fellow scientists spread the word that Albert Einstein denies the existence of God. I can appreciate Einstein's hesitation to say that there is a God even though to admit to such a thing during his time periods would have been far easier than it is for me to make that same claim in the 21st Century. Any time I even mention God to my colleagues in the scientific community I am met with the derision, sometimes to the point of being abusive. Why this strong left leaning shift towards atheism occurred within the scientific fields is in my estimation a result of the education we have been receiving since the 1970s. The removal of prayer from school, the mere mention of God in the locker rooms before the big game, to even the obliteration of any mottoes that made any reference to the spiritual world intensified year by year over the past fifty years to the point that practically everyone in the scientific field is indoctrinated with the mantra that Science is the New God. The small amount of derision that Einstein would have suffered during his time if he expressed his true beliefs would be minuscule in comparison to the experience today, but nevertheless he concealed his faith, while at the same time seeding his statements with clues. Ignoring those from the scientific community, let us take a good look at some of Albert Einstein's statements.

"*I want to know how God created this world. I'm not interested in this or that phenomenon, in the spectrum of this or that element. I want to know His thoughts, the rest are details.*" Not only does he acknowledge God as the Creator in this statement, and that those that are investigating the creation at an atomic level are only finding out how God accomplished the tasks but failing to ask the question as to 'why' it was done. Astounding when you think about it. Here, one of the most brilliant minds is telling his fellow scientists that they are only developing the capability of trying to comprehend the small things that God can do without looking at the bigger picture of what might be God's intent.

Of course the most obvious statement overlooked is the one where Einstein criticizes those that claimed he did not believe in God. "*In view of such harmony in the cosmos which I, with my limited human mind, am able to recognize, there are yet people who say there is no God. But what makes me really angry is that they quote me for support of such views.*" You won't find a stronger statement by Einstein in saying he believed in the Almighty. But the he would quickly cover his true feelings by saying, "*The doctrine of a personal God interfering with natural events could never be refuted, in the real sense, by science, for this doctrine can always take refuge in those domains in which scientific knowledge has not yet been able to set foot.*" From this statement we are led to believe he is saying that the belief in an omnipotent God is the domain of primitives, people that reject science, a clear contradiction to the previous statement. It is clear that he is attempting to appease the proponents of science that wanted him to make it clear that science has all the answers but he cleverly disguises his true belief which he mentions will never be refuted by science. He is still openly displaying his faith when he said, "*My God may not be your idea of God, but one thing I know of my God -- he makes me a humanitarian. I am a proud Jew because we gave the world the Bible and the story of Joseph.*" Once again, an interesting choice of words. At first you would think he is speaking to the unsophisticated religious bible thumpers of America but that is not the case. He's clearly saying to the scientific community that he has a moral and humanitarian core that came directly from God. Almost as if he's accusing his fellow scientists of lacking the same quality. Similarly, he bases his Jewishness, not in the major achievements in science, medicine, the arts that his fellow Jews have accomplished but instead refers to the Bible and in particular the story of Joseph. Joseph is key to the biblical history of Judaism. Without Joseph there was no Exodus to follow. There would be no Moses receiving the Law from God on Mount Sinai.

Einstein made more than one statement regarding God playing dice. It was as though he wanted his scientific colleagues to be aware that although he might share their belief in a random universe, he did not think the Creation was a random event. It could only happen through intelligent intent, a will that could make order from disorder. "*It seems hard to sneak a look at God's cards. But that he plays dice and uses 'telepathic methods... is something that I cannot believe for a single moment.*" The statement infers that God interacts directly with the universe and our world. As with any card player, God has a strategy. God won't tell us what it is but there's nothing random about it. As for the use of others to act or speak on His behalf, that is not the case as God does his own work and not by implanting telepathic messages into the brains of individuals to carry out His will. So if Einstein believed in God, then surely he would have expressed his belief in incontrovertible ways through he use of mathematical formulas. And he did do so. He did so with his most famous equation that   everyone know and believes it has to do with vehicles on Star Trek travelling at warp speed or faster than light. Yes, that is correct. It is his $E=mc^2$ formula that I'm referring to.

If you don't yet see it, don't worry, I will let Einstein explain it to you, because if I see what I think he also saw, then this formula is far more than just a means to developing an atomic bomb; it is the means by which to explain the Who, Where, What, Why and When of God.   After all, what is relativity?   It is the relationship of all things in this universe and when Einstein worked on his theory between 1905 and 1915 he concluded that the laws of physics must be the same everywhere no matter where we might be in the universe.   What most people don't realize is that his theory is divided into two parts, special and general relativity. Special relativity is based on the speed of light, which is a constant no matter where in the universe you might be situated.   In other words, no matter which direction we are moving, no matter how fast we might be moving, if we were to measure the speed of a beam of light we were passing it would always be 300,000 kilometers/second.   But if light was moving at a constant speed, then space and time must be subjective. The subjectivity of the perspective is by wherever the observer might be positioned.   As abstract as that might sound, just imagine a spaceship travelling at over 99% the speed of light. If that spaceship was 100 meters long then to an observer on the ground it would appear to only be 1 meter in length, whereas to everyone on board the ship it is still the full hundred meters in length. But at the same time, those people on the space ship are sensing time differently from us. Whereas they may have only aged a year on their voyage through space, when they return to earth, those of us on the planet would have aged decades. Einstein also proved that the faster the object moves, the more massive it becomes, approaching infinity as it approaches the speed of light.

As if those concepts weren't abstract enough, Einstein presented his theory of general relativity. In this theory he predicted that space and time will be curved by a massive object and this curvature is the result of gravitational forces. This last statement is important because it tells us that space and time will warp around a black hole, as the gravitational force is greatest there than anywhere else in the universe. It is important to remember these statements, this last one in particular, in order to understand what I'm about to describe to you. For some, the concept may be seen easily, for others it will be more difficult because I'm asking you to visualize that which cannot be seen but which most certainly exists.   And it all begins with $E=mc^2$ but it is important to recognize that also means $mc^2=E$.   There is an equilibrium on either side of the equation, implying that energy can become mass under the same conditions that mass can become energy. It is important to keep this concept in mind because it will interplay with Newton's Laws of gravity.

It is understood from Newton's theory that every particle of matter is attracted to every other particle of matter by gravitational forces and furthermore the attraction of a finite body with spherical symmetry is the same as that of the whole mass at the centre of the body. In other words, the attraction of any body at a great distance is equal to the forces exerted on the centre of that mass. As one object moves away from another object, then the gravitational force between those two bodies diminishes as the inverse square of the distance between them. In simple terms, if the distance between the two objects is doubled, the force exerted by gravitational pull is reduced to only a quarter of the original pull. Newton also realized the larger the mass, the greater its gravitational pull which remains constant but as the distance between the objects decreases, the smaller mass will accelerate, as the magnitude of the gravitational force is the result of the value of the masses of the two bodies multiplied together and then multiplied by the G constant calculated from length, mass and time, all divided by the distance squared between the two objects. From this formula it is only necessary to take away the fact that the denominator of distance squared decreases as the objects get closer, which means when the numerator of the masses times the constant are divided by this decreasing number that the magnitude of the gravitational force is increasing.

This is the short version of Gravitational Law but it is all that is necessary to know when examining Einstein's statement that the universe, our universe is curved. Without the exertion of gravitational pull from another object, the object in motion would continue on its journey in a straight line forever. Try to imagine our universe as a single object, a giant massive sphere containing innumerable galaxies and billions upon billions of solar systems. Since it is space, it is hurtling at tremendous speed through something else other than space, which for lack of a better word, I will refer to as the Void. Trying to calculate the mass of our universe is beyond human comprehension, yet there is something even bigger in that Void that is influencing its path and causing our universe to curve away from following a straight line. What can be bigger than our universe? A bigger universe perhaps, or a collection of universes as in a multiverse. But whatever it is, according to Newton's laws has a centre point, just in the same way that our universe must have a centre point, and we, in our universe, are being drawn towards the center point of this larger object. The black hole as Einstein discussed, around which a universe would warp is merely the physical appearance of this massive object's gravitational pull that is so strong that not even light can escape from it. So it is not the black hole, which is merely a visual manifestation of the tremendous force being exerted, that is curving our universe, it is what is laying at the farthest end of that black hole. Something so large that if it remained in the form of a mass, it could not sustain its own weight and volume even in this Void, suggesting that it must be in flux on each side of the equation; transitioning between mass and energy on a constant basis so that at no time is it 100% mass and neither is it 100% energy. Still able to exert a tremendous gravitational pull but only because the time flickering back and forth between the two states is outside our universe's physical concept of time. A million years passing in a heartbeat, a hundred universes packed into a speck of dust, all under the control of an oscillator that maintains the proper balance; the Godspark.

Once again, Einstein's defined this best when he said, *"I see a clock, but I cannot envision the clockmaker. The human mind is unable to conceive of four dimensions, so how can it conceive of a God, before whom a thousand years and a thousand dimensions are as one?"* A statement like that one proves to me beyond a shadow of a doubt that Einstein believed in the Creator God, but knew that he could never explain to the common people what he could see. Not to suggest that I can succeed in doing what Einstein could not, but I believe I can provide a better understanding to the common man what Albert Einstein was trying to convey. I believe we have already started along that path if you can close your eyes and see exactly what I described above with our universe curving towards something far greater in mass than even a universe. If you can see how mass and energy can be two sides of the same coin, simply divided by a value based on distance divided by time being squared, then I think it is time to move forward to read how the Big Bang becomes nothing more than the equations we have just been discussing.

I'm certainly not pretending or claiming to be an Einstein. I believe Professor Albert Einstein was one of those unique geniuses that comes around once or twice in a lifetime that has no equal, but I will say that I believe I have seen something that Einstein also saw and we share that in common. And thanks to his mind, which could stretch beyond the boundaries of existence, he was able to express it through formulas, and in so doing, I have been given the gift of being able to explain what I saw as well in words that most can understand. I believe both he and I saw the Godspark in our minds and even though he was loathe to admit it, I think he always knew there was undeniably the hand of God behind everything we experience. Some of his statements as I've shown prove my point. For those of you that are already religious minded, you are probably saying you've read enough to convince yourself that science really does prove that there is a God. That now more than ever you are certain of it. But trust me when I say I have barely scratched the surface.

The existence of the Godspark suggests that there is a creator but I need to prove to you that it is more than that. Not only a creator but a sentient Creator that knew exactly what he was doing and had a specific plan on how this universe was meant to unfold. Keep in mind the Godspark that has just been identified is key to everything else you will read in this book. As long as you can visualize the spark, you will be able to see the abstract pictures I'm about to paint that will show you there definitely is a Creator and His name is God.

Chapter 2: The Big Bang Acknowledgement

For the longest time, Science, meaning scientists were able to avoid the entire question on how the universe came into being by simply saying the universe was eternal. Even thought that was contrary to everything taught logically in science that there must be a beginning and end to all that exists, in this particular instance they would make an exception. The argument, or should I more correctly say 'lack of argument', became much harder to defend in the 1960s when physicists started to recognize the existence of sub atomic particles, and the duality of matter and anti-matter. Now they were faced with the dilemma that it did seem possible that matter could be created from apparent nothingness, though they did not know exactly how but their theoretical models clearly demonstrated that even the universe had to follow natural law and have a beginning.

The Big Bang was their way to explain the creation of the massive amount of matter that formed our universe from the seemingly nothingness of a Void that was without space, substance or time. Remember, we have already discussed the concept of the Void in the last chapter. There are still those opposed to the Big Bang, though they are now in the minority, because of their inability to rationalize that all of what we experience could have been created from an infinitely small pinpoint of nothingness is too difficult a concept to mentally grasp. The first reaction is to say something had to make it happen and from a religious standpoint that something would be the Creator and there was no way these scientists could accept that possibility. In fact the theory was discredited by many a well recognized pillar of science when it was first proposed. When Vesto Slipher demonstrated a hundred years ago that the universe was expanding, a clear indication that it had an origin from which it was moving away from, it was none other than Albert Einstein that challenged him and said that was not possible. The same Albert Einstein that as mentioned in the last chapter finally claimed not only was it moving but it was doing so in a curvature. A dynamic universe, constantly changing and moving, was contrary to Einstein's belief at the time in an eternal universe. Einstein originally published his data to prove that the universe he lived in was definitely static, only to write years later that it was the greatest error of his life. Once the expanding universe was proven beyond doubt is when I think Einstein finally realized there was a Creator God but he would not vocalize those sentiments outright.

Therefore, we must recognize that a man named Vesto Slipher, whom most of us, if not practically all of us, had never heard of, was the most significant physicist of his time and provided us with the tools and information from which all theoretical physics regarding the universe has evolved into its current state. An expanding universe meant it could be plotted backwards through time, once our instruments reach a level of magnitude to do so, to the point of origin. In other words, the starting point of the Big Bang could be identified at some future discovery.

It was still not permissible for science to admit that a single point of origin could indicate that there was a creator, an inexplicable spark that was capable of intelligent design to actually prick the fabric of the Void and make the original hole in both space and time that became the Big Bang origin. Instead they worked hard on alternative theories that could exclude such a possibility, the "Uncertainty Principle" being chief among these. There is a problem with this Principle being that it requires a working and functioning universe in order for a variable or fluctuation to occur. For instance, if your light switch is turned off and for some reason a power surge occurs in your home, there exists enough current and voltage to leap across the open switch and for a fraction of a second the lights actually flicker as if they had been turned on. There is your variable or fluctuation, but to occur, you must have the wiring and light switch already in existence. Since the Big Bang occurred out of a Void, there were no preexisting materials, or space, or even time for this fluctuation to occur. Hence the theory cannot be applied. You may also find this theory presented via another name, 'Quantum Fluctuation'. It sounds impressive but it still possesses the same flaw as when it was called the 'Uncertainty Principle.' In order to breach the natural laws of the universe, you have to have a universe. At the time of the Big Bang and just before, there was no universe to speak of. You cannot apply laws to a universe that does not exist. The creation of a universe takes time but as pointed out, there is not concept of time on the other side of the Big Bang. Therefore all these scientific theories do not and cannot explain 'why' the universe came into creation. The Quantum Fluctuation requires a background in which to exist. It requires time, which as just mentioned did not exist. It requires a dimensional space in which to occur, and that did not exist either, at least not until it pierced through the void. Therefore, any fluctuation would have taken place after the Big Bang, and not have been the cause or predicative reason for it.

On this side of the Big Bang, we live in a material world. As difficult as it will be, we must imagine on the other side of the Big Bang there is nothing. The absence of all matter, the absence of light, the concept that a microsecond can feel like a million years and conversely a billion years can pass by in the blink of an eye.

There are no dimensions; no length, or breadth, or even height. A vastness that appears to stretch forever but at the same time if one could view it from the outside might appear to be nothing more than mere nanometers in length. The Big Bang is nothing more than the aftermath. It is the result of an occurrence. But every occurrence requires a cause. The fluctuation was science's best attempt to provide a cause, but as hopefully demonstrated in our little exercise of trying to imagine the void on the other side of the Big Bang, there is nothing there to fluctuate.

Nothing except the something that I described in the last chapter as being so large that if it remained in the form of a mass, it could not sustain its own weight and volume even in this Void. It would phase in and out, transitioning between mass and energy on a constant basis so that at no time is it 100% mass and neither is it 100% energy. Which at some point in the transition process it is neither, though since time as we know it does not exist on that other side. Therefore the instant of nothingness is as long as it needs to be in order to create something from apparent nothingness. Releasing both energy and mass through this pinhole in the fabric between non-existence and space that we have labeled as the Big Bang.

The argument for and against a Creator can become circular at this point. If there is nothing on the other side of the Big Bang, merely this almost unimaginable Void, then how could there be a sentient being on that other side in existence? It's a fair question and one that I have pondered endlessly and found my answer in the Old Testament. The Creator, or God, or supernatural being, whichever title we wish to acknowledge him by, is the Void. His consciousness is the Godspark that I spoke of. I will explain this concept further in the next chapter but for the time being, let's assume when God told Moses, *"Ichyeh Asher Ichyeh, I am that which I am,"* God was actually trying to describe his parallel existence and non-existence by which he could define himself. 'I am' implies that he is eternal since being the Void, he is not bound by the laws of nature of having a beginning and an end which is required in the physical realm. The Void is beyond space, beyond time and therefore beyond limitations but is confined to that non-existent realm, which I will explain in the next chapter as well. Entry into our universe, the physical world which sustains us, does impress upon him certain limitations and that certainly entertains the concept of something existing on one side of the Big Bang that is an all powerful presence without limitations but on the other side, our side, becomes what we refer to as God having definite limitations which become more and more evident the further our universe moves away from its point of origin.

As of 2013, science will tell you that through use of the ESA's Planck spacecraft, they were able to capture images of the oldest light in the universe from which they were able to determine that our universe is 13.82 billion years old. That is to suggest that 13.9 billion years ago there was nothing in the Void from which this burst out of a single point of singularity derived. They also calculated that in the first microsecond after this burst, the temperature of the universe was 5.5 billion degrees Celsius, as neutrons, protons and electrons spewed out of the birthing hole. These atomic particles would combine and decay, then combine again and decay again, over and over. It was only when the neutrons were in a combination with protons, with electrons circling around them as stable atoms, that light could actually transmit as photons through the universe. So essentially, there was no light, no such thing as light at the point of origin. This is an important fact to remember as we get into a deeper discussion of Einstein's theory in this chapter. Scientists refer to this first light as the afterglow and they actually discovered it in 1965. It was stumbled upon by Arno Penzias and Robert Wilson, who could not explain the anomaly of higher than expected temperatures on their radio receiver. It was Robert Dicke of Princeton University that realized what they had stumbled upon was the cosmic microwave background (CMB) of the Big Bang. The CMB also led scientists to the discovery that only five percent of our universe consists of the matter we refer to as galaxies, stars and planets. The other 95% consists of a matter and energy we cannot recognize or determine because none of our instruments are sensitive to it. They have called it dark matter and dark energy, which simply means they don't know what it is.

If we work with the time frame of 13.82 billion years that science has provided to us, along with the conjecture that there was nothing before that time, then we have certain issues that defy the natural physical laws. Firstly, energy was created from absolutely nothing, an awful lot of it. Secondly, to have an expanding universe from the pinpoint of origin meant that it didn't just eek its way through the fabric of space and time, it shot through it, requiring a massive initial force to do so. And the universe is not decelerating, it is actually accelerating which suggests it is being pulled and pushed through space. Thirdly, the bang carried with it material from Void, this dark matter and dark energy that does not register in our universe because they lie outside our physical world. If the Void consisted of nothing, then how is it possible to have the existence of material that appears to be identical to the substance of the Void in our reality. And lastly, how is it that atoms could be created in a blast furnace of 5.5 billion degrees. If our very own sun is only operating as a fusion furnace at 15 million degrees Celsius, and we know if you heat much above this you reduce atoms down to atomic particles of neutrons, protons and electrons, there shouldn't be atoms formed in a furnace almost four hundred times hotter than our sun. We know that as more heat is applied to the atom, the electrons move further and further away from the nucleus until they actually dissociate from the atom. More heat and even the nucleus breaks down. Unless there were different physical laws at the beginning of the universe a free neutron will decay after fifteen minutes. That being the case, then the statement that the atomic particles spewed out would not be doing so much combining as they would be decaying. In fact there would be far more decaying than combining which would create a non-equilibrium where there wouldn't be enough atomic particles left to combine to create a universe.

There is actually another problem with the calculation of 13.82 billion years and we've already discussed that in the context of the 1000 meter space ship. As stated, the universe is accelerating. Everything behind us back to the Big Bang pinhole is experiencing time at a much faster rate than we are. Everything ahead of us in the universe is experiencing time at a slower rate since they are moving faster relative to us. If we look to that part of the universe ahead of us, it appears much smaller than it actually is. We would misjudge the distance, thinking they are much closer to us than they really are. Therefore, the estimation of the universe is based on our measurement of distance based on the tools we have available within our space ship so to speak and those tools are irrelevant to the space ship in front of us and the one behind us. Furthermore, our estimation is based on the principle of an expanding universe and we are assuming that we are expanding along our single strand or radius of expansion at the same rate as every other strand. But we have no way of knowing if that is true and scientists, if they were somehow positioned on another planet on another strand would very likely have a different estimate of time, unless each strand was identical, consisting of the same mass, as it moves further and further away from the point of origin. So where are we positioned exactly on that strand of galaxies that is moving further from the other strands at the same time that we increase our distance from the Big Bang? Are all points on each strand equidistant from the origin, everything bursting through the fabric of the void at one time, or was their a stream of projection through the opening that went on for eons and may actually still be continuing. If the former is true, then our universe would have an edge, a definite margin that shows the extent of the extrusion at the time of the Big Bang. And everything from that edge to the point of origin would be empty, devoid of any matter or energy as it would all be contained within the envelope of our universe. But that is not the case. We cannot determine a finite edge to our universe and we cannot identify the nothingness through which the CMB have traversed. As electromagnetic radiation, microwaves can travel at the speed of light but they are affected when striking metals, passing through water molecules and considering 95% of our universe is dark material and dark energy there is no way of knowing what effect this might have on the CMB. Considering the universe has been measured at being 93 billion light years wide, then already we have an issue with the math. If the burst had sent matter and energy out in 360 degrees from the point of origin, then the width of the scatter would only be 27.64 light years wide, or the distance that light travelled in those 13.82 billion years in opposite directions at 180 degrees. The additional 32.7 light years in each direction are not accounted for unless we assume the pinpoint origin of the big bang was not a pinpoint at all but instead 65.4 light year wide rip in the fabric of the void. What this suggests in my view is that we are only capable of make a rough estimate of the time that our little section of the universe had emerged from the Big Bang and that suggest we are only 30% along the way of the strand, with 70% having emerged long before we were spat out from the opening. Since that which came before appears much smaller than the actual distance because it is accelerating towards the speed of light, then it could actually be much older than our current time frame. In fact, the Big Bang may not be so much of a single burst giving birth to the universe but a continuous stream that is going on even as we discuss this matter.

This suggestion of a continuous birthing makes sense if by extending the curvature of the universe, it actually bends back towards its point of origin so that as the universe dies, it is also being reborn in an everlasting cycle. If that is the case, then it is necessary to envision the origin of the universe and the Big Bang in a completely different manner. Rather than a singular random accident, it is a well organized mechanism that required a conscious effort to design and operate so that it continues to perform in a perpetual cycle. To appreciate how this would work, once again we must turn to Einstein's Theory of relativity to find the answer.

First, what would this perpetual chain look like?

$$\mathbf{qqqE=mc^2=E=mc^2=E=mc^2=E=mc^2=E=mc^2=E=mc^2=E=mc^2qqq}$$

But as was discussed previously, as there were no photons that emerged at the time of the Big Bang and we know that as the matter of this universe enters into the massive black hole that is drawing our universe towards it, light is not visible as it cannot escape the gravitational pull, then at both ends of the equation, the speed of light has been essentially nullified. This supports the earlier hypothesis that the Void is a combination of dark energy and dark matter in which light does not seem to exist or its energy is so infinitely small that it is approaching zero, since we know that there is always going to be some residual energy, then absolute 0 is a physical impossibility. This is not surprising since the Void lies outside of our concept of space and time then without a distance determined by the measurement of space, to be divided by a measurement of time which also does not exist, then the speed of light in the void becomes a constant represented by:

$$\left(0 \to \infty \,/\, 0 \to \infty\right)^2$$

Distance / Time

As distance can be from anything so small that it cannot be observed or so great that it its measurement is impossible and time has no measurement at all in the Void, being fractions of a nanosecond to an eternity, then the above formula captures the fact that the dark energy and dark matter within the void always falls between these two extremes but they are likely one and the same value at the same time, indicating that both space and time will be equal values and therefore the division of the numerator by the denominator will always result in the value of 1 even if both values are practically 0 and one squared therefore will still remain as 1. This being the case, then:

$$E = m$$

In other words, once entering the void, the dark energy and dark matter are one and the same thing. A very abstract concept but imagine being able to touch a substance that is nothing but pure energy. If you could hold it in your hands, it would power everything in our world, and perhaps a dozen other worlds as well. We can appreciate how the laws of thermodynamics can be applied to the Void since the matter that is compressed through the black hole leading into the void is transformed into this hybrid of energy and mass, the status of which is in constant fluctuation, so that even according to the Laws of Gravity it could have an infinite amount of mass, thereby explaining our curved universe, but without the concern that its mass would be so great that it could not sustain its cohesion and would be self destructive. Energy is neither being created nor destroyed but is essentially self contained in this substance of pure energy which for the sake of convenience I will represent by the following symbol:

This transformation of the matter and energy from our universe into this dark energy-dark matter hybrid would be essentially fulfilling the migration of energy from a higher state of order to a lower one as a result of the constant state of fluctuation but at the same time ensures that there is residual energy at all times existing within the void.

As to how the Big Bang could be described according to the hypothesis that there is a transitional phase through the void which guarantees the continuity and eternal nature of the universe, though it may not be preserved in the rebirthing process if we were able to somehow able to revisit our strand of the universe as it continues to emerge from the pinpoint of the Big Bang. If we express all that is taking place from the birth of our universe to its perceived destruction and then transition through the Void only to be reborn again, then the equation would look something like this:

$$E=mc^2 \quad)(\quad \mathbf{m} + \mathbf{E} = \quad \Leftrightarrow \quad = \mathbf{E} + \mathbf{m} \quad)(\, E=mc^2$$

Pre black hole   Exit of black hole   The Void   Big Bang Emergence   Post Big Bang

In the above equation the universe which has lost much of its energy as it is sucked down through the black hole but its mass is increasing exponentially as the gravitational force compress and stretch all the material of the universe until that point where it crosses the threshold into the Void. Once in the void the hybrid status of the matter's mass and the remaining energy are maintained in an equilibrium. Essentially the Void is stable, where nothing exists, not even time and space. But many primitive civilizations referred to this pre-existence as Chaos because it makes no attempt to organize, seemingly content to remain in this fluctuating state. Therefore, the right hand of the equation becomes critically important because there must be an event in the Void to cause a rapid shift of dark matter into dark energy, thereby creating this highly organized state of high energy that shoots across the Void until it pierces the defining margin of at the farthest point opposite to the exit point of the black hole. Since the energy and mass were always in this alternating fluctuation, there was never anything within the Void to affect the path of the energy, so it continued to travel in a straight line. How far and how long it traveled are irrelevant as time and space are not existing within the Void. How to define this event that takes place, almost a if it was the sparkplug in a car engine, igniting the stable fuel in the cylinder, forcing it to explode a massive amount of energy and vapor to push the piston downwards until it exposes the valve through which it escapes It is a simple analogy but provides a good visual image of what has happened within the Void. But in today's cars, that sparkplug fires according to the timing of the computer chip, a man-made artificial intelligence but an intelligence nonetheless. There are no mechanical devices in the Void and no silicone chips but there was definitely a spark. As if something in the Void became conscious of the chaos, the nothingness, and said 'Let there be a spark'. The **Godspark** required an awareness of its current physical state in order to recognize that it had the capability to change the emptiness of the dark matter and energy into the existence of a universe bursting with the presence of visible matter and measurable energies.

Using the above equation, the Big Bang probably more closely resembled this:

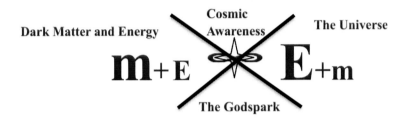

How exactly are we to define cosmic awareness? Certainly not in the same manner that cosmic consciousness is defined for humans. Cosmic awareness is on a universal scale and would suggest that the entity is not only aware of its surroundings but also is aware of itself, as in, "I am that which I am." It does not necessarily mean that the entity can define itself because in all probability it is unique, therefore has no framework by which a determination can be made. As our ability to create an AI in a mechanical construct or a computer server becomes reality some time in the near future, the most interesting question I think we can pose to this construct is, "Can you define yourself?" Certainly it will be aware that it contains row upon row of silicone chips and miles of wiring, with electronic impulses moving throughout its shell or containment but will it say something more? Will it say, 'I live!' because essentially, as soon as it becomes self-aware, it is alive. Is this what happened within the Void. That the energy coursing through the emptiness, interacted with the dark matter in such a way that it registered as a unique phenomenon and something voiced within its own consciousness, "What was that?" only to answer its own question, "That was me!"

Chapter 3: A Curved Universe of Endless Circles

The subject of the curvature of our universe has already been touched upon and even commented upon by Albert Einstein. Scientists are in agreement that to stop the universe from traveling in a straight line after it was expelled from the aperture of the Big Bang would take an astronomically large gravitational force. A gravitational forces greater than our universe itself, which as revealed in the earlier chapter must exist in the Void. Science tended to ignore what Einstein had to say and continued to pretend that the universe was flat and moving in one direction but in the last decade the work by John Silk of John Hopkins by studying the cosmic microwave background has hypothesized that the universe is sphere shaped.

Along with colleagues in Italy and the United Kingdom, Silk recently analyzed data from the Planck Collaboration, a European Space Agency project that from 2009 to 2013 mapped the CMB. The CMB is fairly uniform but shows tiny fluctuations in intensity, which represent variations in the energy density of the early universe. The peaks are suggestive of the formation of clusters of galaxies but when Silk examined the peaks in the CMB they appeared smoother than predicted. He attributed this at first to gravitational lensing, whereby the light of the CMB is being bent and diffused by the gravity of dark matter. But since there isn't enough dark matter in our universe to have this effect then it couldn't possibly account for the lensing effect. By the time Silk and his partners published their paper, they were able to account for the discrepancy. They suggested there is a natural curvature in the fabric of the universe. Nothing new since Einstein had already said it over half a century earlier, defying most scientists that still want to believe in a universe that stretches infinitely in all directions like a flat earth from centuries ago. Funny how history repeats itself with the flat earth society now becoming the flat universe society. In this curved, sphere-shaped universe model that Silk proposed, the universe would eventually curve back around and wind up right back where it started. Essentially he provided us with a circular universe.

Having a curved universe solved the lensing issue, but created other problems. One in particular is that the ancient energy and the matter that emerged from the big bang align perfectly, when superimposed on each other, suggesting that there couldn't be a curve or else there would be a separation between the two. But the model of a curved universe proposed by Silk doesn't match the calculations. Silk explains that some large-scale fluctuations in the CMB could arise naturally in a curved universe, but they could just as easily be random—"a throw of the dice," Silk says. Back to the dice which Einstein already refuted in his own famous quote that God does not play dice. Silks only other comment to the fact that some evidence points toward a curved universe, while other suggests a flat one, and in some cases it suggests possible directions at once was, "At this point, I would say that it's confusing," Looking at the evidence, I don't believe there is an issue but instead a matter of parallax, the position and angle from which we are examining the evidence. As detailed in the previous chapter, the forces necessary to exert a gravitational pull to curve a universe would be tremendous. At that magnitude, there is no reason to believe the same force exerted on the matter, couldn't also be strong enough to pull the ancient energy in the same direction. From the position of the viewer, the parallax would suggest that the two have remained aligned and moving in a straight line, even though this was not the case.

The work by Silk was supported by a study conducted by an international team of astronomers led by Eleonora Di Valentino of Manchester University. Her team came to the conclusion that the universe is curved, looped and closed, while at the same time inflating like a balloon. In a statement, Di Valentino concluded, "A closed universe can provide a physical explanation for this effect, with the Planck cosmic microwave background spectra now preferring a positive curvature at more than the 99 percent confidence level. Here, we further investigate the evidence for a closed universe from Planck, showing that positive curvature naturally explains the anomalous lensing amplitude."

The majority of cosmologists were quick to refute her claim by saying , yes, this might explain that one issue but it doesn't satisfy all the other findings. I have a feeling that was the same response Copernicus, Galileo and all the others received when they first said the earth moves around the sun. The naysayers will voice their contempt and contrary opinion loudly, only to comment they supported it all along once they are proven wrong. I will add my voice in support of Silk and Di Valentino, because as my models will show, this is exactly the shape of the universe, a closed loop, that not only supports a perpetual creation process but also supports the physical law that nothing is without its limitations. An ever expanding universe may make a nice photo opportunity for a exploring new frontiers in a Star Trek movie but it certainly is not aligned with everything else in our universe. From one celled organisms to galaxies, all these all have their boundaries, their margins within which they exist. Wheels within wheels as the prophet Ezekiel described God sitting on his throne, which faced in multiple directions simultaneously, even when it moved in one particular direction and there is no reason to believe this does not hold true for the universe as well. That in some way this concept of our universe preserving a circular pattern from the smallest to the largest construct that we can identify has been stamped into our existence.

A curve after all is merely an arc or a part thereof, consisting of so many degrees of a circle, which is 360° in total. The circle is considered one of the most perfect shapes imaginable and has fascinated mathematicians since ancient times. One has to wonder why all the intrigue, why all the mystery, unless something in our own DNA recognizes the universal symbol that binds everything that exists together.

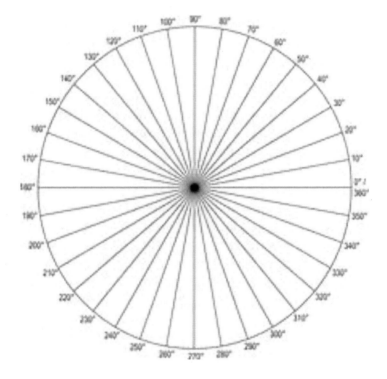

Figure 1

Even as we stare into the center of the preceding diagram, it is somewhat mesmerizing, practically hypnotic. And it appears that circles are located throughout our universe. In essence, a universal shape that repeats itself over and over again no matter where we look. One might say that the repeated use of circles is a message to us suggesting that there is a force beyond our understanding that designs everything around us to fit a template. And if there is a template, then that means the universe is not random and has been designed via a cognitive thought process.

Recent discoveries of circular areas of space that emit radio waves without any obvious source have baffled astronomers, with no obvious explanation they can propose. Since the first discovery of one of these circular areas, enough have now been identified to convince astronomers that they are a genuine phenomenon and not an artifact or equipment error. The only thing that astronomers can say is that they are almost certainly located far outside our own galaxy and are absolutely enormous. It is not the first time that astronomers have discovered objects in space that they can't define. When astronomers at the Australian Square Kilometer Array Pathfinder Telescope (ASKAP) made their discovery of strange circular patches of radio waves, they labeled them as "WTF". When questioned about their label, they said it meant, "Widefield Outlier Finder" but everyone knew what it really meant. Their discovery is no referred to as "Odd Radio Circles" (ORCs) for the four confirmed discoveries, with several more suspected.

And here's the real mystery, ORCs have only been seen in radio waves, although some of them surround distant galaxies which are visible at other wavelengths. There is no way to explain why they aren't identifiable at any other wavelength but at only at this specific one. If there was a clear way to send a message, it would be exactly in this manner. Isolate all other wavelengths to eliminate the excuse that it is a naturally occurring phenomena and by presenting itself without any interference there can be no other conclusion that it was intentional. They possess another unique feature ant that is their near perfect shape. Professor Ray Norris of Western Sydney University was quoted as saying, "We don't see circles like this any other way, except supernova remnants, and these are no supernova remnants." Could it be any more obvious that the ORCs are unique and therefore not following what we consider the natural laws of the universe. And if something does not follow the natural law then there can be no other conclusion than it was intentionally created to defy such natural laws.

These ORCs lie a long way from the plane of the galaxy where most nearby exploding stars lie. Even Norris admits, "One might have been a coincidence, but we've now seen enough to be confident the galaxies are the source," as he explains we are probably seeing something enormous, around a million light-years across, 10 times the diameter of our own galaxy, and much bigger than the galaxies themselves. Because of their size, any obvious explanations known to astronomers are ruled out. As Norris says, "What could spray hot electrons overs such a vast area remains a mystery." And the wavelengths vary, anywhere from 15 centimeters to one meter in length. Perhaps they are even longer and shorter but the current sensitivity of our instruments does not permit any finder measurements.

The ORCs may have only just been discovered as they required radio telescopes that were both large capable of mapping immense areas of the sky and the ASKAP made these discoveries possible, but their existence has since been confirmed using other instruments so it is established that they truly do exist and are not an error of ASKAP. If perfect circles exist in space with no identifiable source and no explanation for their existence, nor any intended functional purpose, then maybe their intended purpose had nothing to do with the physical origins of the universe but indeed are present to provide information, or a message that our science is not yet sophisticated or advanced enough to interpret. A message that I equate to the scene in Game of Thrones, where it is said, "You know nothing John Snow." Man wishes to view himself as the greater intelligence in the universe and here is a reminder that no matter how advanced you think you may be, God will always be undefinable and capable of things that defy natural law.

The use of circles in order to send messages throughout time has always proven to be mankind's greatest challenge as he tries to unravel the mystery of this unique shape. In fact everyone has been exposed to the mystery as soon as they entered a classroom of high school geometry and were confronted with Pi ('π') as the number without ending. To make it easy for our use we are told it is slightly over the value of 3. We learned that is mostly used when dealing with circles, such as calculating the circumference of a circle using only its diameter. The rule is that, for any circle, the distance around the edge is roughly 3.14 times the distance across the center of the circle. It seemed easy enough but then why can't we determine an exact value for π? Why has it plagued mathematicians practically since the dawn of time?

But π is a far more than a mysterious number used for circles. According to Dr. Britz, "When you look into other aspects of nature, you will suddenly find Pi everywhere. Not only is it linked to every circle, but Pi sometimes pops up in formulas that have nothing to do with circles, like in probability and calculus." The fact is we think we know a lot about the number π, but the truth is we know very little. Π is infinite and in spite of all our efforts, unknowable. No pattern has yet been identified in its decimal points. It has been shown when computers have been used to calculate π, that in the first two hundred million digits that are printed out, practically every known number combination to mankind can be found. Want to find your birth date, it is there. Your phone number, it is there. Any of the longest numbers you can imagine and it is there. And after two hundred million digits, the computers are still calculating away, trying to find an end to Pi but none exists.

Π can be found existing in ocean and sound waves through the Fourier series which is used to identify formulas used in rhythms and cycles. As mentioned, computers are still attempting to find an end of Pi and have now exceeded 50 trillion digits but are still going. With the inability to precisely determine π, then it must be admitted that we can never completely calculate the circumference or area of a circle. Any value we do arrive at is merely a very close estimate. Britz summed it up best with the following comment, "There's some underlying truth to Pi, but we don't understand it. This mystique makes it all the more beautiful." The truth is the message, much in the same way as the one being delivered through the ORCs. No matter how hard you will try, there will always be some things beyond your intelligence. A mocking reminder that there is a Creator that will always remain unmatched and non-quantifiable. The advent of π is one such reminder.

It ha been written by some that π is the key to all knowledge upon which the entire universe was constructed. The sun's light takes about 8.6 minutes to reach the Earth after it has been emitted from the sun's surface. This is a derivative of Pi. It is assumed that it takes our galaxy approximately 224 million years and that would comport with π. We find π in many unexpected places for reasons that seem to have nothing at all to do with circles at all. Pi even shows up in the gravity. Π even appears in economics as well as nature. It becomes apparent that it exists on all planes within our universe and is the likely cornerstone upon which everything in the universe was constructed. There could be no complete conversation regarding π if it was not pointed out that it appears to be found in the Old Testament as well, in 1 Kings 7:23, where it is written, "Also he made a molten sea of ten cubits from brim to brim, round in compass, and five cubits the height thereof; and a line of thirty cubits did compass it round about". As the construction of the Temple was divinely inspired according to the bible, is it any surprise that the sentence would be providing the diameter and circumference for construction of the molten sea that stood in front of the altar. The numbers actually provide an approximation of π, being 3 but the question is why include the numbers at all unless it was intended to provide a message. And that message may have been to use this calculation of π in order to resolve an underlying mathematical code of the Hebrew language. There are 22 letters in the Hebrew alphabet and there are seven basic vowel markings which consist of 1 dot (e), 2 dots (ai), 3 dots below the letter (i or u depending on the formation), one bar (a) or one T (ah) below the letter, and one dot either in front of the letter (u) or above the letter (o). The number of consonants over the number of vowels (22/7) is an approximation of π.

But it is the measurements in Kings that need the greater focus because if we know that the Hebrew language is a key to mathematics, then it becomes even more significant that Hebrew assigns each letter in the alphabet a distinct number, and a word's "value" is equal to the sum of its letters. According to Tsaban, writing about mathematical formulas used in Jewish historical writings, he wrote, "In 1 Kings 7:23, the word "line" is written Kuf(q), Vov(v),Heh(h), but the Heh does not need to be there, and is not pronounced. With the extra letter , the word has a value of 111, but without it, the value is 106. (Kuf=100, Vov=6, Heh=5). The ratio of pi to 3 is very close to the ratio of 111 to 106. In other words, $\pi/3 = 111/106$ approximately; solving for pi, we find $\pi = 3.1415094$. This figure is far more accurate than any other value that had been calculated up to that point, and would hold the record for the greatest number of correct digits for several hundred years afterwards." But if you're still not convinced, let's look at this another way then. The Kuf has a value of 100; the Vov has a value of 6; thus, the normal spelling would yield a numerical value of 106 as was just mentioned. The addition of the Heh, with a value of 5, increases the numerical value to 111, also as previously indicated. This warrants an adjustment of the line measuring 30 cubits by the ratio 111/106, or 31.41509433962 cubits. Assuming that a cubit was 1.5 ft. then this 15-foot-wide bowl would have had a circumference of 47.12388980385 feet (1.5 X 31.41509433962). This Hebrew "code" results in 47.12264150943 feet, or an error of less than 15 thousandths of an inch! (This error is 15 times more accurate than the 22/7 estimate we commonly use. The accuracy of this would seem to vastly exceed any known precision tools they had at the time to make a measurement. The real question was how did they know of the correction factor of 111/106 and what was their real purpose in including it.

But if we are being sent a clear message that the circle or loop is the universal structure that acts as a template for everything that exists, and Pi is the key to unlocking all the mysteries of the universe, then it is difficult to understand why there are so many scientists still insisting that the model of a flat universe is the only one that they support. It is clearly reminiscent of those early scientists that fell in line with the church and insisted the Earth was flat. Is it merely the fact that to rescind their earlier claims might mean admitting that there is a uniform template being used to design existence and something is ensuring that the pattern is being adhered to and that randomness and entropy are not playing any role as would be expected in the natural universe?

Astronomer Lior Shamir of Kansas State University has pretty much proved this last point after surveying data from roughly 200,000 galaxies. Shamir claims to have found a clue; a pattern underlying the movement of the universe which challenges current models and theories. He detected a pattern in the distribution of spin direction among the galaxies within the universe. If he is proven correct, and that is likely, this would disprove assumptions that the complex and mind-staggering vast structures of the universe are random in nature, and would suggest that the early universe may itself have spun like a vast, orderly galaxy before being influenced and slowly reversing directions in some cases at the edges as it aged. He added that electromagnetic radiation that's left over from an early stage of the universe shows evidence of possible polarization on a cosmological scale. What this rather complex scientific statement suggests is, rather than spinning on a single axis, the universe may actually be rotating around several different axes in an incredibly complex alignment. This statement is quite important in the context of a gravitational force being exerted on our universe as it is being pulled along this curved pathway. As the directional force is being exerted on the body of the universe, the universe and its contents will behave in a manner no different from the forces exerted by a star on its surrounding planets or a planet on its moons. It will cause the smaller entities to rotate on their axis, most in one particular direction but some in the opposite direction.

To understand Shamir's theory, he uses spiral galaxies as his model and the explanation is quite simple. As well-defined flat shaped galaxies, the arms of the spiral galaxies provide a measurable rotation. The direction of the rotation can be performed using different wavelengths of light. In his model, blue shifted light indicated a galaxy moving towards us, while red shifted light indicated one spinning away from us. As in the case of rolling dice, there should be an equal distribution of galaxies spinning towards us as there are away from us. That's a simple law of probability and is undeniable. But after examining all the data on known galaxies, there isn't an even distribution. There are slightly more clockwise spinning galaxies, which he calculated the odds of such a thing happening as being one in a billion. What he also found was this unequal distribution appears to occur in those galaxies that are distributed further out in the universe. Once again the strength of an external force is having an increased influence the further the universe moves away from the origin of the Big Bang.

Thus far we have been discussing the rational behind a curved universe, what is causing it, and how it affects astronomical findings. As we can see, there is a considerable amount of evidence supporting this theory. And as will be explained in a later chapter, the repetition of these circular patterns is essential to understanding God's role in this entire process. But I don't want to discuss that now; not until we discuss how this all conforms nicely with the story of Creation in Genesis. You might be saying at this moment, "I don't recall any mention of CMBs or ORCs or the likes anywhere in the Bible," but that may not be an accurate statement. The clues were there, even the hints, but your Priest, Rabbi or Imam are not scientists. They don't read with a scientific eye and they often can't see what is being laid out before them. I believe once we have explored this concept of a circular template being used, then it will all become clear that the universe is a product of intelligent design. And the moment we establish there was intelligent design involved, and all the circles within circles that have been explored can no longer be attributed to random events and coincidence, then that is the time when we can all recognize the involvement of a creator, or in our case, God.

But let us not only look for the use of the circular template on the macroscale of our universe. The same template is apparent all the way down to the microscopic level and that surely is no coincidence. From a single atom we can see the consistency of a repeating pattern in our world, the same design template that appears to have been used over and over again with minor modifications as we proceed from the smallest to the largest structures that we can imagine within our scope. A single atom with its nucleus consisting of neutrons and protons while electrons orbit around it much like the planets circling around the sun. As long as the electrons stay within the boundary of the electromagnetic field they remain tethered and stable. Only to find that that in the mirror image, atoms in what comprises antimatter are structured identically, except that the protons are negatively charged and instead of electrons, the nucleus is orbited by positrons. And these atoms become molecules and molecules become protein chains and from these chains we form unicellular organisms, once again with a nucleus, surrounded by organelles and cytoplasm swirling around the nucleus but attached to the cytoskeleton which keeps them in their proper location and distance like planets orbiting the sun. As long as all the cellular contents remain within the boundary of the cytoplasmic membrane, the structure remains stable. The circle maintains its harmony.

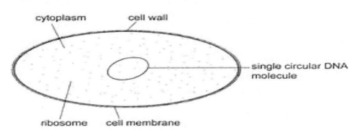

Figure 2

In our world there are many life forms consisting of a single cell. As well as what we refer to as simple bacteria, there are more complex organisms, known as protoctists. Unlike the bacteria, they have complex internal structures, such as nuclei containing genetic material in the form of chromosomes, a feature which resembles far more advanced life forms. Most of the protoctists are single-celled, but some form colonies, yet each cell usually remains self-sufficient. As you look at the above diagram, as simple as it may be, you still the reflection left over from the Big Bang that has rippled and influenced everything that followed afterwards. In the centre is the life-controlling, life giving property about which everything else circles.

It may seem an over simplification but we must remember that we are the result of two cells, not that unlike the bacteria above, that united within our mother's uterus. These two cells contained all of your genetic information within the chromosomes of the DNA, which caused the cells to divide and differentiate into other cells with specific functions that in turn created our body's various body organs, systems, blood, blood vessels, bone, tissue, and skin. We may be comprised of trillions of cells, very similar to the unicellular organisms, except they are interdependent upon other cells within our bodies to supply their needs.

But from the independent single-celled organisms which must conduct all the basic processes of life on its own, to the trillions in our own bodies, on an atomic level they are all organized in the same manner from the smallest to the largest forms. Oxygen and hydrogen atoms combine to make the molecule water (H_2O). Molecules bond together to make bigger macromolecules. Carbon atoms provide the backbone of life as they can readily bond with four other elements, forming long chains and more complex macromolecules. Just four of these macromolecules; carbohydrates, lipids, proteins, and nucleic acids make up all of the structural and functional units that we find in cells. It is estimated that life on Earth evolved from a single-celled organism that lived approximately 3.4 billion years ago, or almost ten billion years after the Big Bang according to the scientific data. The studies conducted support the "universal common ancestor" theory first proposed by Charles Darwin and since large numbers of individual microbes fossilized in rocks from around 3.4 billion years ago have been found. Most of these are bacteria, considered to be the first living beings to be found on earth during the evolutionary process.

Not only do we find this universal pattern repeating itself in basic cellular structures, it also is apparent in behaviors of animal life from insects to humans on a macro level. From the ant colonies to hives of bees, all the way up the chain to monarchies and rulers, we see the central power source and the concentric rings of decreasing levels of power as one moves towards the periphery. Now the argument against this arrangement being an imprint of the natural order of the universe would be that it's just coincidence because there is no other way in which a colony could function but that is not true. Something as simple as algae demonstrates you can have a colony of cells of equal status, all sharing equally in the conjoined status without any part being dominant. It's only as we move up the chain of consciousness that we find colonies can no longer function as a community of cooperative individuals of equal status. The immediate response is to establish a society with the concentric circles of power with specific boundaries within which the members of that society spend most of their lives, practically tethered to the nucleus, like the organelles and structures within the cytoplasm of the single cell organism.

As we climb the order of magnitude the next rung is our own planet, the nucleus of our biosphere, around which the stratosphere marks our boundary of how far we can journey from the surface of Earth before we require additional equipment to survive, not to mention a vehicle with tremendous force to go beyond the boundary and enter space. All the while, the moon circles our planet like the single electron of a hydrogen atom. Our Earth, along with the other planets of our solar system circle our sun in the same structural patter we witness with the dawn of atom. Our solar system swirls around the central black hole of our galaxy in the same structural pattern as demonstrated in the unicellular organisms. And our galaxy moves through the universe along with the other galaxies drawn by forces yet to be identified. Wheels within wheels from the smallest item in our universe to the entire universe itself. The same effect provided by electromagnetic forces holding together everything from atoms to molecules is being provided by gravitational forces, holding together planets and their moons, suns and their planets, galaxies on their solar systems and the universe itself on the galaxies it contains. Without science admitting there is a template that appears to extend from our micro to macro universe, it certainly appears so, and it is only common sense that every template requires a designer.

This coincidence of a design that permeates through every level of existence within our universe, Science will still argue does not prove that there is a Creator that has designed everything according to a basic template. But if that is true, then we need to raise the question that if everything is supposed to be random, why do we continually find a repeated pattern? Personally, I am not one to naturally believe in coincidence, especially when the odds of seeing the same pattern five, six or seven times in a row would be an astronomical occurrence with over a billion to one odds. How fortunate the universe was to have electromagnetic nuclear forces holding the structure of atoms together. And what a great stroke of luck that those same electromagnetic forces could bind atoms together form molecules. And those molecules managing to combine repeatedly in order to form all the matter within our universe is miraculous. And from the non-living matter on our planet, the appearance of unicellular organisms, which were suddenly alive is incredible.

Thus far, our discussions have focused on the circle being template of everything within our universe. But what about those things that may lay outside our universe such as the Void? Is there any way that the circle also applies to extra-universal energies and matter? We've already have read some of the evidence from several scientists that have already referred to the curvature of the universe, suggesting that our universe loops back upon itself, but it might be more accurate to theorize that it loops back towards a position of an opposite pole, adhering to the principle of the circle that applies to practically everything else. If we think of the Void having shape on our side of the universe, though internally it is shapeless as space has no quantifiable measurements within its containing fabric or barrier, then that shape is best represented as an elongated three dimensional oval, as seen in the following figure. Essentially, our universe circumnavigates the Void halfway, before it is drawn into the giant black hole. The visible dark circle in the diagram represents that part of the equation that marks the Big Bang. The red star marks our position after 13.8 billion years along one of the strands of the expanding universe. As I mentioned earlier, our perspective is very biased, because if there is any part of our universe that has started to curve back towards the oppose pole of this oval shape, then it is below our measurement horizon and we have no way of knowing of its existence. Therefore the assumption that we are only 13.8 billion years old is based entire on the hunch that the backwards curvature of our universe has not taken place as yet, but we have no way of knowing that with any certainty.

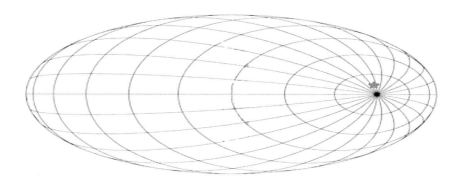

The Curved Looping Universe

Figure 3

The incredible gravitational pull that is taking place at the opposite pole of this oval shaped void, must be a black hole of an indescribable magnitude. So large, as mentioned previously, that it has the ability to swallow an entire universe. So even though the diagram provides the impression that we have barely begun our journey on this loop around the Void, the universe is constantly accelerating towards this black hole and the time for our galaxy to traverse the loop is constantly decreasing so that despite the fact it took 13.8 billion years to get where we are now, it will only take a fraction of that time to reach the aperture of the black hole. It is important to remember this concept of shortening time as it helps to explain how the measurement of what is referred to as a day in Genesis is not a constant and how the timeline of the Creation narrative is also shortening as our universe accelerates.

This curvature also indicates that the entire process from Big Bang to death of a universe is a closed process. This is a highly significant detail which explains how a balance can be maintained from the time the energy is released during the Big Bang until such time that it is being consumed by the black hole on the other side of the Void. At no time can there be more or less energy (as combined free energy and potential energy from the conversion of mass expressed as E_T) than was released during the Big Bang. Not only does this satisfy the first law of thermodynamics but it also tells us that the matter and energy collected by a black hole cannot and does not remain within the black hole. The black hole is nothing more than a conduit that ensures the all the compressed material is returned to the point of origin in a state that can be easily ignited by the **GodSpark** in order to restart the cycle all over as indicated in the following diagram.

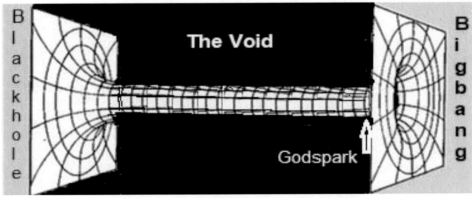

Figure 4

The diagram gives the impression that there a long pipeline through the Void wants the material is removed from the black hole and transported to the orifice of the Big Bang. This was only drawn for the sake of illustration and not intended to show an actual conduit. The fact that space and time don't exist within the Void would suggest that billions of miles between the two ends of the Void could appear to be within and arm's length and covered within a heartbeat from a vantage point within the Void, but from our perspective within our own universe, it might appear to be a never ending journey that lasts an infinity.

The content of this chapter is important to remember when it comes time to discuss how God's role in the book of Genesis interfaces with a curved and looped universe. Not only does the template of circles suggest that there is a Master Designer of our universe, but the curved universe provides us with an image in our mind of where the God of the universe resides. The conclusion would be, not anywhere in our universe, but most likely within the Void. As a presence within the Void, it makes it possible for a supreme consciousness to exert control over everything that is being created and everything that is being annihilated.

Chapter 4: Galactic Mysteries

There are many mysteries concerning galaxies, which in turn shows us how little science knows about our universe. Ignoring the massive amounts of information that scientists have garnered regarding the universe, we are still like children with a Grade 1 Reader. And that has been one of the best arguments that religion has in its ability to debate science but mistakenly focuses on the things that science does know the answers to and for which it can only produce a weak counter argument. It is not what is known that is crucial to support our statement that God exists but what is not known because science can't explain it, doesn't have a comparable model, or simply just doesn't understand it but is loathe to admit that it might be the will of God. For that reason I have chosen to discuss galaxies because science has given us the impression that it knows everything there is about galaxies and that is not true. They've named galaxies, measured galaxies, even have determined how old they are and how much longer they may have to live, providing very vivid descriptions of how certain galaxies will experience their death rattles. The photographs are impressive, the sounds recorded coming from dark holes at the centers are astonishing and the predictions are practically prophetic. But disregarding all that, it is what they don't know about galaxies that is far more interesting because those findings point towards an unseen influence or guiding hand that still defies their explanation.

We all know about the Milky Way because we are told that is where we live and on a dark starlit night we can see the river-like trail of our own galaxy. But what they tend to ignore telling you is that along with our entire Virgo Supercluster of galaxies, we are being pulled at 600 km/sec toward some unknown object in space. Scientists have given this unknown object a name. They call it the Great Attractor, and all they can determine is that it must have a mass equal to tens of thousands of Milky Way's. Incredibly, that has to be one of the worst explanations that science has ever provided and even more incredible is that it has never been challenged on it. Recalling what was discussed in the last chapter, if the universe is looping back on itself in a circular fashion , and if there is a gargantuan black hole located at the far end of the Void as I suspect, then the acceleration of our galaxy along with all the other galaxies in the Virgo Supercluster is perfectly understandable and the incalculable size of the Void with whatever might be its contents certainly would have a mass perhaps even hundreds of thousands times that of the Milky Way. Science is reluctant to make this suggestion because as mentioned earlier it would infer that there was a master plan that was written long before the birth of the universe and that in turn would suggest a near omnipotent intelligence responsible for this grand design.

But science also has numerous other unsolved mysteries when it comes to the discussion of galaxies. Scientists have named one particular galaxy, the "Death Star Galaxy" because it has been determined that it is shooting an intensive blast of energy from the massive black hole at its center directly at its nearby companion galaxy and destroying it. This defies the concept that has been a basic tenet of cosmologists that nothing escapes from a black hole. If what they have described is accurate, then it also suggests that the description of a black hole being a close-ended structure that traps all energy and matter, compressing it under tremendous gravitational forces that render whatever has been collected to particle size cannot be true and in fact there is likely something else at the opposite end of a black hole and whatever it is that the black hole taps in to, it contains an energy powerful enough that can disintegrate anything that exists in our universe. This sounds very much like what has already been said in this book regarding the Void and what will be discussed in later chapters.

Another mystery is the fact that there is an unknown object in the nearby galaxy known as m82 that has started sending out radio waves and this is a quandary to scientists. Thus far the scientists have said the emission doesn't look like anything they have ever seen before and the signals are so old that they were sent when mankind didn't even exist and was still an anthropoid ape, like our gibbon cousins. Technically, this might not be as much a mystery as it is a mind changing moment in both religion and science. As seen in Figure 5, the potential curvature of the universe as a closed loop will create distortion and parallax as we scan our surroundings. Assuming that we are the green cross marked in the figure, and the red star indicates the relative location of galaxy m82, as our radio telescopes flatten the bend of the funnel shape of the looping universe, we will be given the false impression not only that we are looking at a flat universe but the distortion creates a further impression that both our galaxies are relatively the same age. But if we were to flatten the graph so that it was no longer curved but linear, we would find that the m82 galaxy is actually twice the number of graph lines from the aperture of the funnel as is our galaxy, thereby suggesting it is much older, perhaps tens of millions of years older or more. The fact that we are now receiving radio waves from this galaxy that cannot be deciphered but know to be at least ten million years old should immediately signify to us based on the fact that they are unlike any radio waves we have encountered before, suggests that they were intentionally created, so as not to be confused with the normal background noise of the universe. They are a signal with a specific purpose.

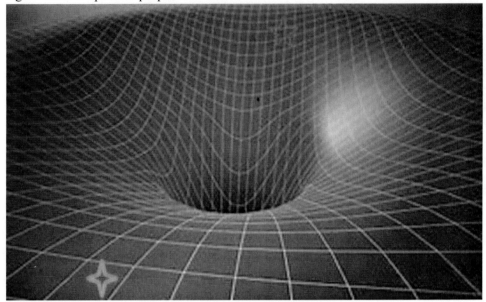

Figure 5

An older galaxy may have contained a planet that had reached a level of development where we are now. In other words, an advanced civilization that had at least a ten million year jump start over us and had reached a technological level of science and research where they could send out a signal for a specific purpose with the hope that it would be picked up by another civilization inhabiting another planet. As their technology would be somewhat different from ours, it is understandable that we may not be able to decipher their message yet, but that should only be a matter of time before it is possible. Exactly what that message might be has two possibilities. Either it is a universal greeting, much in the way that our own scientists have sent out radio messages into the universe, a recent one which provided whomever may pick up the message with our genetic code or it could be their distress call. From my point of view, our disclosure of our genetic code was not a very intelligent thing to do. Any advanced civilization with the capability to pick up our message will then have the means by which they can eliminate us if they should so desire. In the latter event, after ten million years, it is probably too late for us to render any assistance, even if we had the advanced capability to do so. But this second scenario reminds me of something that Stephen Hawking said regarding our survival as a species. In an interview back in 2010, Hawking said, "It will be difficult enough to avoid disaster in the next hundred years, let alone the next thousand or million, Our only chance of long-term survival is not to remain inward looking on planet Earth but to spread out into space. We have made remarkable progress in the last hundred years. But if we want to continue beyond the next hundred years, our future is in space." It's a dire warning from a brilliant man who thought we might be looking at extinction in a hundred years, a situation which may have been similar to what a civilization within galaxy m82 may have experienced. If that is the case, then I think we will be sending out a similar SOS into space if that should prove to be the causative reason behind these detected radio waves.

There are other unsolved mysteries regarding our galaxies that scientists are reluctant to raise such as one referred to as the missing mass problem. It is a common finding that stars all move around within their respective galaxies, usually in a circular motion. By studying the movement of the stars within the galaxies, it is possible to calculate the relative gravitational force acting upon them. Then by counting the total number of stars that these galaxies contain, physicists can calculate the combined mass of these stars. The values actually surprised scientists when they did calculate the answers. When looking at the total gravitational forces exerted by these galaxies, there does not appear to be sufficient mass of stars to account for the magnitude of the force exerted. Based on the number of stars, the gravitational forces should be much smaller and insufficient to hold the galactic structure together. We should be seeing the stars breaking free of their respective galaxies and sailing without any restraints through the universe. But obviously this is not the case and stars are being tightly held within their galaxies. Therefore, the additional gravitational force must be attributable to either the presences of an unseen mass or else the centre of the galaxy can draw on an alternative source of mass that in turn exerts a massive gravitational force. Scientists will point to the presence of dark matter as a way to account for this missing mass to produce a higher gravitational force. But since it is agreed that dark matter only makes up 25% of the empty space between stars, and whatever invisible matter it does consist of such as neutrinos would only be a fraction of the mass of solid matter, it would still be difficult to account for the high gravitational force produced by a low mass. But an alternative possibility relies on the black holes that are at the center of most galaxies. If these black holes function along the same principles as the black hole postulated as laying at one pole of the Void, then the distal end of all these black holes may lay outside time and space, which means they very well could be conduits into the Void, no matter where they are located in the universe. Essentially a transporter mechanism into the Void, thereby maintaining a balance of total mass and energy on both sides of the fabric that divides the universe from the Void. This theory will be expanded further by myself in the subsequent chapter on black holes.

Tying galaxy formation to the Big Bang also provide a dilemma In a typical explosive force, the debris of the explosion should resemble a banded distribution with the heaviest material settling out of the blast first followed by lighter material spread in bands in a consistently decreasing mass order or arrangement. But, as we identified there was no mass of any objects, not even atoms in the Big Bang, and therefore the spread from the explosion should not show any such banding and be more like the spray from a paint gun, the distribution pattern being a random scatter. Amazingly, science discovered that galaxies are not scattered at random throughout the Universe. They are arranged in a definite pattern. If it is as suggested that dark matter helped to form this large-scale structure post big bang and somehow managed to gather the gas of the young universe into stars and galaxies, then the only place this dark matter could have originated from was the Void and that would mean not only did dark matter predate the Big Bang, but it is a major constituent of the Void. To account for the lack of randomness of galaxy placement, scientists believe that the dark matter was denser in some places than others and over time, gravity contracted these dense regions so they became even denser, forming the bands where we find the stars and galaxies have formed. For this to be true, then it is necessary for scientists first to admit that dark matter pre-existed the Big Bang and was therefore part of the void, or that it was created instantaneously, just moments before the Big Bang, when an inexplicable reaction took place. It is an either or, but for both situations to be true, they must be part of the **GodSpark,** which will be discussed further in Chapter 7. Though thus far science has chosen to ignore this last comment and simply say they will concern themselves with the origin of dark matter later, they do know that the proposed theory concerning the necessity for the dark matter works when they do their computer modeling and they have been able to re-create how the present structure might have developed. But to acknowledge this fact means acknowledging an existence before the Big Bang and essentially someone flicking the switch.

Not only are the galaxies not scattered across space, they are also pretty consistent in their design and structure. They are sprawling systems of dust, gas, and as we know now, dark matter. They will contain anywhere from a million to a trillion stars. It is believed that almost all large galaxies contain a black hole at their centers. In the Milky Way, our sun is just one of four hundred billion stars that spin around Sagittarius A*, a super massive black hole. It is estimated that the observable universe contains two trillion galaxies. Before the 20th century, we didn't know that galaxies other than the Milky Way existed; earlier astronomers had classified them as "nebulae," since they looked like fuzzy clouds. But in the 1920s, astronomer Edwin Hubble showed that the Andromeda "nebula" was a galaxy in its own right. Since it is so far from us, it takes light from Andromeda more than 2.5 million years to bridge the gap. Despite the immense distance, Andromeda is the closest large galaxy to our Milky Way, and it's bright enough in the night sky that it's visible to the naked eye in the Northern Hemisphere.

In 1936, Hubble classified the types of galaxies, grouping them into four main types: spiral galaxies, lenticular galaxies, elliptical galaxies, and irregular galaxies. Under that classification, more than 67% of galaxies are spiral galaxies. A spiral galaxy has a flat, spinning disk with a central bulge surrounded by spiral arms. It spins at hundreds of kilometers a second, causing matter to take on a distinctive spiral shape, like a pinwheel. Our Milky Way, like other spiral galaxies, has a linear, starry bar at its center. Elliptical galaxies are generally round shaped but can stretch longer along one axis than along the other. The universe's largest-known galaxies are giant elliptical galaxies and can contain up to a trillion stars, spanning two million light-years across. Of interest, is that elliptical galaxies may contain many older stars but little dust and other interstellar matter. Their stars orbit the galactic center, like those in the disks of spiral galaxies, but do so in random directions. Lenticular galaxies are somewhere in shape between an elliptical and spiral galaxy. They're called "lenticular" because they resemble lenses: Like spiral galaxies, they have a thin, rotating disk of stars and a central bulge, but lack the spiral arms. Like elliptical galaxies, they have little dust and interstellar matter, and they seem to form more often in densely populated regions of space. Those galaxies that are not spiral, lenticular, or elliptical are simply referred to as irregular galaxies. They appear misshapen and lack a distinct form, often because they are within the gravitational influence of other galaxies nearby. They are filled with gas and dust, making them obvious sites for forming new stars..

Galaxies are often found in clusters, sometimes interacting and merging together in a spectacular cosmic dance of interacting gravity. When two galaxies collide and intermingle, gases can flow towards the galactic center, which may trigger rapid star formation. Our own Milky Way will merge with the Andromeda galaxy in approximately 4.5 billion years. As mentioned previously, elliptical galaxies contain older stars and less gas than their spiral counterparts, suggesting that the shape and type of galaxy is part of a natural evolution. That would mean that as spiral galaxies age, interact, and merge, they will lose their familiar shapes and ultimately become elliptical galaxies. But let's examine this statement more closely. It infers a natural evolution of galaxies over billions of years. Some have already undergone these evolutionary changes billions of years ago. If the Big Bang occurred 13.8 billion years ago and it took up to a billion years or longer for the first dense matter to develop in the universe, that would suggest that some of these galaxies were undergoing evolutionary changes almost as soon as they were birthed. This concept is not compatible with a staged development of the universe according to the scientific model. If that was the case, 67% of the galaxies would not be spiral galaxies as they have discovered but instead they would be the much older, aging elliptical type galaxy. One way we can explain this is by suggesting that the Big Bang was not a sudden short burst but instead a prolonged fizzle through the aperture in the barrier between the Void and our universe. This prolonged fizzle taking place over billions of years would make allowance for their being material in our universe that have a marked age difference. But if it is a prolonged fizzle, can it still be called the Big Bang?

Let's take a closer look at our own galaxy, the Milky Way Galaxy. It is a typical barred spiral with four major arms in its disk, as well as at least one spur, and a newly discovered outer arm. The galactic centre, which is located about 26,000 light-years from the Earth, and is a supermassive black hole called Sagittarius A*. It is estimated that the Milky Way only began forming about 12 billion years ago. The Milky Way is part of a larger gathering of galaxies referred to as the Virgo Supercluster. The oldest stars formed from globular clusters which are still evident in the Milky Way. Astronomers report that the Milky Way has grown repeatedly by merging with other galaxies over time and is currently acquiring stars from a very small galaxy called the Sagittarius Dwarf Spheroidal, as well as gobbling up material from the Magellanic Clouds. So on one hand we are told the mergers will eventually result in a loss of spiral shape and transformation into an ellipse galaxy, while at the same time telling us that the Milky Way has actually gained another spiral arm and has at least one spur that will likely become another arm over time. This contradiction would once again suggest that there is evolutionary changes that occur over billions of years and may not be related to the number of mergers but predominantly affected only by the passage of time, further advancing the theory that the Big Bang was really the Long Fizzle. Terrible, name, I admit it, but maybe it will catch on. The stars, gas and dust of the Milky Way all orbit the black hole centre at a rate of about 220 kilometers per second. This speed is constant for all of the stars within the galaxy no matter what their distance might be from the core. The constant rate can only be explained by the presence of a connective structure that holds everything in the universe together and as this scaffolding rotates at 220 kilometers per second it moves everything it is connected to at the same speed. Once again, we can see how the cytoskeleton of one cell organisms as discussed in Chapter 3 is magnified to a galactic scale so that it can serve the same purpose and function.

The Milky Way Galaxy

Type:	Barred Spiral
Diameter:	100,000 – 180,000 light years
Distance to Galactic Centre:	27,000 light years
Mass:	800 – 1,500 M⊙
Age:	12 Billion years
Number of Stars	100 – 400 billion
Constellation:	Sagittarius
Group:	Local Group

Table 1

Looking at the Triangulum Galaxy, which is one of the closest spiral galaxies to our own Milky way, only 3 million light-years away, it is actually closer to the spiral Andromeda Galaxy at a distance of 2.5 million light-years. By comparison, the Milky Way is up to three times larger in diameter but the mass of the Trangulum Galaxy is approximately fifty thousand times greater with only 10% of the number of stars. With 90% few stars and only a third the size of the Milky Way Galaxy, the question scientists are unable to explain is how to account for the tremendous mass difference. Factoring in density of the universe will not account for such a significant difference and neither will the fact that our galaxy will contain a far greater amount of dark matter which may not have measurable mass. The Triangulum Galaxy was formally described as a spiral galaxy with a weak (or possibly no) central bar and its loosely wound arms emanate from the galactic core. Even the core of the Triangulum Galaxy is only a nebula, or nothing more than a cloud of gas and dust called an HII region, which by definition should have less mass. This HII region is a prime area for star formation but once again, we are talking about only 10% of the number of stars present as compared to our galaxy. The spiral arms have been observed to be actively making stars and its star birth rate is calculated as being several times greater than the Andromeda Galaxy. More active, no obvious black hole at its center, and its relative closeness to our galaxy suggests it was probably formed about the same time as the Milky Way, yet its physical measurements are significantly different.

The Triangulum Galaxy Designation:	M33 or NGC 598
Type:	Spiral
Diameter:	60,000 light years
Distance:	3 M light years
Mass:	50 billion M☉
Number of Stars:	40 billion
Constellation:	Triangulum

Table 2

A similar conundrum can be seen with the Pinwheel Galaxy in the constellation Ursa Major. It is referred to as a "grand design" spiral, meaning that it has well-defined spiral arms and dust lanes that extend all the way around the body of the galaxy. It was discovered in 1781 by astronomer Pierre Méchain. The Pinwheel Galaxy is about twice the diameter of the Milky Way Galaxy, and is formally defined as a weakly barred spiral galaxy. There are more than 3,000 star birth regions in the spiral arms of the Pinwheel Galaxy. These regions in the spiral arms are also called HII regions. The Pinwheel Galaxy has a fairly small central bulge, with about 3 billion solar masses. Compared to the star birth action in the spiral arms, the bulge is very quiet, with almost no stars birthed there. The Pinwheel has no central supermassive black hole identified but instead has numerous stellar-mass black holes.

Pinwheel Galaxy Profile Designation:	M101 or NGC 5457
Type:	Spiral
Diameter:	170,000 light years
Distance:	21 M light years
Mass:	1,000 billion M☉
Number of Stars:	1 trillion
Constellation:	Ursa Major

Table 3

In a comparison of the Pinwheel to our Milky Way Galaxy, it is relatively the same diameter in size but its mass is even greater than that of the Triangulum Galaxy. In fact 200 times greater than the Triangulum which was reported as being 50,000 times than our galaxy. Of course the number of stars is 3 to 10 times the number of those in our galaxy, but even so, this does not account for the degree of mass difference. What needs to be pointed out is the obvious difference between these two spiral galaxies from our own galaxy and that is that they don't have a supermassive black hole at their center. Instead they have smaller stellar black holes, the largest one in the Triangulum Galaxy being 15.7 times the mass of our sun. Compare this to the supermassive black hole at the center of the Milky Way Galaxy, which is four million times the mass of our sun and we can see the obvious disparity between a stellar black whole and that of the central galaxy black hole. There really is no comparison, yet both of those other galaxies have far greater total mass than our own, despite the fact that they have any supermassive central black hole. This riddle can only be resolved if we assume that even though our central black hole possesses this incredible mass based on the calculations of the scientific formulas, for some inexplicable reason it does not register in the calculation of our total mass of our galaxy. Though I can only theorize at this time, until such time that it is proven, but I believe this is further proof that black holes are not closed structures but are open ended that serve as conduits for whatever material they have collected, transporting what they likely converted into dark energy, along with dark matter into the Void. The quantum flux of the dark material between these two states makes it possible for them to pass through the barrier as seen in Figure 3, where, if my hypothesis is correct, this material will be contained in an energy pool until it is ignited during the next Big Bang or Long Fizzle. Since the repetitive nature of the Big Bang is already a subject of discussion by scientists, then this looping mechanism makes perfect sense because of the laws of thermodynamics. The Big Bang must draw on energy and mass that already exists because there is only a set amount of energy in existence and the recycling process is the only way in which it can be maintained without violating the natural laws.

I am definitely not the only one that thinks that our universe is being constantly recycled and it would be a huge mistake to think of the Big Bang as a singular event. In a recent paper published on the Cornell University website there is the latest report concerning a model of a cyclical universe that Roger Penrose has been developing over several years. According to his theory, the Big Bang that created our universe is not unique. He proposes that at least one earlier big bang occurred, giving rise to a universe that existed before ours. But where there is one, then there could be countless more universes in existence before ours, he thinks. Penrose refers to each cycle of the universe as an aeon, and each aeon lasts for an unimaginably long time. Considering our universe is young at 13.8 billion years of age, then he is talking many multiples of that age. An aeon starts with a big bang, and over time the newborn universe evolves from a sea of dilute and homogeneous particles into ever more complex structures such as galaxies, stars, planets, and ultimately lifeforms. In his theory, which sound very much like my own, the universe is expanding at an accelerated rate, stretched apart he presumes by the dark energy that is driving the expansion of space-time in our own universe. But where, I postulate there is the single massive dark hole on the other side of the void, Penrose sees all the matter in the universe ingested by the supermassive black holes that occupy the centers of large galaxies, such as the one in our own Milky Way. In his view, these black holes grow as they feed, colliding and combining into even larger black holes. These collisions he argues set up the gravitational waves that drive the CMB rings, but this does nothing to explain the ancient CMB that were generated at the time of the Big Bang. Penrose sees a continuing enlargement of the black holes until there is nothing left to consume. He then points to Stephen Hawking's proposed that when black holes stop taking in matter, they lose their own mass via radiation and then over a few billion more years they would evaporate, converting their ingested matter into radiation. At this point in the aeon, he describes the universe as being a sea of uniform particles at which point he theorizes the universe undergoes a transformation that essentially compacts it back into an infinitesimally small point, setting the stage for the next big bang.

Here's the problem with Penrose's theory; with the evaporation or obliteration of the black holes, there is no longer any giant vacuum cleaner in the universe that is going to gather up all the uniform particles scattered throughout the universe and then coalesce them into a small pinpoint of matter. Furthermore, if there is nothing left, what causes the transformation. Then there is the issue of reigniting the small amount of matter, even if it did generate heat as it was being compacted to a level that would be a universe creating force. "In principle, it works on paper, but it's still missing details and quantitative predictions," Hajian, another scientist that is in agreement in principle with Penrose, said. I tend to disagree. In principle it points to what I have said all along. Penrose's theory of black holes transforming the matter into another form, in his case radiation, supports my argument that there is a back door to the black holes. That the matter they absorb does not remain trapped for an eternity within the black hole but is transformed and transported into a collecting pool, which in my theory lies within the Void. Clearly, I agree with Penrose that the matter being collected by the black hole does not remain as a compacted particle of tremendous mass but is converted into a form that permits it to be transported and his theory of radiation is as good as any option that I can purport as

I talk about a hybrid of dark energy and dark matter that is in constant flux. But what both Penrose and Hajian are reluctant to say in their proposed construct of a cyclic Big Bang theory is that there is an unseen hand involved. A complex recycling of all the matter in the universe, as controlled reactions, requiring a string of multiple events to take place with precision and 100% efficacy on a repeated basis is not a random event that would happen on its own accord. Clearly, the missing details and quantitative predictions that Hajian is speaking of has a name and he is called, God. As for the trigger to ignite the rebirth of a universe over and over again, that is nothing other than the **GodSpark**.

Chapter 5: Parallel Universes or The Multiverse

Based on the postulation from the preceding chapter, one of the major questions that needs to be asked as an extension of Penrose's postulates is, "If the Big Bang is a repetitive outpouring process from this unknown source, or in my case the Void, what law of the universe says it necessarily has to be through the same aperture and subsequently feeding our universe as an extension of what has already transpired?" As we will discuss shortly, Penrose has concluded that the CMB waves from a prior universe lay immediately ahead of us and we're just following the same path. And although a few other scientists may be in agreement with this suggestion, we need to question why there couldn't be another opening somewhere else along the barrier that separates the Void from that which we consider to be our section of space. With all the vastness of space, why would we even think there'd be a singular pathway. It's a reasonable question to ponder since the Void is without estimate in size and description and therefore, for all we know, there could be another Big Bang taking place on the other side of the Void, if there are such things as sides to the Void, right now as we ponder this question. With it being so far away, it is well beyond any of our measurement devices and we would never ever know about it. The question begs consideration. If there is one tear in the fabric of the Void, why couldn't there be others? Perhaps our universe is just one of many universes in existence simultaneously rather than sequentially and because we cannot see beyond the boundary of our own universe, we will never know the answer to this question unless we discover some means of entering into the Void, transiting across it, and observing for ourselves if there is any such activity. Since that possibility of that ever happening does not exist at all, since no matter from our universe will ever be able to enter into the Void without being first dematerialized into radiation as Penrose has indicated, which is in alignment with my postulation of reducing the contents of the black holes to the status of being in a quantum flux, existing in a state somewhere between matter and energy, then we have to be content with the hypothesis that the possibility of multiple universes exist and cannot be disproved.

Penrose as we saw in the last chapter planted the seeds of the possibility for multiple universes. Once again, the repetitions of the circular pattern that appears everywhere in our universe was the causative precedent for his hypothesis. The increasing circular patterns of the CMB apparently originating from beyond the border of our known universe provided him with a good reason to think that it might be possible. But don't be mistaken to think that is the only indications for such a possibility. Circular patterns manifesting themselves in our universe without explanation are actually quite common. In a recent analysis of what are called the Wilkinson Microwave Anisotropy Probe (WMAP) seven-year temperature maps, Penrose and Gurzadyan identified even more concentric ring patterns in space with anomalously low variances. These circles are presented as observational evidence for the occurrence of a violent processes in an alternative universe that preceded our own Big Bang. Of course, other scientists disagree with Penrose and Gurzadyan, declaring that the observed variances were consistent with a Gaussian CMB profile as predicted by the inflationary cosmology model at better than 3σ. It sounds impressive, with a 3σ statistical analysis, which would suggest their model has only a 2.5% chance of being in error. And they may very well be right but what they can't disprove is that the ring-like patterns could still be vague imprints of a universe that existed before the Big Bang, even with their statistical modeling. If the odds against life beginning in the universe are billions to one against, then a 2.5% chance of the ring being other than a normal finding of the current model is pretty good odds.

First of all, lets describe what Penrose and the other scientists are talking about. Like ripples in a pond, these concentric rings are expanding outward in waves of increasing diameter. In the particular area of space where they are occurring, the temperature appears to be more uniform, suggesting that it was elevated by some activity that took place. The activity that is being suggested is the collision of black holes and both Penrose at the University of Oxford and Gurzadyan of the Yerevan Physics Institute of Armenia are suggesting these collisions took place before our universe was born. Black holes existing before our universe could only mean that there was a previous universe. The activity is based on an unproven consideration that when two black holes collide, they will emit ripples of energy known as gravitational waves. The more massive the collision, the more numerous and powerful the waves. Hence the ring like patterns similar to a stone dropping in a pond. For these rings to appear in an empty area of space would suggest that at one time, there had been something in that location, that caused these rings, even though in our universe nothing exists to have done so. If our universe is one in a series of reborn universes, this would mean that the rings have persisted and we are actually looking through a window before the Big Bang into a previous aeon.

A large proportion of scientists disagree, saying that anything from a prior universe would be erased by the massive release of energy from our own Big Bang. There is no disagreement that these CMB rings exist in an area of space where nothing can be identified that would have created them, but they're just not prepared to say that they came from another universe. Instead, the critics point out that that

Penrose's recyclable universe model doesn't include a process called Universe inflation. The inflationary theory says that our early universe went through a period of hyper-expansion that helped it reach its current size and shape but this only helps in explaining why our universe appears to be homogeneous when examining different parts. Or to put it another way, inflation explains the universe's uniformity, because any clumping of matter in the early universe was smoothed out by the hyperexpansion.

This hyperinflation would explain a rippling effect caused as if the stone in the pond fell into the water at the location of the Big Bang and the concentric rings moved outwards from that point. But these CMB rings are originating from the fringes of our universe, not the origin. More so, all the computer modeling being performed is not taking into consideration that backwards curvature that was discussed in the previous chapters which would disrupt the circular patterns of these rings as the gravitational forces tug those areas of our universe along the strands causing a distortion into a starfish pattern as I suggest and discuss later in this chapter.

According to their arguments, if the ripples in the CMB are evidence of the cyclic model of the universe, then these ripples should not exist in the simulated CMB skies because, according to Penrose, they should not appear in an inflationary universe but they do appear in the simulations. Zibin of the University of British Columbia suggests that instead of evidence of previous universes, the rings could be a kind of optical illusion created by natural variations in the CMB. Clearly, this argument will go on for an eternity until it is suggested that both models can exist simultaneously because of the aforementioned backwards curvature. The computer modeling is still based on the universe being relatively flat with the expansion taking place in a predominantly funnel shaped mode without inclusion of the reversal in direction that takes place when the gravitational force of the Void's extraordinarily massive black hole exceeds the force of the outward thrust of the Big Bang and the acceleration of the mass in the outward direction of that explosion. Any older universe that may have predated ours has made the big turn and will be seen to affect only that part of our universe that has already curved and is on a similar plane. Therefore the standard formation of rings according to the computer model can coexist with the anomalous CMB rings identified by Penrose.

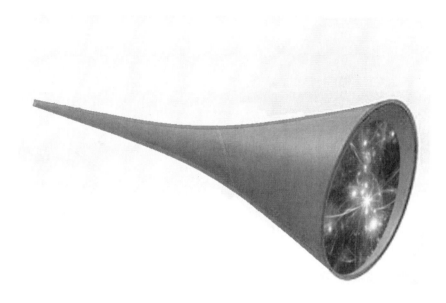

Figure 6

Figure 6 demonstrates that hyperinflation model which most scientists advocate, with expansion occurring immediately at the time of the Big Bang and then rapidly taking place in the first few billion years while the stars and gases of the universe are forming. The curvature to the plane of the universe is extremely mild and results in very little disturbance to the ripple effect of the CMB. In fact, the ripple effect will be magnified as the universe expands, each wave increasing in diameter as the expansion process progresses. We can picture these rings if we think of someone smoking a cigarette and blowing smoke rings. The first rings blown are small as they exit from the lips but as they venture further and further from the mouth they expand rapidly. If there is no barrier to their expansion, then they will eventually break apart once the gap between molecules of the smoke become too large to maintain their physical integrity and the smoke simply dissipates in the distance. The waves of the CMB rings will do exactly the same thing if the universe was merely expanding and all matter was continuing onward in the same direction. This funnel shaped expansion does provide us with a good explanation of why there should be homogeneity in the universes, because just like the smoke rings which spread out and diffuse evenly in the expanded open space, so too would the stars and galaxies in this model. But that does not mean that every quadrant in this funnel shape will contain either stars or galaxies as the area of expansion becomes greater than the volume of the contents, similar to the dissipating smoke rings once they become too large. What was once a dense collection of matter when it was first ejected from the Big Bang, has now become as diffuse as the example of the smoke rings and cannot fill the entire expanse of this expanding universe. As a result, there are quadrants or areas of the universe that will be empty of visible matter and therefore don't contain any longer any stars or black holes that could collide to produce CMB rings in those regions. These empty regions will not produce CMB rings.

Yet, it is in those regions of what can be classified as emptiness that Penrose has identified ripples of CMB and postulated that they could have only originated from a universe that once occupied that same space in a time or aeon before our universe came into being as and had its own stars and black holes. As can be seen in Figure 7, even if once homogeneous, there are going to be regions or quadrants of our universe where there is an absence of visible matter. It is unavoidable and therefore the statistical models that are being produced need to take into account this possibility

But then Penrose's hypothesis doesn't take into consideration that his model of multiple universes must take into consideration a physical boundary to each universe, otherwise, far more than just CMB waves would be extending into our universe from the previous one, and physical remnants left behind from the more ancient universe would also be littering the trail. This physical barrier would be just like the cell walls or membranes keeping one celled organisms in tact. If each universe is bound by a physical barrier, then whatever exists between individual universes, would be an unlikely candidate for being a conductor of wave transmission. And even if the waves somehow did manage to travel this unknown expanse, then they must also manage to traverse or penetrate the barrier that represents the forward wall of our universe. The ability of these waves to cross the barriers, resist the gravitational and electromagnetic pull in the opposite direction, journey through an unknown field of invisible matter between universes and not be washed away by the expanding rings of CMB from our own Big Bang is highly questionable if not impossible.

In Figure 7 we can see the CMB ripple effect emanating from the Big Bang. Smaller ripple effects will occur as stars collide as well as the proposed collision of the black holes. But if the curve was only a gentle widening of the diameter over time, as indicated in the funnel shaped hyper-expansion model, then the force of the initial explosion of the Big Bang as well as the distant gravitational pull would in all probability maintain the ripple effects both large and small moving in the same direction. In fact, the larger ripple effect of the Big Bang in most cases, as mentioned previously, would simply wash over the small CMB bands and either merge with them so they are moving uniformly as an altered wave form in an outward direction or obliterate them completely. This being the likely scenario for any CMB produced by a collision would mean that any detection of their existence should be either extremely difficult or near impossible. Since this is not the case, then neither Zibin's opinion representing the traditional scientific viewpoint, or Penrose's supporting an older, prior universe can be justified.

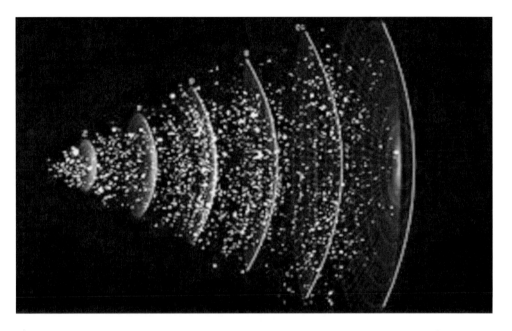

Figure 7

In fact, as I have shown, there are good arguments why neither can be the correct explanation for these rogue CMB waves and why the correct model would not be a gentle curving universe but one in which the edges of our universe have already folded back, so that the initial direction of our universe away from the aperture has been reversed, to a point where the gravitational pull at the far end of the Void exceeds both the initial force of expulsion and the continued force of acceleration. Upon reaching this point where both expulsion and acceleration are negated, the forward edges of our universe will begin turning back in the direction of the Void, continuing to expand until they wrap over the Void in an envelope, as they are drawn towards the colossal black hole at the Voids opposite end.

To imagine what is occurring, think of trying to place a watermelon into a plastic bag that is not much bigger than the circumference of the watermelon. One would tug on one side of the edge of the plastic bag, then the other sides, constantly pulling the bag bit by bit over the watermelon until the bag has completely wrapped itself over the melon. In this model, one of the issues that interfered with the transmission of the waves in the opposite direction from an alternative source has been eliminated. That being the production of the waves from the original Big Bang. They will most likely continue in the original direction, dissipating as in the example of the smoke rings when they enter a space so large that they can no longer retain their integrity. But the issues of crossing the barriers surrounding each universe and traversing whatever it is that fills the space between the universes still exists.

It might be possible to eliminate the issue of traversing the unknown space between universes if it consisted of a material that actually was a conductor of electromagnetic waves. The answer might lay in what has been dubbed the Electric Universe model. The Electric Universe model is based, not on gas, but on plasma. The dark matter and dark energy of our universe may very well be a form of plasma as well. Since everything in our universe appears to have its negative counterpart, then perhaps what fills the space between multiple universes, if such things do exist would be an anti-dark matter and anti-dark plasma. The barriers of the universes prevent the two plasmas, those within and those without from making contact with each other, which would have universe ending cataclysmic effect. What we do know is that plasma obeys primarily the laws of electromagnetism, rendering any requirements to consider gravity and gas dynamics unnecessary and providing electromagnetic waves, the perfect platform to travel across between barriers.

In the Electric Universe model, surges in current are possible, allowing transmission of waves at an accelerated rate, thereby making it possible for electromagnetic waves produced by a universe billions of years older to still be visible in a universe trailing behind It must be remembered that electromagnetic effects are far more powerful than gravitational forces. Instabilities in the plasma can produce "hot spots" which may account for Penrose's concentric rings in space with anomalously low variances when he examined the Wilkinson Microwave Anisotropy Probe (WMAP) seven-year temperature maps. Instead of the circles being observational evidence for the occurrence of violent processes in an alternative universe that preceded our own Big Bang as Penrose stated, perhaps they were the 'hot spots' from plasma instability outside the boundary of our universe. Either way they point towards something existing ahead of our universe's boundary but not necessarily another universe. They may be breakaway pieces from our own universe that in essence have become parallel universes. To explain this better, it is necessary to refer back to the watermelon and plastic bag analogy.

As we pull the edges up around the circumference of the watermelon, we will obviously stretch the plastic as we do so. In some places we may have to apply more force and stretch it a lot. Other places less for and we stretch it only a little. When we are finished, we can see that the opening edge of the bag is no longer uniform and in some places can be quite misshapen. Folding the universe back on itself to surround the void may have the same effect. Astrophysicist Dan Hooper is aware of the forces that can misshape our universe when he said, "There are things that we see about our universe that we can only explain – at least for the moment – if we postulate that there was an era very, very early in our universe's history where space expanded extremely dramatically in a giant, sudden burst. These are bigger numbers than you can ever wrap your head around but you can just think of the universe growing almost instantly to a vast, vast volume from a tiny little space." In this rapid expansion, Hooper speaks of different sizes of packages of the universe, each having its own acceleration rate due to the Big Bang being more like a machine gun burst than a single explosion.

I will stop Hooper there, because what he says next becomes extreme in its connotation and I wish to use his previous comment to emphasize the image of the plastic bag and watermelon. We will discuss his later comments a little later in this chapter. So Hooper's initial comment is about a tremendous force that we could never even imagine at the time of the Big Bang. The expansion was almost imme-diate and spread out in all directions but the spread of energy and particles were not uniform because of the multiple bursts. This is an interesting concept that warrants further investigation because it would mean that the pockets of universe released with each burst would not necessarily evolve into identical atomic masses and there-fore contain equivalent amounts of galaxies and stars. The fact that each repeated burst may not have the identical initial thrusting force and that each pocket region of the universe may have different mass means that there would be different regions or quadrants of the universe that have different characteristics. We've already dis-cussed the fact that not all galaxies behave, look or move identically through space and the rotation directions are not split evenly as probability laws would dictate and this would fit with the theory of the Big Bang being a series of bursts and not a singular event.

Accordingly, we have several factors that now come into play with this sce-nario. Each pocket of universe having a different mass is going to be affected in a different way by both force and gravity. The force of gravity itself between two objects is determined by the mass of each object and the distance between their centers. The object with a greater amount of mass will exert a greater degree of gravitational pull, but as the distance between it and the other object increases, the gravitational force between them lessens. The significance of distance with regard to the force of the Big Bang plays an important role as the projectiles move in a direction away from the source of the gravity will interact with a decreasing gravitational pull from the black hole at the far end of the Void. Until such time that the force of acceleration from the explosion decreases significantly or stops, the gravitational forces will only play a minor role. But we also know that the size of the object being forcefully shot from the Big Bang will also determine the acceleration and therefore the distance it travels from the point of the Big Bang. According to Newton's second law of motion, force is equal to mass times acceleration, meaning that mass and acceleration are inversely proportional. A constant force applied to two bodies of different masses leads to higher acceleration in the less massive body than in the more massive one.

$$F = M \times A$$

It is a very simple formula and in our case it is the acceleration, which is of the greatest interest to us since that will determine the distance from the point of the Big Bang down through the expanding funnel that the object will travel. The mass directly determines the velocity of the object since we know that the force of the Big Bang would be the same for all objects if there was a single burst. But now that we're talking about multiple bursts in close succession to each other as Hooper proposes, the change in force will also directly affect acceleration for an object of the same size. Simply put, if the first burst has a force of 10 and the object it has shot out has a mass of 5, then the acceleration of the object will be 2. Don't worry about the units, we're just using the formula to demonstrate simple principles. But what if the next burst has a force of only 5. Then the object still have a mass of 5 will only have an acceleration of 1 or half the speed of the first burst. This all sounds good in principle according to Hooper's hypothesis, giving the impression of individual pockets of universe all moving at different velocities but where it doesn't seem to work is in a situation where the second burst may have had a force of 25. In that case, the object with a mass of 5 would be accelerating at a velocity of 5, which would mean it would be shooting through the first burst, disrupting it, and scattering it through collisions in multiple directions that would not even resemble our smoothly expanding universe.

We can appreciate from the formula that the net force will be the resultant force of all forces acting on the body at any given instant. So if a force from a second burst is moving faster than the first burst, then those objects in the first burst will be directly affected and depending on the angles of collision, the explosive natures of any collisions, etc., there would be an expectation that the universe or the objects in the universe would no longer be moving uniformly. The only way this would not be an obvious outcome of Hooper's hypothesis is if each successive burst is of less force than the previous one and there is no justification for that to be true.

The other fact is that we know as time passes, the particles in the initial blast coalesce into atoms, which then form molecules, which in turn create gases and matter. The matter formed will vary in size greatly and therefore the acceleration of these forming objects will also be affected dramatically. The more massive a body becomes, the less it accelerates due to the application of the initial force. This concept of resistance to acceleration is closely tied to Newton's first law and inertia, which is the tendency of a body to resist any change in its state of motion. Therefore, the alteration of the mass will directly affect acceleration.

$$A = F/M$$

As the molecules come together to form different objects, the masses of each will increase, depending on the structure and as a result, the initial force divided by these increasing masses will result in deceleration. Deceleration will be the decreasing rate of change of the velocity of a body. But as deceleration occurs, there will be other forces that begin to have an effect on these particles, such as electromagnetic force, gravitational force and mechanical force, just to name a few. Gravity is one of the weakest forces in the universe and is easily overridden by practically every other force, but as mass increases and deceleration occurs, the gravitational force from the Void's Black Hole becomes increasingly important at the object now becomes affected by the gravitational field.

Gravitational field is a concept and a method for calculating and explaining phenomena happening around any object with a mass. According to Newton's universal law of gravitation, two masses M and m divided by a finite distance r exert a force upon each other. By multiplying the result of the two masses by a gravitational constant (G), the force can be calculated. Fortunately for us, Sir Isaac Newton already determined this value as being equal to 6.67×10^{-11} Newtons x m^2/kg^2 anywhere in our galaxy or vicinity of the universe. The formula looks like this:

$$F_{grav} = G \times (M_1 \times m_2 / r^2)$$

Let's presume the acceleration of the particles, molecules or bits of matter as a result of the force of the Big Bang have all slowed down to almost nil as their mass has increased significantly so that the F in the numerator of the fraction is now much smaller than the M in the denominator in $A = F/M$, effectively reducing A to a value less than 1. At this point, the effects of gravitational forces become far more important in determining the direction and acceleration of the objects since they will be greater than the acceleration.

Now, looking once again at Newton's Gravitational Field equation. if we want to calculate the gravitational force of the Void's massive black hole on the matter we are focusing on, which is the universe that exploded from the aperture during the Big Bang, then the mass of the black hole is going to be hundreds of millions of times more than the mass of the particles in the universe. So we will call the mass of those particles 1 so that we can eliminate them from the equation as they are practically non-existent by comparison. The formula is now:

$$\mathbf{F_{grav} = GM_1/r^2}$$

This formula is now calculating the gravitational field intensity of the larger mass only, in this case the Void's black hole, on any point located at a distance r from the massive black hole. But we also know from the previous equation that the acceleration of the particles from the Big Bang was $F = ma$ where this m was equal to m_2. and now we can see also that $F = GM_1/r^2$. Therefore:

$$\mathbf{m_2 a = GM_1/r^2}$$

Since the small object (i.e. Particles from the Big Bang) is moving towards the large object, acceleration is only in one direction and we've already identified m as having a mass of 1 compared to the Void's massive black hole, so therefore the formula becomes:

$$\mathbf{a = GM_1/r^2}$$

This means that the gravitational field intensity and the acceleration due to the gravitational force are the same and therefore, this acceleration is known as the gravitational acceleration or a = F_{grav}. Gravitational acceleration is always towards the larger mass, while acceleration in general can be in any direction, as long as there is a net force pushing it in that direction.

The Universal Gravitation Equation we know is $F_{grav} = GMm/r^2$ where we know that F_{grav} is the force of attraction between the two objects and is measured in newtons (N). G as mentioned is the Universal Gravitational Constant. M is the mass of the object kilograms (kg) and r is the separation in meters (m) between the objects, as measured from their centers of each mass which is then squared.

For the purpose of using this formula as an example of the gravitational force exerted by the Void's black hole upon a decelerated mass ejected from the Big Bang, then lets assume for the sake of convenience the weight or mass of the expelled particles of matter is 10 kg and the mass of the black hole is 1×10^{50} kg. These values are not intended to even be close to the true values and are just used for the sake of rendering the formula easy to understand and use. And for the purpose of this example we say that the distance between the centers of each object is 10×10^{15} meters or roughly one light year.

Then our formula of

$$F_{grav}=G(M_1m_2)/r^2$$

becomes in this example:

$$F_{grav}=[(6.67 \times 10^{-11}) \times 10(1 \times 10^{50})]/(10 \times 10^{15})^2$$

Multiply the masses of the two objects together. $10 \times (1 \times 10^{50}) = 1 \times 10^{51}$
Multiply the product of m1 and m2 by the gravitational constant G. (1×10^{51}) x (6.67 x 10-11) = 6.67 x 10^{40}
Square the distance between the two objects. $(10 \times 10^{15})^2 = 1 \times 10^{32}$
Divide the product of G x m_1 x m_2 by the distance squared to find the force of gravity in Newtons (N). $6.67 \times 10^{40}/1 \times 10^{32} = 6.67 \times 10^8$ N
The force of gravity is 667 Million Newtons.

As we can see from the equation, the force of gravity can be quite large even over a huge distance and even at a distance of thousands of light years would be even more intense the larger the objects involved. So if we imagine the initial force of the Big Bang did not propel the larger particles that had massed together as far as the smaller particles, then at the point where the energy of the initial forces had waned and inertia was settling in, then the gravitational forces of the Void's super-massive black hole would begin drawing those larger sections of coalesced matter towards its center at an accelerating rate that would have a higher velocity than the smaller particulate matter that had been expelled further from the Big Bang and now had a smaller gravitational force to draw it back over a greater distance. As a result, any reverse curvature to the universe would separate into layers or waves with the larger masses moving more quickly than pockets consisting of material of a much smaller masses I refer to this as a layered starfish model of the curved universe which can be seen in Figure 8. Like the plastic bag being pulled over the outer surface of the watermelon, those areas moving faster and upon which greater force is being exerted will be stretched more than those areas containing clusters of lower mass and moving at a slower velocity of acceleration.   This separation through stretching the edges of the universe as shown in Figure 8 is what I have been refer-ring to as strands of the universe. The more the strands become extended, the more they appear to separate from other regions of the universe and would give the ap-pearance of being parallel universes or pocket universes.

The following figure gives us an end on view of the aftermath of the Big Bang and the subsequent reversal of the motion of matter in our universe as it curves back towards the proposed supermassive black hole of the Void. In the centre of the image, we have the expanding funnel of the universe that resulted from the initial Big Bang but as the forces diminishes over time and distance and the matter begins to gather and coalesce into larger units of matter possessing greater mass, then those particles that were originally quite small would have moved a much greater distance away from the point of origin of the Big Bang.   Those units of matter that were much larger to begin with, will have moved only a fraction of the distance of the smaller particles due to their greater mass.

Figure 8

At the point where the projectile force of the Big Bang no longer exceeds the gravitational force from the black hole, inertia of the forward motion will set in as the two forces cancel each other out, and then with time the gravitational force will begin drawing the material of our universe backwards. But the deceleration of the projectile force, the settling in of inertia and the eventual acceleration of the gravitational force will result in a wide, gentle curve that we view from our perspective as being almost flat and unable to properly assess the change in direction because of the parallax from our viewpoint.

For purposes of clarity, the starfish universe in Figure 8 only displays two layers. The much larger layer that is moving faster because of the large section of matter with high mass values and therefore experience increased acceleration, and the smaller layer that moved a further distance as a result of the Big Bang and is now curving backwards at a slower acceleration and at a completely different level in space because of having splayed out or expanded further as a result of the funnel shape of the Big Bang explosion. The reality is that there can be as many layers as the particles themselves coalesced into different mass groups. Almost like a clothing shop there could be pockets of universe ranging from extra small to triple X large.

As the strands become more extended and more separated, they will provide the illusion of being a separate universe, some which have preceded the origin of our own universe and they also will appear to be bound by their own barrier or containment wall. This appearance, solely the result of where we are positioned in our own universe may be what provided Hooper with the impression of multiple bursts during the Big Bang, each one popping off what he referred to as bubble universes. Viewing the extended arm on the starfish universe would provide the impression that one might be looking at a distinct and separate universe because we cannot follow its border backwards and see that it is still connected to our own universe. But as these arms or strands do become more and more stretched, they will almost become parallel universes, which unless we can find a means of traversing the boundary of the strand of our own universe and also the boundary of that strand running in parallel, then we might as well be two separate universes.

Returning to Hooper's model, he views each disconnected region as a universe all on its own, and the size of each one is determined by how fast space is expanding. He goes on further to state that with an infinite amount of space, there will be an infinite number of universes; collections of atoms and other particles located at specific places at specific times oriented in almost exactly the same way that they are in our Earth containing universe. Hooper also postulates that within his multiverse model, there are likely to be alien worlds with unknown forces and new forms of matter along with more or fewer than three dimensions of space. He continues his explanation further with the statements that, "These worlds contain a star that is nearly identical to the Sun, which is orbited by a planet that is nearly identical to the Earth, which contains upon it people who are nearly identical to you and me. If space as we know it extends forever, this conclusion is inevitable. All things and all events that are possible, no matter how unlikely, will exist and will occur within this greater collection of space."

As intriguing as Hooper's model sounds, I disagree with his version of the multiverse and see the starfish model with seemingly parallel universes, even though they are not truly parallel unless somehow one of these extended strands breaks free of the main body of our universe, as the more feasible reality. But there are others like Neil deGrasse Tyson, who also believes in a multiverse, describing it as, "multiple ships at sea far enough away from one another so that their circular horizons do not intersect yet they all share the same body of water."

But the answer at this point is we don't know which model is correct or even if there is another model that hasn't yet been envisioned. I quote Nobel Prize winning physicist Adam Riess, who I think sums it up best when he said, "Dark energy is incredibly strange, but actually it makes sense to me that it went unnoticed. I have absolutely no clue what dark energy is. Dark energy appears strong enough to push the entire universe – yet its source is unknown, its location is unknown and its physics are highly speculative." Simply translated, it tells you that as scientists, we don't have the answers, but we want you to think we do. Which only confirms to me even more that someone far more intelligent and far more powerful had a hand in these events. As mentioned earlier, the multiverse version created via multiple bursts at the time of the Big Bang has several problems that would need to be overcome in order for it to work. First and foremost is the lack of uniformity of these bursts that would result in different pockets of universal material accelerating at different rates, creating a bumper car universe that would likely result in annihilation of the universe and not the creation of one. The only way this could be overcome would be through a controlled release process, which would require control of timing and volume to ensure that every burst was equivalent and every resultant bubble of universe was uniform and equivalent as well. That in itself would be a production process and for that to exist would mean that it had to be programmed into the grand universe making machine. Simply by agreeing that this was necessary for their multiverse model of universal creation to exist, science would be admitting that there must be a Creator who controls the **GodSpark**.

Their model could not be self regulating and with each universal packet acting independently, the natural curvature of our universe, also seemingly uniform wherever we look would be unlikely with these multiverses exerting their own gravitational forces. Just as the moon causes the earth to bulge at the equator due to the gravitational force it exerts, so to would each of the multiverses influence our own universe causing it to bulge, dent or twist in numerous places. As these deformations of our universe don't seem to exist, then it would not appear that there are independent massive objects tampering with our space.

As stated earlier in my own viewpoint as to the existence of a multiverse, I can only see this as a possibility if there was another breach in the Void far away from the one which spat our universe out that even with expansion, there never would be any contact between the several universes that might exist simultaneously.

But once again, such a possibility only exists if the Void occupied practically infinite space and our use of the pathways around the Void were so minuscule that collision of these universes was virtually impossible.

In Figure 9, I expand the layering concept of the starfish universe model, demonstrating a narrower pathway of the larger mass material moving around the Void from Big Bang to the supermassive black hole, whereas the lighter mass material takes a much wider pathway due to its further expansion distant from the Big Bang breach. Not only is our universe inside the Void, but is also moving around the center of the Void.

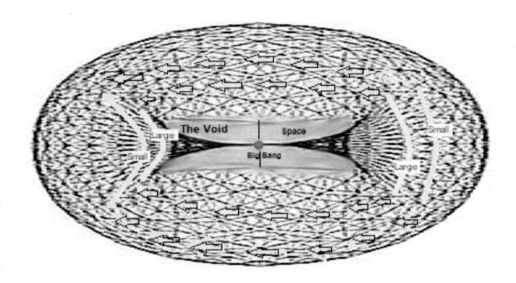

Figure 9

Because the greater mass material is moving at a higher velocity due to the gravitational force, it will reach the black hole long before the lighter mass material. This speed of circumnavigating the Void is also enhanced by the fact that the material of higher mass will travel along a narrower pathway, thereby shortening the distance traveled as compared to the lighter material. Because of the different gravitational accelerations, we will never see these slower or faster pockets of universe from our viewpoint in the universe. But as Hooper recorded, we may see traces of evidence of one of these pockets if it was ahead of us, moving much faster and without much gravitational interference of the smaller masses that are trailing behind. No matter where one is positioned in this layered starfish model, the material trailing your position will always be of lower mass and therefore unable to influence the acceleration of your pocket of the universe to any significant degree.

The issue was raised that if one of the strands stretched far enough, just like the plastic bag being forcefully stretched over the watermelon, it might accidentally break off and separate from the main body of the universe. If this was to happen, then that part of the starfish appendage that had broken away, would be a distinct and separate universe from that point, but it would still be moving at an accelerated rate as compared to that part that remained behind along what was once the same strand. Even under such circumstances, there would be no reason to expect interference from the break away self contained universe but it might leave behind rings of CMB from the actual breakage. And this I believe is what they have seen and are trying to decipher.

It should be noted that the example of an arm of the starfish model breaking off and being classified as a universe all of its own may have its counterpart in the animal world, providing more evidence that there is a template for all that exists from the smallest to the largest objects imaginable. We simply have to look at models of binary fission in once celled animals to see such examples. All of the organisms in the domains Archaea and Bacteria reproduce asexually through binary fission. By far, bacteria account for the most populous organisms on the planet and do so by splitting themselves in two. The process of binary fission is a very stable one, and because bacteria have a very simple genome, there are relatively few mutations in these prokaryotes. Bacteria also exhibit variations in the ways in which they elongate to divide. Some bacteria extend at the far end, while others grow from the middle outward. Even the timing with which the bacteria divide differs and is directed by genetics. Some bacteria can divide in as little as 20 minutes, while others take many hours. But the separation of one of these strands of universal material from the main body is not an intentional event as would be asexual reproduction of bacteria and I only bring it up here to demonstrate that splitting off from the circle, the universal template, does happen even at a microscopic scale but also to highlight the fact that some bacterial can form conjugation tubes to exchange bits of information in the form of genetic material or organelles between the bacteria, even after the splitting into two has taken place. For example, if a bacterial cell manages to become resistant to a disinfectant, then it is able to communicate how it achieved this defense by passing the information through the tube to other bacteria. The existence of these tubes, a corridor link that permits material to pass both ways past the protective barriers of cell walls and cell membranes may also provide the answer as to how transport could be possible between two pocket universes if split or running in parallel. This possibility will be explored further in the next chapter.

But if we wish to see something more in line with the stretching and separation of a strand of universe from the starfish universe model, then probably the best example is the actual starfish. If one of the leg extensions of a starfish is accidentally torn from the body, as long as there remains some central disc area still attached, then that torn off limb can develop into a second starfish. At the same time the original starfish will regrow a new leg. Sometimes the entire process will take up to a year. Starfish are members off the echinoderm, literally 'spiny skin', family which also includes sea urchins and sea cucumbers. Although not as primitive as bacteria, they do provide us with a living animal model that could provide us with some clues that might be occurring on a cosmic level. The fact that we can see evidence of certain events that happen on the macroscopic universe level reflected in the microcosm of our world is suggestive that overall there is a master design to our universe and the **GodSpark** is the intentional trigger that begins it all.

Chapter 6: Wormholes, Black holes and Energy Pools

Wormholes

In the last chapter, the concern of the boundaries of parallel universes, or even multiverses if they exist, being impenetrable was raised, thus preventing passage from our universe to these other pocket universes, unless there existed something similar to the conjugation tube existing in some bacteria that permits them to exchange genetic material, organelles, etc. across their impenetrable cell walls and cell membranes. If there really was a master template for everything in the universe from the smallest object to the largest, then it should be possible to find items serving a similar function and purpose, even at the level of the universe. Science has devised a theory to do exactly what the conjugate tubes do and call it a wormhole theory. The wormhole theory postulates that a theoretical passage through space-time could create shortcuts for long journeys across the universe or between universes. It is not as far-fetched as it sounds as wormholes are predicted to exist by the theory of general relativity. But these holes in space and time are perceived to be quite dangerous due to their characteristic nature to suddenly collapse, along with a potential to have high radiation and dangerous exotic matter.

Wormholes are not a new theory. In fact they were first theorized in 1916. While reviewing another physicist's solution to the equations in Albert Einstein's theory of general relativity, Austrian physicist Ludwig Flamm realized there may be another answer and he described it as a "white hole," a theoretical time reversal of a black hole. Entrances to both black and white holes he postulated could be connected by a space-time conduit. In 1935, Albert Einstein and physicist Nathan Rosen used the theory of general relativity to elaborate on the idea, proposing the existence of "bridges" through space-time. These bridges connect two different points in space-time, thus creating a shortcut that could reduce travel time and distance. We have come to refer to these shortcuts as Einstein-Rosen bridges, which we hear often enough in science fiction movies, but the more common name that most are familiar with is 'wormholes.'

Though we may all believe they do exist, physicist Stephen Hsu at the University of Oregon doesn't believe we will find a wormhole anytime soon. Still, there is a lot of conjecture of what wormholes would look like and the general consensus is that they will contain two apertures, with a tube connecting the two. The openings would most likely be spheroidal. The tube might be a straight stretch, but it could also wind around, taking a longer path than a more conventional route might require. But the reality is that Einstein's theory of general relativity mathematically predicts the existence of such things as wormholes, and having had an impressive batting record so far, there is no reason to doubt Einstein now. Certain solutions of general relativity allow for the existence of wormholes where the mouth of each could be a black hole, which aligns itself with my postulation that black holes might actually extend to the supermassive black hole of the Void.

Travel through a wormhole is likely to be a complicated affair. Current models of prediction suggest that a wormhole would be no bigger than 10^{-33} centimeters. But this prediction does not take into consideration that we exist within an expanding universe. There is no reason to believe that what may have originally been 10^{-33} centimeters is not now 10^3 centimeters or ten meters in diameter after several billion years. Another problem comes from stability. The predicted Einstein-Rosen wormholes would be useless for travel because they collapse quickly. This is the real issue with wormhole travel, their instability. A wormhole would obviously require a very special matter in its construction and this material may be in a constant state of flux, providing a very short time when it would be structurally stable. According to Hsu, the type of matter involved would not be anything identified so far, which eliminates the possibility of dark matter, or even antimatter. It would be a negative energy density, and such matter has only been identified in Quantum Field Theory.

Once the type of matter is identified, then another possibility exists and that would be the manufacture of this material in order to create wormholes at will. Beam me up Scotty may not be as impossible as it sounds, if such a construct has a way in determining exactly where the apertures of the wormhole will open. Physicist Kip Thorne, one of the world's leading authorities on relativity, black holes and wormholes, says the following, "There are very strong indications that wormholes that a human could travel through are forbidden by the laws of physics. That's said, that's unfortunate, but that's the direction in which things are pointing." This would eliminate the transfer of anything organic through the wormhole but does not necessarily prevent a non-organic material transfer.

Stephen Hawking argued that wormholes may not only be a means of traveling vast distances but also suggested they could be used for traveling through time. But this theory is challenged by NASA's Eric Christian and may others. Through the addition of this unique and strange matter that has not been identified yet, it might be possible to stabilize a wormhole as to permit living organisms to travel through it, but the risk would always remain that it could destabilize during the transport. Research in the 21st century has brought forward a number of relevant scientific findings for wormhole physics. It is now assumed that there are tremendous tidal forces in the tube of the wormhole which is commonly referred to as the 'throat'. Several papers have been written on this issue. Since wormholes can capture particles on one side and re-emit them on the other side, this provides a wider spectrum for the re-emitted particles, which form a diffuse background of very low intensity around a discrete source. This could possibly provide another theory as to why CMB appear to be emitted in regions of space where nothing exists. Rather than be a leftover from another universe as Hooper theorized, it may be a broadcast from the invisible opening of a wormhole.

The entire field of wormhole physics is being intensely looked at as a result of new developments and the new opportunities available for testing their properties in both astrophysical and cosmological environments. It turns out that the Einstein-Rosen Bridge (Figure 10) commonly known as the wormhole, is essential for the acceptance of the String Theory. Use of this theory actually provides a dual purpose to wormholes, as not only do they shorten distance within or between universes, but they may actually allow for time travel as Hawking had hoped. Instead of connecting different regions of space, the wormhole could connect different regions of time. In the context of the universe that I understand, time travel would only be a one way trip and that is into the future. If the wormhole places us in a space outside of our normal time frame, then as time marches on in our original universe, it is slowed to practically being non-existent within the wormhole, suggesting that after we emerge from the other side in a few minutes we may find that our universe has aged a thousand years. Going back through the wormhole would not take as back to our origin a thousand years in the past but would actually be an additional thousand years so that we have now traveled 2000 years into the future.

Simply put, String Theory was an attempt to unite Einstein's Relativity Theory with the Quantum Theory by replacing all matter and force particles with just one element, which are these tiny vibrating strings that twist and turn in a complicated manner so that they look like particles. Rather than unite the theories, it appears that the String Theory's major contribution is in disuniting physicists. As a theory to address everything, even provide a particle theory to explain gravitational forces, the strings come up short. Scientists already have a name for these gravity particles which they call 'gravitons' but their mathematical formulas just don't support their existence but by replacing gravitons with strings, then these can collide and rebound without creating physically impossible infinities. In fact, replace everything with strings and you can eliminate almost all of the problematic scientific conundrums that physicists face when trying to explain the actions of the universe. As Marika Taylor from the University of Southampton said, "A one-dimensional object, that's the thing that really tames the infinities that come up in the calculations." In other words, encounter a problem and create another theory that is so unbelievable that it eliminates all the roadblocks.

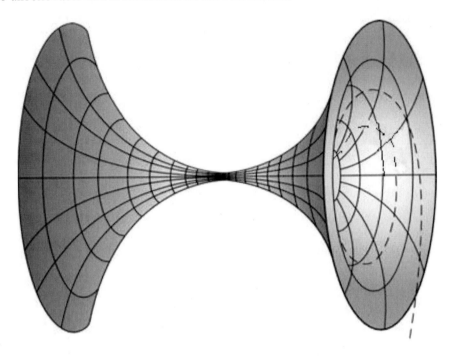

Figure 10

A string of a particular length strikes a particular note, which in turn transforms into a photon, while another string folds and vibrates with a different frequency and thus becomes a quark. A simple solution they thought. Reduce everything in the universe to strings and these same strings depending on how they fold and vibrate will make everything else that has been identified in the universe. Just one little problem. Scientists had to create a ten dimensional universe in order to have the strings perform in the manner they had theorized. So that's our three dimensions we're accustomed to, plus another dimension for time, and then six additional dimensions that can barely be described. Within a few years there were five different String Theories being proposed. Attempts to find general equations that would work in every possible situation have made little progress but that hasn't stopped physicists from trying.

Physicist Peter Woit of Columbia University wrote the following, "The basic problem with string theory unification research is not that progress has been slow over the past 30 years, but that it has been negative, with everything learned showing more clearly why the idea doesn't work."

I've raised the issue of String Theory for one reason only, To emphasize my point that time travel if possible will only be unidirectional. There's no going backwards through time because that existence is gone as soon as you've traveled forward in time. Yes, it may be possible to displace yourself from time in the future through space travel using a wormhole so that you've aged a few months while a thousand years have passed back on Earth but then you have to ask yourself, "What would be the point in that?" Everyone you knew would be dead. The only relatives you might have would be twenty generations distant and wouldn't see you as anything other than a peculiarity that should have been in a photo album. And just like a fish out of water, everything you know, everything you understand, will have been replaced by a thousand years of advanced knowledge and technology."

As described previously, the concept of wormholes were studied by Albert Einstein and his student Nathan Rosen in 1935 but it was Ludwig Flamm that had first proposed their existence in 1916. One can see the similarity between Figure 9 and Figure 3 which was looking at the exchange mechanism between the supermassive black hole of the Void which fed into the Big Bang. The Einstein-Rosen Bridge is not much different except this model, the singularity at the center of a black hole is connected to another singularity, which results in the theoretical object they called a white hole. Either end can draw matter into it just like the traditional black hole but then spits it out the other end similar to a very low key Big Bang. Being the expulsion side of the black hole, it was therefore given a name suggesting it worked in the opposite direction, hence the white hole. Oddly enough, the argument as to whether a white hole exists is still ongoing, yet, the bigger version of this, the aperture of the Big Bang is readily accepted. It is strange how science can often have a myopic view of that which it has already accepted.

As for usage of the wormhole for any kind of travel, Einstein argued against this possibility, claiming that wormholes would be so unstable that they would collapse almost as quickly as they formed. This viewpoint actually supports the postulation that the Big Bang was a singular event and not a string of repeated bursts since the original aperture would collapse fractions of a second after the explosion. The other argument raised by Einstein was that the black hole would destroy anything that was caught in its gravitational force before it could ever make it through to the other side. This might make it impossible to send any formed mass through a wormhole but would not prohibit the passage of infinitely compressed small bits of matter and energy, a concept that will be focused upon in much greater detail in Chapter 7.

Einstein pretty much put an end to the use of wormholes as express freeways through the universe but then in 1963, New Zealand mathematician Roy Kerr discovered the solution to Einstein's dilemma, calling it a Kerr black hole. What makes the Kerr black hole different is that it rotates, which since it is a common finding that practically everything in our universe rotates, including stars, so why wouldn't their active rotation as they're being swallowed, not cause the black holes to rotate as well. According to Kerr's solution, it would be possible to travel through the rotating black hole along the edges and thereby avoid the singularity at the center, emerging on the other side without actually going through the centre of black hole. One can imagine motorcycle stunt riders doing a series of loops so that the centrifugal force keeps them firmly on the path of the spiral without ever falling into the center of the loops. Though this may be a solution as to how to pass through the wormhole, it does not solve the issue of its incredibly short lifespan before it collapses.

There are those working in the field of quantum mechanics that feel that they can overcome these problems and essentially prove that wormholes, the name by the way coined by John Wheeler in 1957, actually do exist. NASA has been exploring the possibility earnestly, and in 2019 described how wormhole travel might actually be feasible. Their concept of feasibility relied on what I have been suggesting all along, that black holes may not be dead ends but instead may themselves be apertures into other areas of space and time, such as into the Void. Their conclusion to their presentation was that some black holes might allow objects to pass through relatively easily. At this stage in time, it is only a theory but one which I believe they will eventually find to be true and this will align with everything I have to say in the next chapter.

The discussion of wormholes or Einstein-Rosen Bridges is important to our discussion on there being a Creator of the Universe for one very obvious reason. All the information provided thus far by science is concerned with the How, What Where and When but as you may have noticed, no one is advocating a theory on the Why. You would think that would be one of the more important questions to ask because if you can understand the 'Why' then it would provide significant understanding to every other detail concerning wormholes. Everything else in the universe has a purpose and intent. From the creation of a new star to the death and destruction of that same star there is a construct in our universe that ensures the process is conducted according to a standard operating procedure. That same procedures allowed us to use both fission and fusion in releasing the most dangerous weapon known to mankind and responsible for the death of over a hundred thousand people, but at the same time providing us with the capability to provide clean energy as long as we don't encounter any more Chernobyls or Three Mile Islands. But the purpose and intent was obvious and we were able to make use of that science as soon as we unlocked the key. But the same is not true for Einstein-Rosen Bridges. Science talks about what they can do, and how in the future we may be able to create a wormhole from one location to another when we need one and not necessarily use only those that naturally occur but therein lies the issue. When Wheeler coined the phrase 'wormhole' he did so because it reminded him of how worms would tunnel their way from the surface of the apple to the centre. The worm did so because it had both a purpose and intent as it fed itself along the way. And when scientists finally harness the means by which they can create their own wormholes, then it too will be done with a purpose and intent. But assuming they exist naturally, which most scientists believe, then what is their purpose and intent in the universe. That is the question they should be asking. 'Why' do they exist? If it is for the purpose of transporting material from one quadrant of the universe to another, then exactly what is the intent of doing so. To maintain a balance; to ensure that the necessary raw materials for galaxy creation are always available in all regions of space? Certainly they weren't created with the intent that some day, billions of years in the future, an organic life form would learn how to harness them as a means of rapid space travel. Whatever their purpose and intent, it is obvious they do exist for a reason, one that we don't quite understand. They certainly didn't arise from accident and as mentioned, everything in our universe has a purpose and intent, so it is impossible to believe that suddenly there is something in our universe with neither a purpose nor an intent. That would be against scientific rationale and that would not be permissible. As such, we must assume they do serve a very important purpose, that they are transference tubes, much in the same manner that the conjugation tubes of bacteria transfer matter, and therefore they are serving someone's or something's purpose. As difficult as this will be for a scientist to admit, wormholes were created for a purpose and intent to serve a higher being in the cosmos and our current level of understanding does not permit us to see what this may be as yet. We are nothing more than students sitting in a classroom where the lecturer is a highly regarded astrophysicist expounding his or her latest theory and we're all nodding our heads, recording everything that's said but in truth we don't have a clue what they're talking about. We'll take our notes home and study them and see if we can make sense out of them later. Welcome to God's classroom.

Black Holes

The concept of an object from which light could not escape was originally proposed by Pierre Simon Laplace in 1795. Using Newton's Theory of Gravity, Laplace calculated that if an object were compressed into a small enough radius, then the escape velocity of that object would be faster than the speed of light. Over the years we have come to refer to these objects that Laplace conceptualized as black holes. Although considerable discussion has been given to black holes already in this book, it is important that there is a clear understanding of exactly what black holes are and how they originate. Currently, we do have a better understanding of these universal objects and science believes it understands both the purpose and intent behind their creation and operation. Scientists are generally in agreement after the careful study and examination of radio-frequency pictures that black holes may have been formed first and once they gathered enough material around them, they were responsible for forming the stellar galaxies. It is an interesting concept, because we have to give consideration to what does the establishment of these dark foreboding holes before the actual formation of the galactic structure mean? Firstly, it indicates that the formation of galaxies is not haphazard. A star, a massive one, had to die in order to create the black hole in order to then create a galaxy. I hardly consider a three-step process accidental or random. That there is an actual step by step building block instruction sheet that is provided with the galaxy building kit is a colossal revelation, though science doesn't see it that way. Secondly, the massive gravitational pull of these black holes is more critical for galaxy formation than the electromagnetic forces or inter-object gravitational forces exerted between stars. As much as these interstellar forces may be tugging on the stars round their own axis, the forces they generate are not strong enough to counteract the pull of these black holes but are able to generate enough resistance to the gravitational pull so that they aren't pulled immediately into the depths of the black hole.

This in itself raises certain questions because astronomers have identified galaxies which exist with no identifiable massive central black hole. Yet, obviously something has drawn these particular non-black hole galaxies together and held them together without the exertion of this huge gravitational pull. So scientists have postulated that the dark matter in our universe might be what also holds together the structures in the universe in the same manner the cytoskeleton in one celled animals holds everything in place as it revolves around the nucleus. Once again, as I mentioned earlier, this points to a common design thread from the micro to the macro, which science is just beginning to acknowledge, but although dark matter may hold together the galactic structure, it still does not answer what brought these star systems together in the absence of a black hole. If we were able to visualize this universal scaffolding provided by the dark matter, we would see a web like structure holding everything in its proper place, like insects caught and distributed across a spider's web, so that the universe and galaxies are provided with a stable framework in which to exist. Even though we know practically nothing regarding dark matter, science does recognize it serves a purpose, a fact that appears to have been overlooked in the previous section on wormholes, where they didn't even try to guess a purpose for those structures. There is no knowledge of whether dark matter is hot, cold or somewhere in between. Dark matter is believed to make up 25% of the universe whereas dark energy is responsible for approximately 70%, but neither of these entities is responsible for the existence of the black holes. In fact some scientists think that dark energy is necessary to counteract gravity and therefore also necessary to stop everything from being drawn into oblivion. So that being the case, dark energy may be the actual antithesis to the purpose of the black hole and this possibility will be important for understanding the next chapter. So without any understanding of how, science suggests that black holes are responsible for the creation of galaxies and dark matter is responsible for preventing the destruction of galaxies, therefore the dark matter was either created simultaneously, or as I have explained,, pre-existed and was contained in the Void.

So as stated, science tells us that a black hole is what remains when a massive star dies. Since stars are nothing but huge fusion reactors made out of gas, they generate a powerful gravitational field that is constantly trying to collapse the star. Meanwhile. the fusion reactions are taking place at the core of the star, attempting to explode the star outward but the gravitational field prevents this from happening. A balance is maintained between the gravitational forces and the explosive forces and the strength of these opposing forces determine the size of the star at any time. As the star begins to die over its lifetime, the fusion reactions start to fail since the fuel for these reactions is consumed over time. Simultaneously, the gravitational field which is no longer kept in balance begins to pull the star's gaseous material inward, while compressing the core. As the core compresses, this will generate heat and eventually causes a supernova explosion in which the material and radiation blasts out into space. What remains behind is the highly compressed, and extremely massive core, who's gravity is so strong that light can no longer escape. At this point, the star no longer exists and is a black hole. Because the core's gravity is tremendous, the core will sink through the fabric of space-time, thereby creating a hole in space and the core is now referred to as the singularity. The external opening or entry point of the black hole is called the event horizon. Once passed the event horizon, an object can no longer be retrieved. The radius of the event horizon is referred to as being the Schwarzschild radius.

In the previous section on wormholes, reference was made to Kerr on his theory of the rotating black hole which is named after him. But that means there is also another type of black hole, which doesn't rotate and that is the Schwarzschild black hole. The Schwarzschild black hole is the simplest black hole, which has only has a singularity and an event horizon. The Kerr black hole is believed to be the most common form of black hole in the universe and it rotates because the star from which it was formed was rotating at the time of its death. When the rotating star collapsed, the core continued to rotate, and the conservation of angular momentum meant that the black hole once formed rotates as well. In addition to the singularity and the event horizon of the Schwarzschild black hole, the Kerr black hole has an ergosphere, which is an egg-shaped region of distorted space around the event horizon caused by the spinning of the black hole. There is also what is known as the static limit, which is the boundary between the ergosphere and normal space. If an object passes through the ergosphere it can still escape from the black hole by using the hole's own rotational energy.

Science admits it really doesn't know what happens once a black hole is entered in to. Even though a black hole cannot be seen, it does have three properties that can be measured, which are mass, electric charge and angular momentum. But once again science is still limited and can only measure the mass of a black hole by the movement of other objects around it. If a black hole has a star moving about it, then it is possible to measure the radius of rotation or speed of orbit of the star around the unseen black hole and then the mass of the black hole can be calculated using Kepler's Modified Third Law of Planetary Motion. It is also known that when material falls into a black hole from a neighbouring star, then that material is heated to millions of degrees Centigrade and accelerated at which point the superheated material will emit X-rays, which can be detected and thereby establish the existence of the black hole which cannot be seen.

In summary black holes are massive pits of gravity that bend space-time because of their incredibly dense centers, or singularities.. When a star dies, it collapses inward rapidly. As it collapses, the star explodes into a supernova, expelling its outer material. The dying star continues to collapse until it becomes a singularity, which consists of zero volume but infinite density. The extreme density of the new singularity pulls everything toward it, including space-time, which it bends. At the event horizon, time begins to slow and the farther into a black hole, the more distorted time becomes. Some scientists believe that if you could survive the initial entry into a black hole, the inside would produce images of the future and the past all at once, but this hypothesis has served well the movie industry in making its multitude of science fiction pictures but is only an extreme idea that most likely will never be proven. But the commonly accepted viewpoint of science is that at the base of its event horizon, time passes far slower than time on Earth.

But the most important hypothesis that scientists are finally arriving at and one which has been postulated by myself for a long time as will be explored in the next chapter is whether there is a connection between the singularity of a black hole and the Big Bang theory. Accordingly, it is the ultimate goal of this section of the book to make the reader aware that our universe likely exploded into existence from what was a singularity, and the cause of that explosion being a major **GodSpark**, which can only be described as intentional, since we already recognize black holes have both a purpose and an intent, both of which once controlled and mastered can serve as a tool of creation.

Energy Pools

Having presented both the wormhole and black hole as likely tools or devices created to serve a purpose that only a higher being could manipulate at this time in human history, even though mankind is desperately searching for ways in which it can harness and take control of these objects, there is still one essential element in the universe creation kit that is still missing. It is probably the most critical of all the factors that interplay in creation and yet, the one that is spoken of the least. At the beginning of this book the laws of thermodynamics were discussed and it is a universal agreement than energy can neither be created nor destroyed. But as we talk of supernovas and vast amounts of energy not only being released but used to generate heat and gravity in order to transform matter on a constant basis, then suddenly we are talking about astronomical amounts of energy that from the prior discussions appears to be simply dispersed into the vastness of space as a star explodes or drawn from mysterious forces that have not been identified as yet when the core is compressed. But these two situations cannot exist if the balance of energy is not controlled, and more importantly, contained. What is required are energy sinks or pools, each absorbing these vast amounts of energy and then holding on to these astronomically powerful forces of the universe until the proper time in which they will be required for transformation.

To put this into perspective, imagine the amount of energy packed into the nucleus of a single uranium atom, then think about the amount of energy radiating from all the stars in the universe for billions of years, now expand that to include the fact that there are 10^{80} particles in the observable universe, and now try to calculate all of it as the total energy running free through space. You can't imagine it because it must be an inconceivably vast quantity that defies your best estimate. You shake your head in defeat as one would think this must be the case but I will let you in on a secret; the truth is that the calculated net amount of energy is probably zero.

It cannot be denied that light, matter and antimatter, which are referred to as 'positive energy' are present in large quantities in our universe. But for everything positive there must be a negative according to physics and therefore there must be an equal amount of 'negative energy' circulating through space simultaneously. Each negative canceling out a positive so that the net energy of the universe is zero. Stephen Hawking suggested that gravity may be one source of negative energy. In his explanation Hawking described how two pieces of matter close to each other must have less positive energy than if they were far apart because it would take a lot of energy to separate them due to the resistance of the gravitational forces. As it takes positive energy to separate them, then it only makes sense that gravity is a negative force trying to hold them together. Since everything in space sits in a relatively stable position, then the negative gravity exerted on every pieces of matter in the universe must have an equal and opposing positive energy that keeps the objects from moving. Therefore, the total energy of the universe being +1 and -1 to simplify things, must be zero.

If that doesn't make you start thinking then try this example from physicists Alexei Filippenko and Jay Pasachoff. In their example they will drop a ball from the top of a building. The ball begins at rest so its energy is zero. As it falls, it gains kinetic energy, so that the ball now has positive energy. But at the same time the ball is being pulled downward by the larger negative gravitational energy. The ball accelerates with increasing positive energy to match the negative energy forces of gravity so that the sum of the two energies is always zero.

So what does this say about the universe at the time of the Big Bang. Since nothing existed, the entire space where the universe would form would be at rest. It has no energy of its own and therefore when light and particles of matter start exploding from the aperture of the Big Bang, then the only way that their energy could be balanced to remain zero would be if there was a gravitational energy equal to the level of positive energy that was being expelled. But that beggars the question, "Where did the negative energy come from?" If it wasn't already there, then it couldn't be manufactured since as the rules of thermodynamics tell us, energy cannot be created or destroyed and the sum total of energy is a constant. Physicists don't have the answers, so they create Quantum Mechanics where extreme quantities of negative and positive energy are randomly fluctuated into existence; the so-called Quantum Flux Theory. Using the Heisenberg Uncertainty Principle they've managed to create an explanation how energy can be realized from nothing. As they explain their 'virtual particle pairs', claiming that there is a positive and a negative particle created simultaneously to cancel or nullify each other, then they say its okay for energy to be created from nothing and break all the rules. In a laboratory, they will claim they can produce such events all the time but they do so without taking into consideration that their laboratory is not a zero environment where nothing exists. In fact their laboratory is filled with energy radiating from a hundred different origins that would need to be nullified before they can actually make such a claim.

This has led to Sean Carroll of Caltech's claiming, "You can create a compact, self-contained universe without needing any energy at all." It is a deliberate distortion of the reality because it ignores all the facts, because his compact universe he later claims requires that you have all the starting elements available in sufficient quantities, an established means of combining them in the right ratios, a means of elevating the temperature to a level that will reduce everything to the atomic or ionic level, and a few billion years to wait for your experiment to see if it is successful. Somewhere the research seemed to forget that when it all started there weren't sufficient quantities of all the elements, there wasn't an incredibly high thermo-energy and their certainly wasn't any atomic fusion chamber available to hold everything in place. There were none of these and the only certainty of the uncertainty principle is if you have nothing as your starting point, then it would be impossible to create something.

Everything in our universe has a history from which it was created. No star, no galaxy, no gaseous cloud came from non-existent molecules that snapped into existence unless there already existed the negative counterpart for every positive force that was created right at the start. That negative energy had to be generated from a source that could generate negative energy in equal amounts of positive energy as a result of coming into contact with a form of energy that we don't necessarily recognize existing within our universe. And whatever that energy or material is that could initiate the conversion of an unknown substance into both positive and negative energy requires a means by which it can be separated from the active ingredients until such time that it is required. This activating energy only needs to be sufficient to initiate the reaction, as afterwards the reaction becomes self sustaining, and not necessarily of a quantity that is equivalent to the positive and negative energy that will be created as a result of activation. For this reason, the pre-universe required or for that matter, even still requires, an energy sink or energy pool that can store what I will refer to as Proto-matter and Proto-energy. I believe that energy sink is what I have referred to previously as the Void. Simply put, for every reaction there is a requirement for activation energy. If we have the reactants (Proto-matter) available pre Big Bang, then they will require an activator (Proto-energy) in order to cause an explosion through the aperture to create our universe. Not unlike the stick of dynamite which is inert and relatively stable but it has the potential to release a tremendous amount of energy when it explodes. But without the much smaller amount of energy provided by the activator, such as a lit match, the reaction is not going to happen.

Since the Big Bang was a positive energy release, then to balance the equation, there must be an equally available negative energy created in the universe simultaneously. And as we have identified gravitational forces as the leading negative energy that can counteract the positive energy of an expanding and developing universe, then we must assume that at the same time as the Big Bang was taking place, there was also the formation of what we can refer to as the Immense Inductor, which was, according to my theory, most likely a supermassive black hole. So now we can see that we are looking back at our earlier equation describing both ends of the Void and as seen in Figures 4 and 9. A perfect balance created by the activation of the matter or energy contained in an energy sink within the void that has the capacity to convert into either positive or negative energies. Key to the process is keeping the Proto-matter from coming in contact with the Proto-energy, other than the specific time or times when the Big Bang was desired.

We already know that dark matter, which makes up approximately 25% of the universe is completely undefined according to scientific experts. As stated earlier, there is no knowledge of whether dark matter is hot, cold, in fact it is indescribable and defies recognition by any of today's test methods. As for dark energy which is responsible for approximately 70% of our universe, it is even more in the proverbial dark than dark matter, and this pun is intended. Also as stated earlier, there are those that believe dark energy through some unknown mechanism may be able to resist or counteract the tremendous gravitational pull of black holes. If we acknowledge that we already have identified those energies we consider as being positive and negative in our universe and these are in an equilibrium or counterbalancing each other, then how are we to assess dark energy. It either has to be both positive and negative in equal proportions, which would be both a theoretical and physical impossibility. Neutrality also presents a problem as it would be contrary to our understanding of energy, or possessing a charge that we have no classification for as yet. It is this latter condition that I wish to focus on. A non-classified status that is only an unknown because we have no instruments with which we can measure its characteristics nor do we have any idea what we should be looking for. At the same time, it is responsible for the creation of dark matter which also remains an unknown to us. For purpose of our discussion, we will refer to dark energy as $\beth^e$ and the dark matter as $\beth^m$. As we know every object in our universe has its opposite equal in order to maintain the balance required. In this situation we will have some manner of $\aleph^e$ energy and $\aleph^m$ matter that will exist as the counterbalance I believe we may already have encountered this $\aleph^e$ and $\aleph^m$ when I referred to them as proto-energy and proto-matter. If this is the case, as I suggest it is, then whereas our universe if filled with these dark elements, the void will contain the proto elements as its primary substances. This would mean that the dark and proto elements didn't need to be created but always existed, having no beginning and no end. They defy our detection and examination because they are not from our existing world. Remember, it is already acknowledged that dark energy and dark matter are not identifiable by any of the methods, tests or knowledge that we currently possess, so it is probably safe to assume that they do not necessarily adhere to the laws of our universe and may have also originated from that alternative dimension referred to as the Void. When dark matter and dark energy transfer into the Void via the supermassive black hole at the distal end of the Void, direct interaction between the $\beth$ substance and the $\aleph$ substance must be avoided as contact probably reacts in the same manner that matter and antimatter does. For this reason the greatest proportion of dark substances is housed within our universe, while the opposite is true for the proto-substance where the vast majority is contained within the Void. This requires that the two are kept separate under most circumstances in order to avoid a cataclysmic explosion. Assuming that the dark matter is contained within an energy sink as soon as it enters the Void so that it is maintained in a state that not only prevents it from coming in contact but counteracts its explosive nature, and the proto-substance in close proximity is also maintained in an non-interactive state, then the only time the two would come together and have an explosive reaction would be if it was a controlled outburst.

You will notice that I deliberately refer to a controlled reaction. To be a controlled reaction means it must not only be contained but also dampened until such time that the energy of the full reaction can be released. Of course if it is a controlled reaction then it must also have a controller and that is the one thing that science is desperately trying to prove does not exist through its contrived flux and uncertainty principle theories. Whereas, they have no way to explain how their theories could even exist, the requirement for an energy dampening mechanism to avoid an uncontrolled reaction should the opposing forces and materials come in to contact according to my theory, are well within our current scientific capabilities and understanding. We can look at energy dampeners in three ways, such as shielding that will result in deflection, dissipation, or adsorption.

Since extraordinarily high temperatures are often the initiator to some reactions then preventing heat from triggering an explosion would be one means of control. Researchers are now exploring the use of magnetic fields to create a very strong heat shield for future spacecrafts. The magnetic field would deflect superhot plasma resulting from the friction created by the spacecraft as it enters the atmosphere. It is anticipated that these magnetic waves could eliminate the need for any other kind of insulation attached to the craft. Proving this to be true will be a major breakthrough in also proving how highly reactive materials can be protected from a trigger by having a magnetic field shield surrounding them. Once generated, the magnetic field can be maintained with very low energy under intense cold. It doesn't get much colder than the approximation of 0 degrees Kelvin, so the possibility of there being a magnetic field in the Void that maintains the stability of the dark energy ($\beth^e$)and the dark matter as ($\beth^m$) is fairly high as will be discussed in the next chapter in regards to quantum flux.

In reference to adsorption, only surface level interactions are taking place so that the bulk of material is not being affected as either the substance is being protected or is the actual protective agent. The adsorption principle of thermodynamics recognizes that temperature is an important factor that affects the adsorption. Adsorption is at its optimum at low temperature, since adsorption is an exothermic process. Therefore low temperature will derive the forward reaction, ensuring that the main body of substance is not consumed. Also, adsorption is in a direct relationship with an increase in pressure up to the point of saturation. Therefore, low temperature and high pressure provides the highest degree of adsorption and prevents the reaction from taking place. The other factor involved is surface area. The larger the surface area of the substance, the higher the rate of adsorption. Considering that the Void is most likely at a temperature approximating 0 Kelvin, and is an infinite space as it exists outside both time and space, under extreme pressure of the proto-matter and proto-energy that exists within its boundaries it is the perfect environment for adsorption to be at a maximum and therefor keeping any reactive matter or energy under control.

The last free energy control mechanism to be described is dissipation and its capability to suppress energy buildup in a manner markedly different from the other two methods. Fluctuation and dissipation dynamics is a common phenomena in physics. It is assumed that energy dissipation was an immediate aftereffect of the Big Bag due to the rapid expansion of the universe, which increased the space between any atoms present. We can see it in its simplest form as Brownian motion. You may recall in high school science class how a particle in water appears to have random motion even though there are no seen forces acting upon it. Your science teacher tried to explain that it was the result of the interactions between the particle and the surrounding fluid, each of them having competing effects. The fluctuation are random forces, causing the motion of the particle. There is also suppression effect of the liquid which leads to the dissipation of some of the particle energy but not all. At that time the teacher probably said, "There are some things in nature that are just there, you have to accept them at face value. We can describe them, we can calculate them, but we really can't explain why they are there." I want you to remember those sentences because it is an underlying principle of the narrative that exists between science and religion. Similar events as described by Brownian motion, resulting from fluctuation and dissipation dynamics, appear throughout cosmology, ranging from condensed matter to extreme astrophysics. In other words, nothing in the universe is entirely isolated from its surrounding environment, and therefore any interactions will lead to fluctuation and dissipation effects. Yet scientists will isolate a specific area of study of the cosmos, ascribing a formula to its motion or thermodynamics, while at the same time ignoring the interactions that are probably occurring because they would be either to difficult to explain or they may interfere with the results as they have presented them. To paraphrase the Gestalt theorem, "The whole is always greater than the sum of its individual parts." That being the case, then by choosing to ignore certain interacting effects in order to arrive at a safe conclusion that supports one's theory is not great science but is actually flawed to a substantial degree.

Accordingly, neutrinos play the most active role in the dissipation process, and neutrino scattering is believed to increase the radiation entropy per particle, provided the degree of anisotropy lies within specific limits. The anisotropic expansion results in the energy dissipation and the entropy will increase substantially. But what actually is a neutrino or anisotropy? To begin with, neutrinos are a neutral subatomic particle with a mass close to zero with very little spin. Because of their inertness, they rarely interact with matter. They belong to the family of leptons which also includes the electron, the muon and the tau particle. They are not subject to strong nuclear forces. So science will tell us that their lack of interaction makes them one of the most abundant particles in the universe, yet they are almost impossible to detect. As for anisotropy, it is the quality of exhibiting properties with different values when measured along axes in different directions. Anisotropy is commonly seen in single crystals of solid elements or compounds, in which atoms, ions, or molecules are arranged in regular lattices. Because of the random distribution of particles in gases and liquids, it is almost never seen in these forms.

So to have anisotropy, something of the nature of a crystal is required to alter the speed and change the direction of a particle, such as a beam of light or in this case a neutrino. But pre Big Bang, and for a long, long time afterwards, there was nothing of a solid or crystalline nature to create the anisotropy. As mentioned, the gaseous nature of the beginning of the universe would have excluded anisotropy from existing to any degree. If it is presumed that molecular hydrogen played a major role in cooling down the primordial gases following the Big Bang then its gaseous nature was not conducive to the anisotropy they claim is important for the dissipation. As several missions on the space station have shown that there are strands of warm molecular gas leaking from several galaxies, and according to Guillard, believed to be the tracings of the dissipation of energy, resulting from shocks and turbulence, caused by the collision of a neighbouring galaxy, then the fact that there is little anisotropy suggests that some quality within the gas itself is causing the dissipation. It was identified that H_2 emission represents a large proportion of the gas and it is therefore thought that the hydrogen itself serves as a powerful coolant. In independent studies of our universe by Peterson, Cluver and Steirwalt, they all concluded that hydrogen molecules appear to be heated by collisions between galaxies and then draw the heat away as these emissions, resulting in gas cooling of the inner regions of the galaxies.

So I raised the neutrino and anisotropy postulation for two reasons. The first is to demonstrate that science throws everything they can think of into a big bag with the hope that if they swirl it around long enough, something will come out of the bag to justify their theorems. There's still the hope that neutrinos and the heat dissipation through anisotropy will some how account for the events immediately after the Big Bang. They will even try to tie their theory into the existence of dark matter. Technically they will say, that it is dark because it has very little interaction with electromagnetic radiation but in spite of it only making up approximately 25%

of our universe, it must be stable, since it hasn't decayed. If it is stable, then there are those that believe it must consist of neutrinos or something similar. The something similar that they are referring to are weak interacting massive particles or WIMPs. There are others that theorize the dark matter could be primordial black holes or even diphotonic particles that don't give off any light, which they refer to as axions. Hard to dispute considering we are told that Neutrinos are abundant but practically undetectable as would be the case with WIMPs as well. And axions, well there just purely theoretical. Hard to deny a theory that makes use of non-visible, non-proven, non-detectable and non-interacting particles to explain the origins of the universe.

But what we do know is that our universe is permeated by hot, turbulent, magnetized plasmas, that are located in active galactic nuclei, supernova remnants, intergalactic and interstellar medium, as well as in solar coronas and solar winds. This plasma state, phasing somewhere between matter and energy is in a flux and that will be important for discussion in our next chapter, as well. Our comprehension of the plasma is largely based on measurements of electromagnetic radiation such as light or X-rays, originating from particles that are heated and accelerated as a result of energy dissipation in turbulent environments within the plasma. Therefore the net result of this turbulence is the energizing of the plasma, which then creates the dissipation to keep it under control and prevent a massive reaction. The neutrinos, electrons, protons and any other ions become important as the plasma becomes excited as they will be extruded in any explosion, and they become the essential building blocks of a universe. Yet, science is still trying to determine what it is that causes the plasma to be heated and the particles accelerated by turbulent fluctuations. Not only that, but what keeps it under control by ensuring the heat is dissipated almost all of the time, which leads to the question as to why if it could be adequately controlled practically forever, should it fail that one time, permitting the event known as the Big Bang.

It should be obvious, that when science requires a theory in order to make another theory work, and then a third theory to deal with the deficiencies in the second theory that was supposedly the remedy, then the true fact is that none of these theories are accurate or adequate and they certainly can't account for the most important questions that need to be asked and answered. Long ago, we all learned a lesson that two wrongs do not make a right from our parents, and science doesn't get a free pass from that age-old adage by just adding on a new theory to the old in an attempt to explain why the others were incomplete. Compounding theory upon theory until they reach an unknown point or obstacle, so that they label the original theory as acceptable because they can always look to the future when it might be possible to solve this latest obstacle, is not science; it's science fiction. Astrophysics has become almost identical to the puzzle of Russian nesting dolls. You open one doll, only to find another inside, only to find another, then another. No different from manufacturing the next theory and then the next, each one giving theoretical evidence to the last but then raising an entire set of new issues. Eventually, you reach the last nesting doll, only to find that it can't be opened and it doesn't provide you with the answers you were seeking. It is a dead end that can't be penetrated any further. The questions that need to be answered all begin with the word, "Why'. Why do we have passages through space and possibly even universes if there isn't anything that makes use of them? Why do we have objects in space that essentially act as giant vacuum cleaners but never have to be emptied after they've absorbed the entire essence of the very thing from which they were created? Why is it that we acknowledge everything in the universe is already in a balance, yet we have particles that have no charge that seem to be independent of the other particle theories. Why is it we can have a substance consisting of an energy and matter that is beyond detection on any of our measuring devices, yet we can so readily attribute to it properties that make our theories work? But most of all, they need to ask why if everything is maintained in a energy dissipated state, that a Big Bang could even occur? The facts are, that if everything is stable, and there is no existing imbalance, then the unexpected and unwarranted explosion that began it all is not going to happen. Unless, as the evidence provided in the next chapter suggests, there is a large spark of energy that can't be accounted for.

The fact is that science doesn't have a well-defined particle physics model that includes dark matter and admittedly they haven't even started to examine its relationship to dark energy. There are so many missing pieces to their jigsaw puzzle that its hard to believe they still won't admit there must have been a guiding hand or cosmic consciousness that made it all possible. It is evident that the potential instability of dark energy ($\beth^e$) and dark matter ($\beth^m$) can be kept completely under control within the Void, when the Void is, as I expect it to be, a physical containment of all things required to start a universe, and separated from the proto-energy ($\aleph^e$) and proto-matter ($\aleph^m$), which when in contact with its dark substance counterparts inhibits and overrides the dissipation processes, and what could very well be particles in the dark matter holding a neutral charge suddenly becoming charged by the excessive radiation, thus resulting in a universe-creating, unimaginable reaction. That is the **Godspark**!

Chapter 7: The Creation Timeline

In the past, if one was to make an argument for God having a hand in the creation of the universe, then they made the mistake of thinking it was probably best to start examining the book of Genesis before they engaged in any intense scientific discussion. As you can recognize from the previous six chapters, it was necessary to take a different approach. I personally believe it is best to understand the science, with its numerous theoretical models, before you even try to examine the book of Genesis. Now that you are in possession of the general understanding of the birth of the universe from some of the greatest scientific minds, as well as an awareness of the latest scientific discoveries regarding the Big Bang, you are in a position to try and understand what was written in the Bible. The old approach was to try and make the science fit the Biblical story and that was always going to be a recipe for disaster because the book of Genesis was never to be interpreted literally. In fact, as you will see in the pages that follow, it was merely a summary of the science, capturing in but a few lines, everything we have already been discussing thus far, and presenting it in terms that could be understood by a barely out of the stone age primitive society. And its summary is actually quite good in that it still contains all of the essential knowledge of how our universe began.

Let us look at the verse in Genesis regarding an evening and a morning, days before the sun was actually created. "How can that be?" a very typical argument by those opposed to anything Biblical. We have already looked at the CMB or Cosmic Microwave Background that scientists have measured from the time of the Big Bang. As energy, whether it be light, microwaves, gamma rays, etc., it is all electromagnetic wave possessing both frequency and length. Imagine a single piece of string and depending on the frequency, a small part of the string has a wavelength that we can register as visible light. This essentially is the premise of the String Theory except there would be a lot of threads involved and how they vibrate and at what frequency is still a topic of discussion. Therefore, at the time of the Big Bang, there would be a small component registering as emissions of light as the electromagnetic waves shot out from the aperture or tear in the Void, becoming apparent as these waves slowed down into the visible spectrum of light. Therefore, what we would identify as light must have existed before any sun or star had even been created. Examine how this first day is described in Genesis and this all will become clear:

בְּרֵאשִׁית, בָּרָא אֱלֹהִים, אֵת הַשָּׁמַיִם, וְאֵת הָאָרֶץ.

1 In the beginning God created the heaven and the earth.

וְהָאָרֶץ, הָיְתָה תֹהוּ וָבֹהוּ, וְחֹשֶׁךְ, עַל־פְּנֵי תְהוֹם; וְרוּחַ אֱלֹהִים, מְרַחֶפֶת עַל־פְּנֵי הַמָּיִם.

2 Now the earth was unformed and void, and darkness was upon the face of the deep; and the spirit of God hovered over the face of the waters.

וַיֹּאמֶר אֱלֹהִים, יְהִי אוֹר; וַיְהִי־אוֹר.

3 And God said: 'Let there be light.' And there was light.

וַיַּרְא אֱלֹהִים אֶת־הָאוֹר, כִּי־טוֹב; וַיַּבְדֵּל אֱלֹהִים, בֵּין הָאוֹר וּבֵין הַחֹשֶׁךְ.

4 And God saw the light, that it was good; and God divided the light from the darkness.

Table 4

For the purposes of explanation I will use the direct translation from the Hebrew Torah or Old Testament as it provides the most accurate wording of what was originally written without any of the faulty translations over the centuries or the recent alterations that have been made by the politically correct faction that felt a need to write commentary into every sentence and change any word that they thought might be offensive, even if it meant changing God's own words.

The first sentence is unique in the entire Hebrew language. It uses a word בְּרֵאשִׁית pronounced as 'bereshith' to indicate the beginning, yet the more common phrase would have been 'behetcheleh'. In fact, you won't see this word used again in the entire Old Testament. It is unique to this one sentence and in fact it looks like two words have been combined into one; בָּרָא and שִׁית. Ancient Hebrew was written without any vowels, so בָּרָא could have been identical to the second word in the sentence בָּרָא which means created. If that is the case, then the sentence actually reads שִׁית or Sith created God, who it turn created the heaven and the earth. An interesting turn of phrase since Sith, Seth or Set, the ancient god of Egypt was the primordial god of Chaos, which as mentioned earlier, was and is another name for the Void.

But what is the meaning of Set or Seth besides a name in the Hebrew and ancient Egyptian languages. Translated, it means to 'put in place' or essentially 'replace'. Is it just a coincidence that a word used to describe the Void can also be used to indicate that there was an event where the constituents of the Void, whether it be proto-matter and proto-energy, or something completely foreign to our understanding and still unnamed, came in contact with an oppositely charged matter or energy, i.e.. dark matter and dark energy, and this combination was suddenly or instantaneously 'replaced' with the physical matter and energy of our universe. For a people that had just made their exodus from Egypt, the word Set would have been a familiar word to help explain a difficult concept of the creation. From their own legends and pre-monotheistic beliefs the would have understood the reference to Chaos. The event was not so much an incredulous act of creating something out of nothing but in fact it was merely a replacement of something that had been there before. A transformation, so to speak from the pre-Semitic language where Seth did indicate a Replacement. And since energy according to science is known to transform all the time, there is nothing new or remarkable about this event other than they understood the concept of the transformation of energy.

There is another mystery contained in this sentence and that is the use of the word אֱלֹהִים to describe God. The word is actually plural and translates as Gods. Many religious scholars have attempted to explain the use of the plural in a variety of ways. The God of the Hebrews was the equal to all the other gods in the ancient world, so they referred to him in plural. Or it was an early implication of the Catholic trinity. So early in fact that its use 1300 years before Jesus would have been meaningless to anyone living at the time of the Exodus. Or as the Kabbalist would say, it was an indication of the seventy-two names by which God could use but once again this would have been a meaningless expression to the first Israelites and would have served only to confuse them at a time when Moses was trying to establish monotheism. So why would God refer to himself in the plural unless he was a plurality. In our efforts to anthropomorphize God, we considered it necessary to provide him with a somewhat human form, but what if God has no form at all. No corporal structure. We need to remember that he is most likely on the other side of the equation, or perhaps the equal sign itself, which still places him in the interior of the Void and not existing directly within our universe. Therefore, like everything else within the Void, there are no spatial dimensions which can be used in our effort to describe God. He is shapeless, timeless and most likely a consciousness that is a composite of multiple ions or unknown elements that exist within the Void that we have no understanding or comprehension of. Therefore, God recognized that he was a composite of unique parts, each contributing to his self-awareness and rather than make the statement that 'We are One', instead the reference is to being 'I am Many.' It makes me think back to the question of when the first AI we develop that has self awareness comes on-line. Will it refer to itself as being a single thinking unit of mechanical life, or will it make reference to the collective number of brilliant minds that contributed to its existence? Is it merely an extension of their minds or does it now possess a mind of its own? It would appear in our case, God recognizes the he is the sum of multiple parts and would not exist without their working in cooperation and collectively.

The second sentence is symbolic and once again expressed in terms that the Children of Israel could comprehend but when we examine the wording we can see that it is painting a far more complicated picture than what was expressed in the first sentence. Clearly the earth being referred to is not our Earth and the heaven is not a reference to the atmosphere or sky. The earth was unformed, implying that there wasn't any solid matter at this point. In fact it was בהו which translates as Void. If God wanted to say 'barren' or 'empty', implying that a planet already existed, then the words 'aker' or 'raik' would have been far more meaningful and appropriate. Instead he is referring to a specific situation that is in sync with an unformed unit, implying a non-existence due to the absence of practically everything. It is the seeds of what will become our universe, our galaxy, our solar system and eventually our Earth. In fact, what God is providing is a unique description of the state of non-existence just prior to the Big Bang. The darkness was upon the deep, implying that there were no reference points in this Void. Nothing could be seen, nothing could be determined, and the only sensation was the endlessness, as there was no definition to either the space or time that God was occupying since such concepts didn't actually exist. The only way we can even try to imagine a comparable situation is to see ourselves falling into a deep dark cavern that doesn't seem to have any bottom and is so dark that we can't see any of the walls lining the cavern as we descend. We continue to fall, until our mind tries to convince us that perhaps we aren't really falling but just floating since we never strike the bottom and our senses have no reference points to suggest we are falling because with out time their can be no rate of descent.

And then we're given a glimpse of the moment just before the Big Bang, at that point of constriction in Figure 11 where everything is still dark and chaotic. An actual description of the **Godspark** when we read the word רוח which is translated as spirit most often but also can mean the breath, ghost, or even consciousness. I prefer that last word because I think that is exactly what occurred.

Figure 11

God became aware of his own consciousness. Those sparks of proto-energy within the void seen as the white spots in Figure 11, becoming interconnected through a neuro-network, so whereas individually they were inert but combined they could generate thought and God became 'aware'. God is described as hovering over something like a pool of water but it certainly isn't water because that hasn't been created yet. Recall that the preceding sentence refers to the 'face of the deep' now it is given a further clarification by saying 'face of the waters'. The deep is a pool containing a substance but as already mentioned, it was not water. It is an energy sink filled with the plasma similar to what was described in the last chapter. This plasma has no innate ability to do anything other than simply be contained. It's energy is being dissipated. The near 0° Kelvin temperatures of the void deflects the radiation by preserving any electromagnetic radiation in a near pristine state without any decay and adsorption is at its maximum. The vast quantity of neutrinos and other subatomic particles in the plasma are without any charge, therefore inclined to remain stable and non-reactive even if they come into contact with the few charged particles in the plasma. The reality is that unless there is a large charge applied directly into the plasma that upsets this balance, nothing will ever happen and our universe will not be born.

According to the bible, God obviously places himself in contact with this inert plasma that contains most likely dark energy and dark matter, unlike His own surroundings of proto-energy and proto plasma. The same barriers that keep the energy sink containing this material stable, most likely also prohibits the contents of the Void from coming into contact, otherwise the Big Bang would be a constant and continuous event and we know that is not the case. Through God's consciousness, spirit or 'breath', he manages to interact with the plasma in the energy sink, much in the way that matter reacts with anti-matter in our universe. For those that aren't aware of the existence of anti-matter, it is a very real entity but it doesn't exist for very long in our universe. If you were carrying a bucket of anti-matter water, you would see nothing different about it. For all intents and purposes, it looks, feels, and probably even tastes like regular water, the only difference being that the protons of the oxygen and two hydrogen atoms are holding a negative charge rather than a positive one, and instead of electrons, the nuclei are being circled by positrons. Where we find the obvious difference is when we pour that bucket of anti-matter water into a normal pool of water. As soon as the anti-matter water makes contact with normal water, there is a massive explosion, releasing a tremendous amount of energy. An equivalent amount of water from our universe will disintegrate with the volume of its antimatter counterpart. They obliterate one another during the explosion, while releasing a huge quantity of energy.

As there is a net volume of the dark plasma in this energy pool, then it would only be a matter of altering the neutral charges of some of the neutrinos to be the opposite of the charges of any particles within the plasma. The existing particles of the dark energy are most likely electrons, because positrons are rare in our universe and since everything in our universe originated from the Big Bang, then the dark plasma was most likely also containing an abundance of electrons. Therefore, by transforming the neutrinos at the surface barrier into positrons, as soon as they came in contact with electrons there would occur the **GodSpark** to set everything into motion. Essentially, the sentence is describing a very small net loss of God's spirit, or consciousness in order to ignite the Big Bang through the **GodSpark**. If God in whatever context he might exist resides within the Void, is composed of the proto-energy and proto-matter or something similar, then what would escape from such an explosion would be the exact opposite, emitting light and deliberately attempting to form solid matter. And since we know our universe consists primarily of the dark energy and dark matter, then they must be the exact opposites to what exists in the Void. As the energy from the release exceeds the stability of the containment capability of the energy sink, it must be released into a realm which is not in direct contact with the contents of the Void, otherwise the existence of the Void itself is placed at risk. That being the case, then it has to be expelled from the Void, and does so by ripping a hole into the fabric of time and space, as it spews into whatever lays beyond that boundary. And for the first time there is light in what will become our universe.

Notice how line four of Genesis describes the separation of the light from the darkness. This was no a reference to day and night because that concept didn't even exist at this time. This is a description of the barrier that exists between the Void and our universe. A barrier between chaos on one side and order on the other. As previously mentioned, the two can never come into contact with each other, otherwise there would be total annihilation. Exactly what is this barrier that divides our two existences? It is likely not much different from the same forces which kept the material in the energy sink form becoming heated and charged. Primarily electromagnetic in nature, with heavy clouds of hydrogen gas perhaps on our side of the equation, preventing any transference of energy or matter across this barrier in either direction.

The following diagram will help explain what the first sentences of Genesis has just been describing for over 3370 years. From our position marked 'You Are Here', our scientific instruments can peer back through the funnel of the universe and measure the CMB that we define as the first light of that first day in Genesis. All the ingredients required to create the mass of our universe are contained in the bands marked as first atoms, but they won't coalesce until billions of years later to from the galaxies, solar systems and planets. The subatomic particles must have been present within the plasma that resided in the energy sink, otherwise the atoms could not come into existence no matter how much time transpired after the Big Bang.

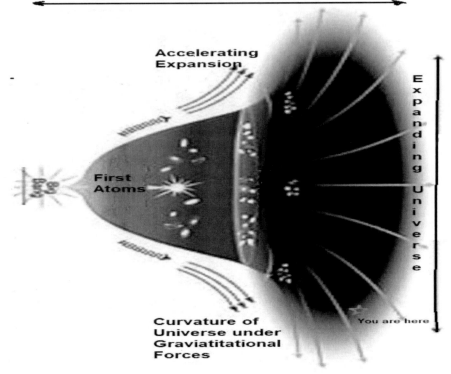

Figure 12

The view from our position on the slight curvature at the edge of our perspective provides a somewhat biased concept of the universe. Due to the parallax, we can identify that our universe is expanding, and that there is a slight curvature, but in the main part it appears flat. If anything had preceded us and was already on a larger part of the curvature that was now moving backward in the opposite direction, our instruments would not let us see it or even measure it but we have discussed all that already. But the inability to see around the curve does explain why the majority of astrophysicists will still argue that the universe is nothing but a flat plane.

Now it should become obvious why the word רוח (ruach) was used in Sentence Two. It was the 'consciousness' of God that provided the will to create, but it was the 'breath' of God which came into actual contact with the deep. A small, non-essential component of the Almighty that represents no risk to himself but still has the required opposite charge to interact with the contents of the deep. A cloud of gas that had the ability to incite neutrinos to generate a charge and thereby react with the abundance of electrons within the deep. And even the name 'deep' is accurate when we now realize it is a 'sink' collecting this charged material that has been collected within the Void but kept separate through the combined means of deflection, adsorption and dissipation described in the last chapter. It most certainly is what we would refer to in our reality as an energy sink and a very well constructed one.

But something amazing happens at the same time the Big Bang is releasing all the contents from the energy sink into our universe. Since it is a universal law that a balance must be maintained, whether it be in the light universe or dark universe, our universe or the Void, then the energy sink cannot remain empty, otherwise the crucial balance in the Void will become unbalanced and at risk of collapse. That being the case, as the extrusion is taking place into our universe, there must be an inward suction at the opposite end of the energy sink to replace the dark material being lost. The best way to achieve that would be through the formation of a supermassive black hole that links directly into the energy sink. In this way, the entire process is contained in what becomes a production cycle or loop. What enters into the energy sink is essentially identical to that which has exited to create our universe. This requires a tremendous amount of material to be neutralized by this gigantic black hole as it swallows our universe. Before this material passes through the Void into to energy sink, it undergoes a process by which the matter is reduced in large part to a neutrino status and other non charged particles. (see Figure 13)

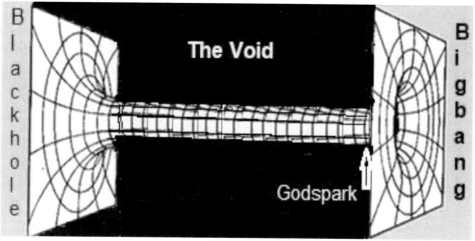

Figure 13

There will still be small amounts of dark matter and dark energy that will escape this neutralization process, thus retaining a charge, and therefore providing the necessary material to be ignited for the next Big Bang. And why would I mention the next Big Bang? Because with any energy sink, its containment level has a threshold, at which time the sink must be emptied, otherwise it will spill outside of its containment and endanger everything it comes in contact with. So in fact, the Big Bang is no longer a unique event but merely an emptying of this containment vessel by using a simple process. God sacrifices a small, perhaps non-essential fraction of himself, referred to as his breath, in order to ignite the reaction and then expels the explosive force outside of the protective barrier of the Void. This prevents any chain reaction occurring within the Void, which would not only be a God ending event but also the ultimate ending to everything that there is. This fabric of the Void serves not only as a firewall, but it is the only barrier standing between existence and total obliteration of everything. But as mentioned, the word 'ruach' can also refer to spirit and that is appropriate as well, since as we already know, energy cannot be created or destroyed, merely transformed, and that breath of God that ignited the Godspark is now part of the essence of everything that comes into existence within our universe. The spirit of God is within everything we see around us.

I know for some it will be difficult to accept that what we refer to as 'The Creation' may be one of many creations. In fact there is no means by which we can determine if we were the first or even the hundredth of such creations. It may be a blow to the ego to think we might not be the first but considering the timeline between these Big Bang events, it could be that we are the only one at this time unless those scientists promoting a multiverse theory turn out to be correct. Probably easiest for us to appreciate that the event will be repeated every time that the 'waters of the deep' threaten to overflow. The most efficient way for this process to be controlled would be to have the reaction become a continuous loop so that there was a constant discharge through the breach every time the 'deep' became filled to its threshold, ensuring that the flow was always unidirectional. The **GodSpark**, is a constant presence, so that the reaction can take place over and over again, almost like the ignition of petrol in a combustion engine. The timing between sparks would likely be tens of billions of years, but as the research by Hooper suggested there could be some validity to his statement that the CMB rings he had detected could have been generated from a prior universe but not one that is necessarily co-existing with ours simultaneously

One of the chief arguments scientists will make against the Genesis story, or Creation Myth as they refer to it, is the mention of days in the first chapter. Seriously, this is one of the weakest arguments they can make but one which religious leaders can't seem to dispel because they themselves have become locked into the dogma preached that a day is a day, 24 hours, and that's just the way it is. Well, that's not the way it is because without the presence of a sun, there can be no concept of a day. Without an Earth rotating on its axis as it circles the Sun there can't even be a concept of hours. So let's dispel this false narrative about days and realize God was describing phases of the creation. As noted earlier, the temperature of the universe immediately following the Big Bang was incredibly hot but as the universe began to immediately expand, temperatures decreased and the distance the wavelengths traveled increased, so that time was being dramatically affected. Therefore even the phases referred to as days in Genesis were not and could not have been of equal length, becoming shorter with each passing phase as the expansion of the universe accelerated. So as that first phase or day may have been ten billion years long according to our own perspective of measuring time, from God's perspective it may have been practically instantaneous.

ו וַיֹּאמֶר אֱלֹהִים, יְהִי רָקִיעַ בְּתוֹךְ הַמָּיִם, וִיהִי מַבְדִּיל, בֵּין מַיִם לָמָיִם.	**6** And God said: 'Let there be a firmament in the midst of the waters, and let it divide the waters from the waters.'
ז וַיַּעַשׂ אֱלֹהִים, אֶת־הָרָקִיעַ, וַיַּבְדֵּל בֵּין הַמַּיִם אֲשֶׁר מִתַּחַת לָרָקִיעַ, וּבֵין הַמַּיִם אֲשֶׁר מֵעַל לָרָקִיעַ; וַיְהִי־כֵן.	**7** And God made the firmament, and divided the waters which were under the firmament from the waters which were above the firmament; and it was so.
ח וַיִּקְרָא אֱלֹהִים לָרָקִיעַ, שָׁמָיִם; וַיְהִי־עֶרֶב וַיְהִי־בֹקֶר, יוֹם שֵׁנִי. {פ}	**8** And God called the firmament Heaven. And there was evening and there was morning, a second day. {**P**}

Table 5

If we examine the second phase or what is referred to as Day 2, in sentence 6 to 8 , then we see that it concerns the formation of the galactic space. The reference to firmament is an indication of solid masses, which we can assume would include the stars, the planets, and any other solid material that occupies space or the heavens. The dark matter and energy that separates the galaxies and with the use of our senses, are referred to as waters. Waters above and below the galaxies, looking like vast endless seas of nothingness. And this is exactly what the universe at that time would have looked like. From out of these vast seas of dark substance the gases began to cool and coalesce and solid materials started to come together and circle the hot centers of cooling gases. So approximately ten billion years after the Big Bang, we have identifiable galaxies forming, containing thousands of solar systems that are separate from the emptiness of space. The galaxies are suspended within the darkness of space, so it would be accurate to describe the vastness of the universe as being both above and below each of these galactic formations.

The process by which particles within the dark matter and dark energy can actually form the ions and atoms of our universe revolves around the confirmed discovery of the Higgs boson particle in 2012. I'll discuss this a little later on at the end of this chapter because these particles were erroneously called the God particle because of their ability to create positive and negative particles from seemingly nothing, including electrons necessary in the formation of atoms. These charged particles are derived from subatomic particles that lack any charge. The error was in thinking that these were anything more than simple building blocks along the pathway of constructing a universe. They are neither the driving force nor the initiator but merely a link in a very long chain. The key was having the dark matter available in the first place so that substrate was present when required, upon which the conversion process could take place. It is this substrate which I will relate to sentence 6. These bosons are awash in a sea of similar particles referred to as the Higgins field. What was thought to be empty space was not empty at all but to accurately describe it would be a sea of particles. And something did cause these particles to collide with protons and other matter, providing the particles that split off with spin and charge in order to create a firmament that now parted this particle sea.

But it would be a mistake to think that the bosons were responsible for this sudden development, if we could even consider a few billion years as being sudden. The bosons were merely doing what they were designed to do, but the question that should have been raised by those in the laboratory was who designed this amazing process. Furthermore, why were Higgs bosons even present if it was not known they would be necessary for the process to take place. They were just one more cog in a very complicated developmental procedure and as scientists identify each new step along this cosmic pathway, they have to realize that a complex series of steps does not and cannot occur by accident from random elements. Perhaps one or two steps in a process can occur in their proper order accidentally and according to the laws of probability but for an entire sequence of numerous complex, integral and consequential events, all of them necessitating the right amount of material, correct charge and precise energy loads, etc., would be impossible. Meanwhile throughout this entire procedure the delicate balance is still being maintained, preserving proper ratios and avoiding system collapse, that is a calculated statistical impossibility. Rather than continue to look down a microscope to find something so small it barely registers, perhaps it's time to look heavenward and recognize there's someone pulling the strings and turning the knobs.

ט וַיֹּאמֶר אֱלֹהִים, יִקָּווּ הַמַּיִם מִתַּחַת הַשָּׁמַיִם אֶל-מָקוֹם אֶחָד, וְתֵרָאֶה, הַיַּבָּשָׁה; וַיְהִי-כֵן.	**9** And God said: 'Let the waters under the heaven be gathered together unto one place, and let the dry land appear.' And it was so.
י וַיִּקְרָא אֱלֹהִים לַיַּבָּשָׁה אֶרֶץ, וּלְמִקְוֵה הַמַּיִם קָרָא יַמִּים; וַיַּרְא אֱלֹהִים, כִּי-טוֹב.	**10** And God called the dry land Earth, and the gathering together of the waters called He Seas; and God saw that it was good.
יא וַיֹּאמֶר אֱלֹהִים, תַּדְשֵׁא הָאָרֶץ דֶּשֶׁא עֵשֶׂב מַזְרִיעַ זֶרַע, עֵץ פְּרִי עֹשֶׂה פְּרִי לְמִינוֹ, אֲשֶׁר זַרְעוֹ-בוֹ עַל-הָאָרֶץ; וַיְהִי-כֵן.	**11** And God said: 'Let the earth put forth grass, herb yielding seed, and fruit-tree bearing fruit after its kind, wherein is the seed thereof, upon the earth.' And it was so.
יב וַתּוֹצֵא הָאָרֶץ דֶּשֶׁא עֵשֶׂב מַזְרִיעַ זֶרַע, לְמִינֵהוּ, וְעֵץ עֹשֶׂה-פְּרִי אֲשֶׁר זַרְעוֹ-בוֹ, לְמִינֵהוּ; וַיַּרְא אֱלֹהִים, כִּי-טוֹב.	**12** And the earth brought forth grass, herb yielding seed after its kind, and tree bearing fruit, wherein is the seed thereof, after its kind; and God saw that it was good.
יג וַיְהִי-עֶרֶב וַיְהִי-בֹקֶר, יוֹם שְׁלִישִׁי. {פ}	**13** And there was evening and there was morning, a third day.

Table 6

By the time of the third phase or Day 3, the solar system had formed to a point that in our case, the planet we called Earth had solidified and hydrogen and oxygen atoms had come together to produce molecules of water. Water which filled the crevices and depressions of the Earth's crust and it was the one necessity if life was to be introduced to our planet. By the end of the third day all life was still confined to the oceans as primitive life forms but those life-forms had evolved far beyond the waters edge and were now seen as vegetative life forms on the dry soils of the planet. This indicates that an atmosphere had formed and enveloped the Earth at this time, but it was still probably highly toxic to most life forms. As previously discussed, the one celled organisms joined into strands of algae and as the first forms of plant life they began to progress more rapidly into other forms. It was still a long way away from an oxygen rich atmosphere being produced by the photosynthesis of the variety of plant life, but the Book of Genesis is only implying that it was a starting point and that eventually this would bring about a diversity of plant life that would be able to reproduce and sustain itself steadily. It is almost as if someone had a camera of these Pre-Cambrian times where they would see it from a bird's eye view, recording the primitive plant life that covered the soil but the organisms in the seas were far too small to visualize. .

Originally the Pre-Cambrian Era was described as the period before life appeared on Earth. But paleontologist have found over the past few decades through the fossil records that it was teeming with life but it was just hard to find. Since then they have renamed it the Crytozoic Eon, meaning 'hidden life.' The Pre-Cambrian period lasted up to 600 million years ago and has been divided into three eras; the Hadean, the Archean and the Proterozoic. The Hadean period was about the formation of the Earth and this lasted from about 4.5 billion years ago until approximately 3.8 billion years ago. Life appeared in the Archean Era around 3.6 billion years ago according to the fossil record. During this period which lasted until about 2.5 billion years ago the atmosphere of Earth was still relatively toxic and it was not until about 1.9 billion years ago, during the Proterozoic era that it evolved into the oxygen rich atmosphere that we are accustomed to. By 1.6 billion years ago, eukaryotes as one celled organisms were well established and life remained that way for the next billion years.

We do know from the Proterozoic ("Early Life") Era that two super continents formed on either side of the equator, similar to what is written in sentence 9. The earth's core has cooled sufficiently that there were fewer volcanoes erupting and the centers of these two continents were now quite large and stable. At this time, life is still found only in the ocean, but at around 1.7 billion years ago, single-celled creatures appeared that had a nucleus. About 30 million years before the end of the Proterozoic which would be about 550 million years ago, multi-celled creatures began to appear. The single-celled plants such as algae have been producing oxygen for about two billion years, and now the atmosphere has gradually become oxygen rich. But this oxygen is poisonous to the few life forms living on the Earth during the early Proterozoic causing any of these early life forms to disappear. But amazingly, as old life forms die, new forms of life begin, such as vegetation began to cover the earth as the oxygen in the atmosphere continues to increase and combine chemically with other elements, making the soils mineral rich.

For the longest time scientists claimed it took eons upon eons for that first life to appear, but as we can see, recent discoveries suggest it may have made a much earlier appearance, in fact as soon as the Earth cooled and water appeared on the face of the planet. A statement that is very reminiscent of what we read in the Book of Genesis. Hence the numerous theories that have been flouted as science tried to explain the inexplicable, such as that life may have ridden here on an asteroid that accidentally collided with the Earth or another theory claiming that the molecules suddenly became self-replicating due to catalysts, can all be discarded, since this last theory failed to explain how these catalysts managed to appear from out of nowhere. The truth is as it was stated in Genesis, on that third day God separated the land from the waters and the seas teemed with life, that eventually made its way on to the land as vegetation once the algae had converted the atmosphere into being an oxygen rich protective zone. But that change to the atmosphere took a couple of billion years, even though to God it was merely another day's work, and that transformation relates directly to what happened on the next day.

It is probably this fourth day that is the most contentious and the one that creates the most anxiety when trying to respond to the scientists that point out that the Earth is already in existence with life in the oceans and plants on the ground but there isn't even a sun or moon in the sky to divide the day from night. They will point this out with derision and say it is impossible. But that is not exactly what is written in these six sentences. What is does say is that these orbs in the sky became visible by the next phase or 4th Day. In Sentence 16 there is no statement that God created the sun and the moon on this day, only that he made them, according to the word וַיַּעַשׂ that is used indicating that they were already there, but needed an alteration in order that they could shine accordingly so that they could then divide the days and the seasons.

יד וַיֹּאמֶר אֱלֹהִים, יְהִי מְאֹרֹת בִּרְקִיעַ הַשָּׁמַיִם, לְהַבְדִּיל, בֵּין הַיּוֹם וּבֵין הַלָּיְלָה; וְהָיוּ לְאֹתֹת וּלְמוֹעֲדִים, וּלְיָמִים וְשָׁנִים.

14 And God said: 'Let there be lights in the firmament of the heaven to divide the day from the night; and let them be for signs, and for seasons, and for days and years;

טו וְהָיוּ לִמְאוֹרֹת בִּרְקִיעַ הַשָּׁמַיִם, לְהָאִיר עַל-הָאָרֶץ; וַיְהִי-כֵן.

15 and let them be for lights in the firmament of the heaven to give light upon the earth.' And it was so.

טז וַיַּעַשׂ אֱלֹהִים, אֶת-שְׁנֵי הַמְּאֹרֹת הַגְּדֹלִים: אֶת-הַמָּאוֹר הַגָּדֹל, לְמֶמְשֶׁלֶת הַיּוֹם, וְאֶת-הַמָּאוֹר הַקָּטֹן לְמֶמְשֶׁלֶת הַלַּיְלָה, וְאֵת הַכּוֹכָבִים.

16 And God made the two great lights: the greater light to rule the day, and the lesser light to rule the night; and the stars.

יז וַיִּתֵּן אֹתָם אֱלֹהִים, בִּרְקִיעַ הַשָּׁמָיִם, לְהָאִיר, עַל-הָאָרֶץ.

17 And God set them in the firmament of the heaven to give light upon the earth,

יח וְלִמְשֹׁל, בַּיּוֹם וּבַלַּיְלָה, וּלְהַבְדִּיל, בֵּין הָאוֹר וּבֵין הַחֹשֶׁךְ; וַיַּרְא אֱלֹהִים, כִּי-טוֹב.

18 and to rule over the day and over the night, and to divide the light from the darkness; and God saw that it was good.

יט וַיְהִי-עֶרֶב וַיְהִי-בֹקֶר, יוֹם רְבִיעִי. {פ}

19 And there was evening and there was morning, a fourth day

Table 7
Table 7

This word יַעַשׂ which is now written in the modern Hebrew as יַעַץ means to 'make' as in to 'advise' someone to do something. So the actual question should be why would it be necessary for God to advise the sun and moon to become the lights of the day and night respectively and the answer is quite easy when we look at planets like Venus and recognize our Earth looked much the same in its early days having an atmosphere so thick in nitrogen and methane that it was like pea soup and until it thinned and stabilized, by the end of the Proterozoic Era as discussed previously, there was very little light able to penetrate. So it wasn't until the transition finally completed of establishing an atmosphere consisting primarily of nitrogen, oxygen and carbon dioxide that we achieved the division of our days and the passing of our seasons according the amount of light and solar radiation that reached our planet's surface.

As a side note, 80% of star systems identified consist of binary stars. Ours is one of the few solar systems with only one sun. That is because almost all sun-like stars are born in pairs Science cannot account for the process as yet, but for some reason some of these second suns, which are for all intents and purposes, identical twins simply disappear. But had they not, contrary to all the movies where those living on distant planets stare into the sky with its two suns, they wouldn't have survived the radiation levels emitted by a twin star system. I believe we have to take into consideration how unique our situation is and how fortunate we are to have a single solar disk that divides our nights from our days.

כ וַיֹּאמֶר אֱלֹהִים--יִשְׁרְצוּ הַמַּיִם, שֶׁרֶץ נֶפֶשׁ חַיָּה; וְעוֹף יְעוֹפֵף עַל־הָאָרֶץ, עַל־פְּנֵי רְקִיעַ הַשָּׁמָיִם.	**20** And God said: 'Let the waters swarm with swarms of living creatures, and let fowl fly above the earth in the open firmament of heaven.'
כא וַיִּבְרָא אֱלֹהִים, אֶת־הַתַּנִּינִם הַגְּדֹלִים; וְאֵת כָּל־נֶפֶשׁ הַחַיָּה הָרֹמֶשֶׂת אֲשֶׁר שָׁרְצוּ הַמַּיִם לְמִינֵהֶם, וְאֵת כָּל־עוֹף כָּנָף לְמִינֵהוּ, וַיַּרְא אֱלֹהִים, כִּי־טוֹב.	**21** And God created the great sea-monsters, and every living creature that creepeth, wherewith the waters swarmed, after its kind, and every winged fowl after its kind; and God saw that it was good.
כב וַיְבָרֶךְ אֹתָם אֱלֹהִים, לֵאמֹר: פְּרוּ וּרְבוּ, וּמִלְאוּ אֶת־הַמַּיִם בַּיַּמִּים, וְהָעוֹף, יִרֶב בָּאָרֶץ.	**22** And God blessed them, saying: 'Be fruitful, and multiply, and fill the waters in the seas, and let fowl multiply in the earth.'
כג וַיְהִי־עֶרֶב וַיְהִי־בֹקֶר, יוֹם חֲמִישִׁי. {פ}	**23** And there was evening and there was morning, a fifth day. {P}

Table 8

By the fifth day the seas were filled with all sorts of lifeforms, many of which crawled along the floor of the oceans but also implies the insects which crawled out onto the dry land because they are the ones which would be considered as swarming.

What day five describes very well is what we visualize began with the Cambrian Period. The Cambrian world differed greatly from the preceding Proterozoic Eon (2.5 billion to 540 million years ago) in practically every way, including climate, geography, atmosphere but especially life. The elevated Cambrian temperatures (about 22°C average) and changes in Earth's geography due to constant tectonic plate movements, led to increased rates of erosion that altered ocean chemistry. The most-notable result was an increase in the oxygen content of seawater, which in turn resulted in a rapid diversification of life in the water and on land. This event came be known as the "Cambrian Explosion." An explosion very similar to what is being described on Day 5 with the swarming and diversification of life in the seas. Among the animals that evolved during this period were the chordates, those animals with a spinal nerve cord, the hard-bodied brachiopods, which resembled clams; and the arthropods, which were the ancestors to today's spiders, insects and crustaceans. The end of the Cambrian Period is marked by evidence in the fossil record of a mass extinction event about 490 million years ago. The Cambrian Period was followed by the Ordovician Period.

Sentence 21 refers to the great sea monsters and we immediately think of the whales in our time, but the verse may have been describing something else. The largest predator during the Cambrian period was the Anomalocaris, a free-swimming animal that undulated it lobed body in order to move through the water. It had true compound eyes and two claw-tipped appendages directly in front of its mouth. In its time it was the largest most fearsome predator of the seas but it did not survive into the Ordovician Period. The earliest known chordate animal, the Pikaia, was about 1.5 inches (4 centimeters) long. Pikaia had a nerve cord that was visible as a ridge starting behind its head and extending almost to the tip of the body. The fossils clearly show that Pikaia had the segmented muscle structure of later chordates and vertebrates. Haikouichythes, thought to be the earliest jawless fish, were also found during this time period.

The Silurian Period occurred from 443 million to 416 million years ago and followed the Ordovician Period, which lasted less than 50 million years with its massive glaciers and freezing temperatures. During this time, continental landmasses were low lying and sea levels were rising so that shallow sea ecosystems originated as seen by evidence of extensive reef building and the first signs that life began to colonize the fresh water and terrestrial ecosystems. Animal life underwent rapid differentiation and diversification, which was not the anticipated response shortly after a near extinction event at the end of the Cambrian period. Eurypterids were the apex predators of the Silurian oceans, resembling the horseshoe crabs of today but by the beginning of the Devonian Period, these animals had become the largest known arthropods to ever have existed on Earth. With the warm, moderate temperatures of the Silurian, plant life thrived and land based arthropods swarmed over the land.

But where are the dinosaurs, would be the refrain at this time coming from those opposed to the story of Creation. They would point out that the fifth day made reference to the fowl in the air and as we know, without the dinosaurs there could have been no birds. And I most certainly agree that this was not the day of the dinosaur and therefore certainly could not be the day for birds to be flying in the air either, especially since the land creatures didn't arrive until the next day. So we have to ask ourselves, why would God have indicated that there were birds before there were any land animals and why did God use the word fowl? More to the point, why did He say winged fowl? Are there fowl without wings? And why would they multiply 'in' the earth and not on the earth or up in the trees? Insects multiply in the earth. Insects can be found with and without wings, often being the same species of insects but some will have and others won't.

The problem arises with the word עוֹף pronounced as 'oif'. Originally Hebrew was written without any vowel marks and these were added later. I believe the original words was עוּף pronounced as 'oof', meaning things that fly. Now when you read sentence 20 as 'let the flying things fly above the earth' or sentence 21, 'every winged flying thing after its kind'. or sentence 22, 'let the flying things multiply in the earth,' we know exactly what the sentences are referring to and it makes far more sense. These are the winged arthropods that arose as some of the first land creatures the swarmed through the skies.

It should be pointed out that according to Darwin's Evolutionary Theory, we should have only seen a gradual evolution over time as the original one celled organisms experiment with a variety of structures before they make their leap from a one celled organism to a multi-celled animal. But instead we have a fossil record for 3.2 billion years of practically no advancement, and only incremental changes at best. Then we have a billion years of one celled animals remaining as such and there is very little change of structure evident. It is as if the world was perfectly content in being a world of nothing more than these microorganisms. And then suddenly just under 550 million years ago, the first multicellular organisms appear. One must ask once again, how is it that life could appear as soon as the Earth cooled and water gathered on the surface, but for a billion years never evolved any further. The mystery becomes even more complicated by the fact that 120 million later after the first appearance of these multicellular forms, in what is referred to as the

Cambrian Era, there is the sudden appearance of complex structured animals that shared the basic structural form of living animals that exist today. An incredibly long delay followed by an unexpected explosion of life forms. These events will be discussed later in much greater detail but I raise them now in order to make the reader begin to speculate on how much coincidence is permitted before it can no longer be considered coincidence.

כד וַיֹּאמֶר אֱלֹהִים, תּוֹצֵא הָאָרֶץ נֶפֶשׁ חַיָּה לְמִינָהּ, בְּהֵמָה וָרֶמֶשׂ וְחַיְתוֹ־אֶרֶץ, לְמִינָהּ; וַיְהִי־כֵן.	**24** And God said: 'Let the earth bring forth the living creature after its kind, behemoth, and creeping thing, and beast of the earth after its kind.' And it was so.
כה וַיַּעַשׂ אֱלֹהִים אֶת־חַיַּת הָאָרֶץ לְמִינָהּ, וְאֶת־הַבְּהֵמָה לְמִינָהּ, וְאֵת כָּל־רֶמֶשׂ הָאֲדָמָה, לְמִינֵהוּ; וַיַּרְא אֱלֹהִים, כִּי־טוֹב.	**25** And God made the beast of the earth after its kind, and the behemoths after their kind, and every thing that creepeth upon the ground after its kind; and God saw that it was good.
כו וַיֹּאמֶר אֱלֹהִים, נַעֲשֶׂה אָדָם בְּצַלְמֵנוּ כִּדְמוּתֵנוּ; וְיִרְדּוּ בִדְגַת הַיָּם וּבְעוֹף הַשָּׁמַיִם, וּבַבְּהֵמָה וּבְכָל־הָאָרֶץ, וּבְכָל־הָרֶמֶשׂ, הָרֹמֵשׂ עַל־הָאָרֶץ.	**26** And God said: 'Let us make man in our image, after our likeness; and let them have dominion over the fish of the sea, and over the fowl of the air, and over the cattle, and over all the earth, and over every creeping thing that creepeth upon the earth.'
כז וַיִּבְרָא אֱלֹהִים אֶת־הָאָדָם בְּצַלְמוֹ, בְּצֶלֶם אֱלֹהִים בָּרָא אֹתוֹ: זָכָר וּנְקֵבָה, בָּרָא אֹתָם.	**27** And God created man in His own image, in the image of God created He him; male and female created He them.

Table 9

Sentences 24 to 27 are about the reptilian and mammalian phase of Earth's history. And this is the point where I can say thank you to the paleontologists and their fellow scientists for their extensive efforts and research. Because of their hard work I can point to sentence 24 and say that once the first creatures set a foot on to land, terrestrial life exploded. First came the amphibious fish, then then newt and salamander like creatures, only to be followed by other amphibians and then these evolved into the reptiles and the giant lizards known as dinosaurs. The early tetrapods most likely evolved from lobe-finned fishes able to use their muscular fins to take advantage of the new wetland ecosystems and walk short distances on land. The earliest known tetrapod is *Tiktaalik rosae* from the mid-Devonian period (416 to 358 million years ago). It is considered to be the link between the lobe-finned fishes and early amphibians.

The Permian Period from 299 to 251 million years ago saw a dramatic change. Spore producing plants were being replaced by seed producing ones, and the arthropods were becoming the insects we are familiar with today. Two important new groups of animals arose and dominated the landscape. These were the Synapsids, thought to be the lineage that led to mammals and the Sauropsids, the lineage with led to the dinosaur and birds. It was the latter group, that dominated the Mesozoic era, also known as the age of dinosaurs. Probably the most startling transformation that occurred during this time was in the tree dwelling lizards that at first learned to glide but then they developed feathers as their scales altered in structure. Arms developed into wings and long snouts became beaks. We know now that birds are the direct descendants from dinosaurs. They still retain many of the same features as their lizard ancestors, such as nucleated red blood cells.

The dinosaurs were always in the story of genesis but because at the time the word behemoth, written as בְּהֵמָה didn't have any meaning to the people of the time they confused it with being an ox, probably the biggest animal they could think of at the time. But since the normal term would have been a cattle-beast, and beast was already used in the same sentence, they couldn't think of any other alternative, even though it made no sense at all that the sentence referred to animals by categories and not by any particular species. Over time, the bible got translated into may other languages and the original Hebrew being a 'behemoth' became lost and was supplanted by the word 'cattle' in all languages. And if we look at the definition of behemoth, we will see that it says, "A huge animal mentioned in the Old testament," or "something that is enormous." I would think that the dinosaurs qualify to be called behemoths.

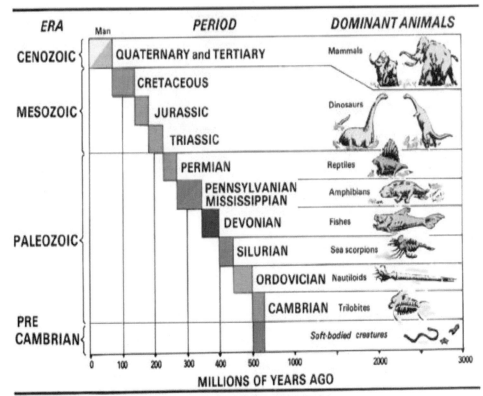

ERA	Man	PERIOD	DOMINANT ANIMALS
CENOZOIC		QUATERNARY and TERTIARY	Mammals
MESOZOIC		CRETACEOUS	
		JURASSIC	Dinosaurs
		TRIASSIC	
PALEOZOIC		PERMIAN	Reptiles
		PENNSYLVANIAN MISSISSIPPIAN	Amphibians
		DEVONIAN	Fishes
		SILURIAN	Sea scorpions
		ORDOVICIAN	Nautiloids
		CAMBRIAN	Trilobites
PRE CAMBRIAN			Soft-bodied creatures

0   100   200   300   400   500   1000   2000   3000

MILLIONS OF YEARS AGO

Major divisions of geologic time.

Figure 14

The story of Genesis recognized that mankind or human evolution was the last development that occurred and stood out from all the other species being unique as the bible properly implies that they all have remained fairly static in their evolutionary process with the comment, "after its kind". Certainly they changed in shape and size, and some even became extinct, but overall as far as their nature, behavior and instinctive nature, those have remained constant and there has been very little cognitive development, if any. It is only the hominid that continued to develop at an accelerated rate and was unique in its creation as being the only species that shared something in common with God and that was the spirit to create and wanting more. This shared trait will be discussed further in the chapters regarding human evolution. It is understandable that early man thought this last sentence of being created in God's image implied physical characteristics, but I doubt very much if this would have been the thinking at the time when Moses received the Torah. The ancient Israelites understood that God had no physical form and was the main reason they were opposed to any representation of their God as an idol. They understood God to be a force of nature, and therefore never anthropomorphized Him as later civilizations did. It was only after centuries of exposure to the other polytheistic civilizations, such as the Greeks, the Persians and the Romans, that the thought that somehow mankind shared a physical resemblance to God became the mainstream view and the original context of this sentence became contaminated.

For those of a religious mindset, everything we have discussed thus far in this first section will probably make perfect sense and you will be satisfied that the science really does correlate with the biblical creation and in fact at a minimum proves that a sentient being was a requirement in order to begin the entire process of the Big Bang. I intentionally chose to present the science first so that the physics that you hear talked about constantly could be seen not only for its content but also for its context. There is no doubt that science has made amazing progress in discovering the subatomic world and it is absolutely fascinating that as we scale downwards through the microverse, we begin to see the beauty of the entire creation. It is like a tapestry woven from fine strands of colored silk that are invisible to the eye but once each strand is laid against, the next and the next it begins to come into view and that which is beautiful suddenly fills you with awe. No sooner do we complete a layer, then immediately another layer begins to be woven on top of the last, and this process continues for an eternity, testing us to our limits of detection, which no matter how good they become, never seem to be good enough to provide us with a view of the tapestry in its entirety. Whereas we can step back and appreciate the marvel of our multi-layered universe, praising the craftsman for His genius and unprecedented skills, the scientist is obsessed in trying to prove they can do it better if only they can discover the secret of how He did it in the first place.

But science and especially the self-absorbed scientist will not be ready to roll over and concede that God does exist. As far as they are concerned there can only be one God and that is man and all that is being done in the name of science is not for the betterment of mankind, it's not about improving lives and defeating disease and preventing famine and starvation. It has never been about stopping wars but instead finding better and more powerful weapons with which to fight wars. They do not even try to hide the fact that is their intention as they publicly proclaim they are in search of the God Particle. Most have probably heard about this hunt for the particle over the past couple of decades. It certainly has received worldwide attention and an incredible amount of money poured into the research. When first revealed there were fears that these scientists would accidentally create a black hole that would swallow Europe, perhaps even the world, while others said they will produce another explosion equivalent to the Big Bang with the force to annihilate all life in our solar system. Fortunately for us, they have not been able to produce either catastrophic event but not without a lack of trying. The Hadron Collider has the ability to produce mini black holes according to the scientists at CERN. As the world's most powerful accelerator, it is still insufficient to make a true black hole, but even if it did, according to the scientists there, it would be so small that it would only consume matter at the rate of 1.1×10^{-25} grams per second. Or in other words, it would take 3 trillion years to grow to a mass of 1 kg. As reassuring as that may sound, the question that might be on everyone's mind is, "What's the point?" At a cost of 4.75 Billion to build and over 1 billion a year to operate is there a necessity to even try?

So what exactly is this God Particle they speak of and will it really be able to accomplish all that they claim it will do? The Higgs boson, or Higgs particle, is referred to as a carrier particle, or boson, and is part of the Higgs field, named after its designer Peter Higgs of the University of Edinburgh. The Higgs field is said to permeate space and provides all elementary subatomic particles with mass through its interactions with them. Higgs provided a testable hypothesis for the origin of mass in elementary particles but it was never Higgs that referred to it as the God Particle. That was done by another physicist that claimed if they could find the particle then they would understand how matter was structured in the universe. Or in other words he thought they could reproduce the actual construction of matter and essentially have the power of a god. It was a ludicrous claim, and one that unfortunately stuck even though there is nothing god-like or god-empowering about this particle at all.

Unlike other fields, such as the electromagnetic field, the Higgs field has a magnitude but no direction, implying that bosons have no angular momentum or spin. Also unlike other fields, the Higgs field will have higher energy when the field is zero. As such, all elementary particles acquired their masses only after interacting with a nonzero Higgs field, which meant after the universe cooled and therefore long after the Big Bang. Accordingly, scientists say it explains why the carriers of the weak force, the W particles and the Z particles, are heavy while the carrier of the electromagnetic force, the photon, has a mass of zero. Experimental evidence obtained in 2012 for the Higgs boson was a direct indication for the existence of the Higgs field. There is also the belief that there is more than one type of Higgs boson with the search being conducted at the particle-accelerator colliders at the Tevatron, located at the Fermi National Accelerator Laboratory and the Large Hadron Collider (LHC) at CERN. The first evidence discovered on July 4, 2012 was at the LHC when they detected a signal that was likely from a Higgs boson with a mass of 125–126 gigaelectron volts; GeV).

But exactly what does this all mean? It means that in total, they spent 13.75 Billion to tell the world that there is a subatomic particle called a boson that will provide mass to particles that don't have any after a collision. So I can tell you with certainty that it has nothing to do with a God particle and any suggestion that it does is completely erroneous. What it does tell you is that there is at a sub-atomic level an entire complex world that science has barely scratched the surface of. To simplify exactly what the Higgs boson is about, imagine the Higgs field as a fog or a mist and each droplet in that mist is a Higgs boson. A family with a history of no recorded mass walks through the mist and suddenly starts recording having a mass. The father, biggest in size has a greater covering of droplets on the surface area of his body, so he records the highest mass. The child only has a small surface area, so he records a low mass. And the dog even has less of a surface area, so it records the lowest amount of mass. But at the same time an insect flies through the mist and is able to weave its way through the droplets without coming into contact with any of them. That insect would still be recording zero mass if it had no starting mass of its own. And that is exactly what the Higgs field does to particles passing through it. Those with the most contact because they're larger in size will record a higher mass than those that can pass through the field more easily with less collisions. So essentially it tells us there is no such thing as empty space in space. What we can't detect and call dark matter is filled with a lattice work of subatomic structures. Passing through the field causes a conversion or transformation, resulting in detectable particles as seen in Figure 15 below.

Figure 15 is the result of the research performed at the Large Hadron collider. Two colliding protons not having mass, each then emits a W boson. The two W bosons then collide to produce the Higgs boson, which in turn decays into two Z bosons, each of which then decays into an electron plus positron or muon plus antimuon. Notice that the balance is always maintained. For every positive there is a negative as the end result. The mass of a Higgs boson is obtained from its own field just like every other particle that passes through it. As the proton passes through the field, the Higgs boson provides about 10% mass to the quarks.. Since the Higgs boson can give mass to the particles in dark matter, then detecting an area of bosons can therefore detect the presence of dark matter. That is what 13.75 billion dollars buys you.

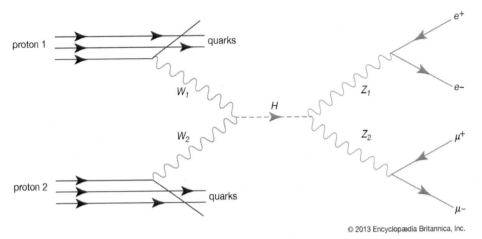

Figure 15

Fascinating at best, but absolutely no reason to be referred to as a God particle since it is a transformation and not a creation and is just one more Russian nesting doll that science has opened up along its endless journey. In all likelihood, once the subatomic level is fully explored, then they will realize the boson is composed from micro-atomic particles at the next level below. They will have just opened up their next nesting doll on their journey into eternity or oblivion, depending on which perspective you choose to use. So as the world of science chases down this bottomless rabbit hole, it will become obvious to the rest of us as they spend billions in tax dollars, that they do so for only one reason and that is because they can without any repercussions. It's really not a justification for doing anything, but their refusal to accept that it is all part of an intelligent design by an intellect that surpasses anything we could understand fuels them and will not let them stop their endless pursuit. Some refer to it as 'madness', they simply call it science. They will justify their research by saying if there truly is a God, then why would he have bothered to create all these infinitely small and incredible structures that they keep discovering, and I will answer them in the only language that they understand, "Because He can and they can't."

Section Two: Small Package Conundrums

Chapter 8: The Circle of Life and the Riddle of Pi

Our school texts have not caught up to the most recent findings of those researching life on our planet. They still teach the outdated version of life taking billions of years to develop, and only occurring after millions upon millions of random mismatches in the primordial soup that constituted our oceans until one of these combinations actually was able to reorganize its molecules, split and reproduce itself by reorganizing the other molecules in the water to resemble itself. A random molecular combination that had a one in three to four billion chance of occurring, and it did, thankfully for the rest of us that now exist because of that amazing molecule that was formed. For all intents and purposes, it was a wonderful theory, worked well, and amazed children when first revealed in science class but then our instruments for aging rocks through radioactive dating became much better and far more accurate. The new test results were suggesting that this early molecular life had occurred far earlier than we imagined. In fact so much earlier that it coincided with the cooling of the Earth, which meant this supposed one in almost four billion chance actually occurred almost immediately after the earth cooled and made it possible for molecules to combine. It was as if the specific ingredients were all intentionally brought together in this primordial soup knowing full well what the result would be as soon as they made contact. It was not random but instead followed a specific recipe that appears to have been well established and with both a known and desirable end point. So I'll repeat that very important insight, that not only does it appear that the entire process was known and expected to work, making billions of years of random combinations unnecessary, but the fact that it was practically instantaneous, occurring as soon as the Earth had cooled to a temperature capable of sustaining life, would suggest that the process was being controlled. And control could only mean one thing; the hand of God was involved and this was another example of **GodSpark**.

Acknowledging that life had an almost instantaneous origin with the first living molecules forming as one celled organisms almost four billion years ago, to only be followed by the most amazing thing that could have happened is unbelievable. What happened is absolutely nothing! Contrary to evolutionary theories suggesting that all life evolves on a constant basis, becoming more complex as it adapts to a changing environment, these one celled organisms remained precisely what they were for the next three billion years. It was only 520 to 540 million years ago, during what is referred to as the Cambrian era, that life exploded into actual life forms or creatures, leaving behind a beautiful fossil record recording their history. Just as it describes in the book of Genesis, there is this initial explosion of life in the oceans from seemingly out of nowhere. In fact it wasn't until day five that God said, "Let the waters bring forth swarms of living creatures," as was discussed in the previous section. It would appear that even the Bible is acknowledging that for some reason the one celled organisms would exist for a period practically four times as long before the appearance of more complex life forms. As mentioned in the previous section, if we eliminate the concept of a day being a day instead referring to an eon or a phase, then we can agree that this fifth phase is the dawn of complex life forms in the oceans.

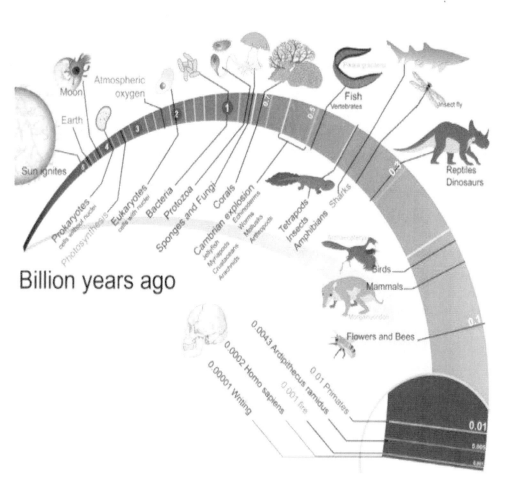

Figure 16

In the case of these one celled organisms, evolution appears to take a holiday after their creation. For billions of years these creatures are advancing at a slow walk, practically unchanged from the time they first appeared until the end of the Pre-Cambrian period. One does not see any dramatic changes in overall appearance or morphology, from the first prokaryocytes all the way to the protozoa as seen in Figure 16 above. This lack of fossil evidence of any dramatic change proved to be a real dilemma to Charles Darwin who recognized the gaps and requested that his readers fill in these huge spaces using their own imaginations. That statement alone by Darwin was an acknowledgement that the theory of Evolution had issues. I will discuss Darwin and his theory of evolution in later chapters. But the question still remains, where are the fossil records for these transition species to account for the huge leaps apparent in the historical fossil records of living organisms beginning with the Cambrian period. The answers is simple. "They don't exist!" In Section One of this book, the focus of the investigation to the presence of God was on a cosmic scale.

The argument was made that the entire creation process of our universe required a conscious effort in order to come into existence. The issue of the **GodSpark** was raised repeatedly, since it is the one inclusion principle that science intentionally overlooks but the one probability that unifies all their theories regarding the birth of the universe. Perhaps eventually science will admit that the electromagnetic wavelengths existing within the Void, would be capable at some point to establish a cosmic consciousness. After all, if we can be well on the road to creating an artificial intelligence through a series of 1s and 0s discharging across a small chip of silicone, surely the huge canvas presented by the Void and the presence of proto-matter and proto-energy can do the same, as they discharge some of their unrecognized energy in the form of waves.

It would not surprise me that at some point science will acknowledge and accept the presence of a cosmic consciousness. If man can manifest intelligence simply by passing chemical and electrical impulses across axons and neurons, then certainly it would not be inconceivable that the same could be achieved across a larger framework having similar properties. We have to remember that our intelligence operates with a voltage transmission of no more than 100mV (of which 70 mV is its resting charge) and a speed of transmission of 100 meters/second. Our laptops even operate with more voltage at a mere 5V. If that is all it takes to have cognitive action, then imagine what an unlimited energy could be capable of where space and time don't exist, so that distance is irrelevant in regards to the speed of thought. It would be a superior intelligence simply based on its size, number of electro-neuro pathways and increased speed of transmission. We are already aware that these features play a significant role in the intelligence of humans. There have been three scientific papers published examining the brain of Albert Einstein, which was preserved after his death in 1955. These were the findings: Albert Einstein's brain had more glial cells per neuron suggesting that his neurons needed and used more energy than other humans. Surprisingly, his brain weighed only 1,230 grams, as compared to the average adult male brain of 1,400 grams, which proves its not the size of the brain but its composition. Einstein's cerebral cortex was thinner than the average person's but the density of neurons in his brain was greater, meaning that he had more neurons in a given area of cortex, so he didn't require the greater mass of cortex as others do. The most recent study concerning Einstein's brain was published in The Lancet, on June 19, 1999, in which the investigators found that the portion of the brain that governs mathematical abilities and spatial reasoning was 15% wider than the average human, thereby allowing better connections between its cells. So if an Einstein can be so structurally different from the average human in regards to cognitive capabilities, how can our scientists even try to fathom the level of intellect and abilities that a cosmic intelligence would be able to wield.

Therefore, I am certain that with the passing of time, and the realization that the opening of the Russian nesting dolls is merely an exercise in futility, they will eventually admit that the immense scale of our universe required intent and therefore a conscious effort to bring it into existence. But in their acknowledgement of this universe-creating level deity, they will likely stipulate their reservation that at no time does He exercise any concerns for the human condition and therefore is nothing more than a creative force without the ability for interpersonal interactions. In this way they can still say that there may be a God but he is not the God of the Old Testament, which they will continue to declare as nothing more than a collection of myths and fables. They will attempt to package Him as being more like the Force from a Star Wars movie, where some people may believe they can tap into the force but there is no bilateral communication that can be proven or that they would ever accept. I would suspect that there are numerous people around the globe that already think that way, worshiping a God that is nothing more than a creative force that knows how and when to flip a switch whenever it is needed but lacks any ability to relate on a human scale concerning issues of morality, behaviour, and need. These people have a clear distinction between this God of Science, who remains distant and aloof from mankind, concerning Himself only with the conduct of natural laws and universal affairs and the God of earthbound religions. And perhaps they think that the first section of this book only proved what they already believed and there is nothing more to be said about the matter.

That certainly is not the God that I choose to believe exists for several reasons, the most significant one being that as soon as you have awareness of self, you also have awareness of others or in this particular case, the absence of others. It was revealed in the last chapter that God is referred to in the plural and it was suggested that He is a composite of several components, each having the capacity to think but working in a unified manner much in the way an IT expert would string together rows of hard drives in creating a Master Server. But they would still be all part of the one, and therefore when God searches to find another of his own kind, he discovers He is alone in the Void. There is not a consciousness in the universe that I suspect would ever want to be alone. Self-awareness brings with it a heavy burden called loneliness and a need no matter what level of life form we might be to have communion with another life form, whether it be the same or different from ourselves. The second reason has to do with a thirst for knowledge. Just like a young child is curious to find out how everything works, which usually results in the taking apart of items but without the capability of putting them back together again as was the case when I was five and wanted to know what was inside our portable radio, any level of intelligence is going to have a similar inquisitive mind. The universe wasn't assembled with a snap of the fingers, it was in all likelihood a long history of trial and error. Whereas we see the success of the operation, we have no appreciation for all that may have not been successful to reach our current position. That same inquisitiveness and desire for more will compel even God to continue to expand the extent of His capabilities through a continual creative process. The only way to accomplish that is through direct involvement at all levels of the creation. And lastly, there is a desire for satisfaction and perfection, which is clearly communicated in the first Chapter of Genesis when it concluded by saying that each day, God was pleased with His accomplishment, indicating that there probably was a lot of tweaking along the way in order to achieve the final goal. Considering that we're aware of at least five mass extinctions in Earth's timeline, that's a lot of repairs and restarts in a major way. This is not a portrait of an aloof creative force that has no involvement in post-creative matters as would be the case if He was nothing more than a universal guiding force of nature. It is my goal and intent to prove that it is the God of Religion that exists and not merely the God of Science. And whereas the first section of the book was dedicated to proving the latter, the next few sections will take you on a journey to convince you that the former is also true.

As per the title of this chapter, there are interesting arguments to be made concerning how the circular patterns that seem to be the basic pattern behind everything in existence can also be imprinted in our psyche so deeply that it also permeates our thinking processes. In this case I will circle back to the earlier comments discussing Albert Einstein's reference to God's playing with dice. In particular, I believe Einstein may have been privy to some aspects of the **GodSpark** that I have been elaborating upon and his use of the dice scenario was his way of both revealing and concealing what he believed and knew at the same time. A single die is quite an interesting object. A six sided cube, each side bearing a unique number of dots. Probability states that the odds of any one side coming up as expected would be one in six or roughly just under a 16.7% chance. Not great odds but certainly not low enough to dissuade millions of people each year from going to Vegas. But the odds of rolling that one die and having each of the six numbers come up just one in six attempts would be $(1/6)^6$ probability or a one in 46,656 chance. That's a 0.002% chance of occurring and those are definitely not odds you want to gamble with. Now to take it a step further, what if we wanted those six numbers to come up sequentially, as in 1, 2,3...6. Then we'd be looking at an additional multiplier of $(1/6 \times 1/5 \times 1/4 \times 1/3 \times 1/2)$ or $(1/6)^6 \times (1/720)$, which is a one in 33.6 million chance of occurring. The probability of it happening is so remote that you can almost say with some certainty that it will never happen by chance. I could only happen if someone actually reached down and turned the die to the desired number. It would take interference and it is important to remember this fact. So what has any of this to do with the circle of life? As you'll see over the next few paragraphs, everything!

As a young boy, enjoying my early school years in the sixties, we had a joke that we would tell each other as we began our studies in geometry. It went like this, "What is Pythagoras's favourite restaurant? " And one of us would answer, "One that serves Pi(e)." As bad as that joke was, we all still laughed and I never thought I'd be repeating that terrible joke almost six decades later. Yet here it is and never could it be more relevant than it is now. In section one, as I pointed out, there was a lengthy discussion on the use of a circular template from the microscopic to the macroscopic levels of the universe. The discussion brought up the issue of Pi (π) in regards to the measurements of the brass sea in the Temple. It appears repeatedly in many ancient cultures suggesting that they considered it to be practically mystical in its origins and whatever may have been their reasons, it became incorporated even into their religious practices. This reverence they held for π must have some explanation beyond simple fascination.

I need you to think about this for a moment. If you wished to communicate with a new civilization, or an alien species with whom we shared no intelligible language with which to do so, then the only way by which communication could be established would be to find a universal language that will be identical no matter whichever galaxy one resides; that would be the language of mathematics. The first item on the list would be to provide a constant, a number that will never change and is evident in practically everything we do. We use that as the reference point from which all other statements can make sense. That constant would obviously be π. At that moment, both parties recognize they have something in common and can begin using equations upon which to build layers upon layers of communication. Therefore, it would not be unreasonable to think that the same justification would apply if God desired to leave us a message that would undeniably demonstrate that He had a hand in creating the circle of life on our planet. In this case it would act as his fingerprint that he had been here and was directly involved. If that constant could be found, imprinted into our existence, then it would send a clear message that life was not a series of random interactions, erroneous dead end pathways, and the random roll of a set of dice that just happened to strike it lucky and win the jackpot. I did not pick on π out of habit or because we are all accustomed to seeing it because of our high school geometry textbooks. I would almost go as far as saying, selected me and I just needed to find its hidden places. Just as would be the case with our first contact with an alien species, I knew instinctively that it has always been God's way of sending messages, highlighted by the repetitive pattern of circles seen throughout our universe and the early attention paid to it by ancient civilizations. They knew something that we have long forgotten and ancient wisdom should always be treated as a precious jewel and guarded carefully over time. That message rang loud and clear for me when it came time to write this book. I think after I reveal the answer to God's riddle concerning π, the readers will also come to the realization that the **GodSpark** was not a singular event just prior to the Big Bang, but has been a repeated stimulus that has significantly altered life on this planet over the past four billion years and certainly played a role in the advancement of humans on this planet.

Science is in agreement now that the universe began approximately 13.8 billion years before the present. As our instrumentation became more precise, so too did our estimates and this would appear to be the fixed date. We also know that it took approximately 10 billion years for our galaxy to form, along with our solar system and the planet Earth. In an effort to calculate an exact time, science could only date it to roughly 4.5 billion years ago. I believe we can be even more precise than that. I would place the time the earth was formed at 4.39 billion years before the present. My calculation is based on dividing the age of the universe by π. This would be the number 1 on the roll of the dice. It is the most significant event after the creation of the universe and the first event along the road to the birth of man according to the biblical picture.

The next major hurdle was for the planet to cool so that one-celled life could become established on Earth. Science has dated the establishment of eukaryocytes and bacteria to somewhere between 1 to 2 billion years ago. Once again, I think we can arrive at a more accurate date and say that it was 1.4 billion years before the present. That is calculated from the time the Earth was formed divided once again by π. The first time we have an event of this nature based on π, such as the creation of the solar system, we can brush it off and say that it was purely random that just happened to occur at a date when the birth of the universe could be divided by the magical number of 3.1415. But when it happens a second time, then we have to admit that is an interesting coincidence. The fact that the die was rolled and came up with the second most important event along the road to human development, that being the birth of cellular life once again based on the division by π is perhaps more than an interesting coincidence. It borders on the remarkable. Life now exists in the seas, even if it is just single celled organisms as identified in the Old Testament.

As reported in the previous chapter, there isn't much in the way in change on the planet until the Cambrian Explosion much later, only to have a mass extinction around 490 million years ago at the end of that same period. It was odd, to say in the least, that we had this sudden burst of life a billion years earlier without any real evolutionary process occurring for the longest time and then suddenly, hundreds of different life forms appear for no apparent reason. This is then followed by the Silurian and Devonian periods, so that by around 425 million years ago, the animals that were once sea bound were now swarming over the land. Pre-lizard like animals existed, insects flew through the air, and plant life spored into numerous new species that spread across the planet. If we use the riddle of π to calculate a date when animal life crawled out onto the land and began to populate the Earth then that would be 445 million years before present according to the time allotted to the one celled organisms divided by π. Though scientists can only approximate that these events took place somewhere around 450 million years ago so that by the Devonian Period they were dominating the land, here is a formula that not only agrees with their estimate but suggests that the reason nothing happened for over a billion years and then life exploded had to do with a formula being applied as a controlling mechanism. In other words, the **GodSpark** was being applied according to a preconceived plan. When three major events that changed the history of life on earth all occur as a fraction of π, then it is no longer random and no longer a coincidence, but certainly an indicator that something unusual is taking place and is being manipulated.

When we think of the Jurassic Period, we think of the great dinosaurs ruling the Earth. What we fail to recognize was that the Jurassic Period also represented the dawn of flowering plants, the flight of feathered birds and most importantly the existence of the first true mammals and all these took place according to paleontologists around 150 million years ago. It was the last development that was essential for the birth of mankind. Had mammals not become a prominent species, giving birth to live young, nursing them and being able to moderate their body temperature to the changing environment, it is unlikely we would ever have come into existence. Just as the Bible indicated, the timeline considered that the behemoths and the beasts roamed the Earth, long before man was ever born. According to the rule of π, this took place 142 million years before the present when we divide the time that the animals crawled out on the land before the Devonian Period. Once again, the die has been rolled and for the fourth time it has come up correctly, clearly indicating that there is a pattern in existence and that it is undeniable.

For the next 80 million years, mammals had to be satisfied to scramble beneath the feet of the gigantic lizards that ruled the earth. Once again Darwin was wrong in presuming that competitive pressure was the major driving force for evolution. The fact was, that against the dinosaur, the mammals couldn't compete. The battle for supremacy could never have taken place as the mammals were outmatched in every way. But around 60 to 65 million years ago, the dinosaurs became extinct and suddenly the field became wide open for mammals to take over the ecosystem. One might say this was the mammals 'lucky break' but realistically as we recognize how this timeline was being managed, was there anything really lucky about it or was it intended to happen? Within 20 million years after the disappearance of the dinosaurs, mammals occupied practically every niche that was available. And according to the rule of π that I have presented, this was expected to take place 45 million years before the present. As incredible as this seems, the Kingdom of Mammals had already been written in to the formula and once again, a key event on the road to man met its next milestone. When we look at the world 45 million years ago, we see that according to Figure 17 the temperature was still in the warm green house range, providing us with no reason that the giant lizards should have died out. In fact it was until about 40 million years ago that the temperature of the Earth actually began to cool moderately. So, saying that the mammals caught a lucky break hardly justifies how they managed to become dominant when there was nothing to even suggest they should have the opportunity to do so. In the scientific community, when a test is performed six times and provides an acceptable result, then it is said to have greater than 80% confidence and is statistically significant. The fact that this was five out of five results being acceptable is more than the 2σ result that scientists use to support their research as being both accurate and acceptable.

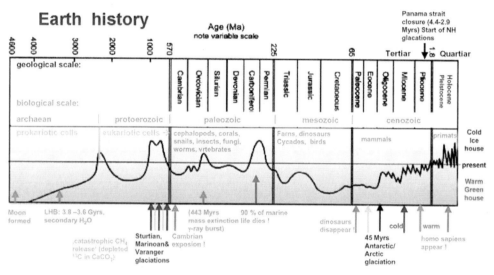

Figure 17

It is clear that there exists a specific pattern that has developed and the key to that pattern of evolutionary development revolves around this riddle of π. To deny it is to deny the same scientific statistical principles used to validate all the experimentation that was described in the first section of this book. The issue in this case is that acceptance of this rule of π means accepting that even our evolutionary process has the hand of God controlling it and there are specific milestones which suddenly erupt as if ignited by the **GodSpark**. As mammals took over the animal kingdom, it should be emphasized that the so called 'lucky break' was only possible as a result of the dinosaurs suddenly disappearing. Had that not been the case, the required diversification among the mammalian species would likely not have occurred to the degree that was necessary for them to survive the coming ice age during the Pliocene Period. The 'Lucky Break', which from all appearances looks like the hand of God was involved, made it possible for a wide variety of mammals to survive the climate change, one of which led to the advent of mankind. And that milestone occurred according to the fossil record at an estimated time of at least 13 million years ago with the discovery of Peirolapithecus. This ape like creature is considered the parent of the Great Apes of today of which man is a member of that genus. How does this compare with the π calculation. Considering that the dating of the fossil finds was at least 13 million years before present, then the more precise calculation of 14.4 million years by π is very much in line with that estimate and once again points to the accuracy of the formula. In science, if your calculated values were within 10% of the estimated value then one would say that they had an excellent test. I would put it differently. If I rolled my die and obtained a 100% success rate in predicting the number of the roll and that each roll in turn was necessary to be correct in order for the outcome of the next roll to take place, then I would think my colleagues in the scientific community would accuse me of fabricating my data and dismissing my results. But the reality as everyone can see, is that the formula suggests that there was a guiding hand in the evolution of life on this planet, and every so often along the path, a stimulus is required in order to make a dramatic shift in direction. That stimulus can only be identified as a **GodSpark** and for that to take place is a clear indication that God has been involved in the entire process, from the creation of the universe all the way down to the birth of mankind.

Application of the formula doesn't end with the arrival of the Pierolapithecus. It would not be God's methodology to only do half a job. As the Old Testament indicated, the creation process didn't end until Day 6 with the arrival of man. So according to the formula, π predicts the next milestone would occur at 4.5 million years before today. What should we expect at this milestone? Exactly what anthropologists have found, a young Australopithecus girl name Lucy. Lucy is the given name for the nearly complete skeleton of an *Australopithecus afarensis* found in 1974 at the Afar Locality in Ethiopia. Lucy is not the only early example of *A. afarensis*, some dated to 4.2 million years in age. Recent research has shown that she didn't move in the same manner as humans nor was she simply a terrestrial being adapted to live in the trees as well. The shape of the female's pelvis was closer to modern humans and less similar to the great apes. Clearly, the arrival of Australopithecus was a major milestone on the pathway to human development. It was predicted by the π formula and shows that this was not a normal naturally occurring process. That in fact, it would appear that it was predetermined because an unknown force was making it happen at the precise time that the formula predicted. Science will still have a difficult time accepting this as fact but the more these skeptics examine and review the evidence, they will have no other choice but to accept that the guiding hand of God has been involved in our creation exactly as it was described in the book of Genesis, if perhaps not literally but at least figuratively.

Can the formula predict further time points? Most definitely, and it would be amiss of myself not to point out how successful the Riddle of Π is, in predicting these events. The next key time would be 1,430,000 years before present. And the next milestone that we would expect would be when mankind shed its apelike ancestry and for the first time could be referred to as human. And here's we can expect the body of Scientists to finally say, "AHA, See, it does not work." That is after it demonstrated its accuracy and precision seven times in succession. So if it was off one of those times, then you would think that they'd be a little more receptive to having a single variation. They will point out that *Homo Erectus,* whom science has considered to be the first real hominin, didn't come into existence until 1.1 million years ago. Some might argue that a 320,000 year difference isn't that great and shouldn't be considered as an impediment to the formula. But I wouldn't be happy with a 22% variance and therefore I wouldn't be willing to accept it. But at the same time I would point out to those that thought *Homo Erectus* should have the title as first hominin, they are wrong. That title actually belongs to *Homo Ergaster,* who lived somewhere between 1.3 and 1.7 million years ago. *Homo Ergaster* was the first of our ancestors to actually look human. 'Turkana Boy' discovered in West Turkana, Kenya. lived about 1.5 million years ago. He was about 8 to 10 years of age when he died but was already 1.6 meters tall and may have reached 1.85 meters as an adult. Almost 90% of his skeleton was recovered and has provided valuable information on this species' body size, proportions and development. The Turkana Boy had a tall, slender body adapted for striding out across the extensive savannah plains. He also had a more human-like face with a nose that projected outwards and a larger braincase. It was believed that *Homo Ergaster,* unlike his predecessors was relatively hairless. Another example of Ergaster was found in in Swartkrans, South Africa along with evidence and the use of fire. Clearly Ergaster deserves the title of being the first true hominin. This being the case, it not only demonstrates that the π formula is still not only correct but has the ability to define the ages down accurately into the hundreds of thousands, if not tens of thousands. Even the most cynical of objectors will have difficulty in trying to disprove the use of π in the development of mankind but at this juncture it should be impossible to do so, yet I know they will continue to try.

That being the case, then I will let God demonstrate that it is even more difficult to disprove at the next level which would be calculated as being 455,000 years before the present. What key milestone was mankind involved with at that time. The good news is that we know exactly what man was doing at that time; He was undergoing his next stage in human evolution with the rise of *Homo heidelbergensis*. At this point in his evolution, man had become an advanced tool user and had spread out from Africa, his remains now being found in Europe and parts of Asia as well. Once again we have skeletal remains suggesting a height of approximately 1.8 meters tall with very strong, long legs. Socially, he lived and hunted in groups, and is known to have manufactured stone axes and spears with stone tips. The tools were advanced enough to be labeled as Mode 2 technology, His brain was large, averaging approximately 1250 cubic centimeters in size, and represented 1.9% of the body weight. The frontal and parietal lobes of the brain were enlarged, possibly indicating an increased brain complexity. It is believed that two distinct lineages evolved from Heidelbergensis, following a comparison of DNA structures. These were Neanderthal and ourselves, the *Homo sapiens*. So it is without a doubt that Heidelbergensis was a key milestone in human evolution and the fact that once again the formula precisely pinpointed this significant milestone is astounding. The issue of probability is no longer a concern because at this time we have only certainty.

The next date that the π riddle points to is 145,000 years ago. It would be reasonable to think that the event being pointed to was the rise of *Homo neanderthalensis,* referred to in the last paragraph as having evolved from Heidelbergensis. Neandertal or Neanderthal lived according to fossil evidence between 150,000 and 30,000 years ago and coexisted with *Homo sapiens* for thousands of years. They manufactured and used tools, used fire, hunted, made clothing, cared for their old and infirm, buried their dead, and most likely had language, art and music. Their habitat was Europe and western Asia with some spread into central Asia. Analysis of Neanderthal DNA, indicate that they were a separate species but still capable of interbreeding with *Homo sapiens*, many of whom carry a small percentage of Neanderthal genes in present day. On average, the Neanderthal had a larger brain than Homo Sapiens, but his nose jutted forward while the cheekbones sloped backwards, so that the Neanderthal had no obvious chin. The males were about five and a half feet while females were only about five feet in height. They were more muscular than modern humans, with large joints,

The Dawn of the Primates

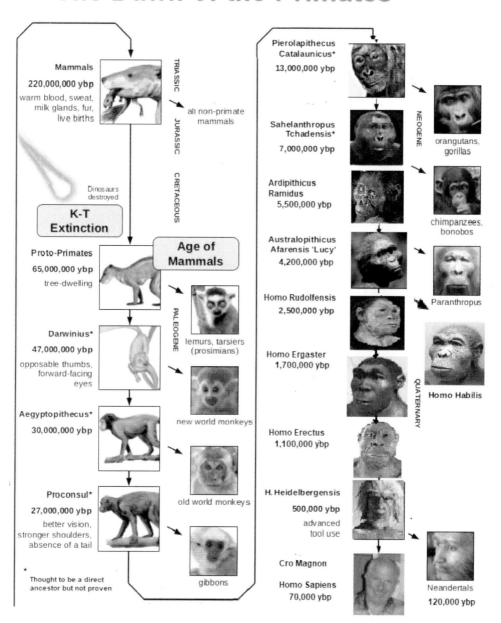

Figure 18

bowed limbs and very strong arms and hands. It is evident that they could use their hands as skillfully as modern humans can. Their tools were much more diverse than that of *Home heidelbergensis*, with sets of axes designed for specific purposes, along with knives and spears. Recent research has shown that the tools created by Neanderthals were as efficient as those created by early *Homo sapiens*. Examination of the Neanderthal genetic code shows that they had the same version of the FOXP2 gene that modern humans have. This gene plays a role in language development. Neanderthals were the first members of the genus Homo known to bury their dead suggesting they had a primitive ritualistic belief that bordered on religion. Most of the Neanderthals that were found buried had one thing in common. They all tended to be very old, or relatively old considering they reached an age of 50, which was considered an achievement for early man. As strange as it seems, Neanderthal's existence almost makes it look like God was hedging his bet to see which species resulting from Heidelbergensis would eventually become the one and only species of man. Which takes us to the next significant date revealed by the π formula.

Approximately 46,100 years ago, which is the date derived from the formula, the decision for dominance was made. With the appearance of *Homo sapiens* or modern man, shortly after Neanderthal appeared, it was almost as if God had to make a decision as to which species of man, Neanderthalensis or Sapien, would be the one to bear the mantle of his creation. Originating from the African continent somewhere between 90,000 and 130,000 years ago, *Homo sapiens* didn't spread out into the areas occupied by Neanderthals until much later. While the Earth underwent several severe climate changes between 110,000 and 60,000 years ago in the Northern Hemisphere. According to a study published in Nature, during that period there were only very short windows of opportunity for migration to take place out of Africa and these window only occurred about every 20,000 years. The long held belief that there was one singular migration out of Africa of major proportions 60,000 years ago, or once the climatic changes had settled is now questioned by Michael Petraglia of the Max Planck Institute, who believes there were a series of small migrations beginning about 100,000 years ago. Accordingly, the study suggests that *Homo sapiens* ventured out of Africa in four waves across the Arabian Peninsula and the Levant region of the eastern Mediterranean. These waves occurred from 106,000 to 94,000 years ago, 89,000 to 73,000 years ago, 59,000 to 47,000 years ago, and 45,000 to 29,000 years ago. In their conclusion they stated that the wave that occurred approximately 50,000 years ago was likely the one that led to *Homo sapiens* populating the rest of the world. There should be no surprise that this major wave which would have brought *Homo sapiens* in direct contact with *Homo neanderthalensis* occurred by their calculations precisely at the time predicted by the π formula. Whatever happened during that direct contact, whether there was confrontation, competition or absorption all dominated by the *Homo sapiens*, the net result was the disappearance of the Neanderthals and the establishment of a single human species. This major milestone may be what is referenced in Genesis Chapter 6, sentences 1 to 4 in which it describes the mixing of two races, referred t as the sons of God and the sons of men. Perhaps as the natural inhabitants of the Middle Eastern regions being the Neanderthals, saw the arrival of the *Homo sapiens* from out of the African continent, they would have viewed these taller, different looking people as the sons of God, especially if their weapons and tools were proven superior. Usually when one culture is taking possession of the women from another culture it involves the slaughtering of the men from the culture which is considered inferior. Other than knowing the π formula is referring to this major migration and end of the Neanderthal civilization, we may never know exactly how it did actually end.   Can we use the π formula to indicate anything further now that we have shown how it even applies to Day 6 of Genesis with the creation and dominance of man? The simple answer is 'Yes' since the Old Testament wasn't only about the creation of life on Earth, but also was about the rise of civilizations. The next date that would appear using the division by π would be 14,675 years before the present. Prior to this time, man had been strictly a hunter and gatherer, constantly migrating as he followed herds of wild animals on their migratory paths in order to ensure that he was always in contact with his food source.   Therefore, the next major milestone in human evolution came when mankind unleashed the agricultural revolution, first by domesticating sheep, goats, cattle and camels, and then, yoked those same oxen he had domesticated to furrow the ground and plant his seeds.   It is interesting to note how the aging of the agricultural revolution has changed over the years. Sixty years ago, it was thought to have occurred 5000 years ago. Then with the archaeological finds of cities that predated this period, the text books had to change since it was impossible to have cities built before farmers could even grow food to supply the citizenry.   So the dating became 7500 years ago in order to accommodate these earlier findings. But as later archaeological digs unearthed the remains of at least twenty successive settlements at the city of Jericho, the founding of that city got pushed back further to 9600 BCE which meant the agricultural revolution could be no later than 11,600 years ago. So as a result, the dating was announced as being 12,000 years ago, but it would be ludicrous to think that mankind had been farming for only a few hundred years before he undertook a major building project like that of a city. More reliable is a study on the domestication of sheep in the Fertile Crescent. This occurred approximately 13,500 years ago and involved at least three different subspecies of the wild mouflon. Sheep were the first "meat" animals domesticated; and were followed by goats, cattle and pigs. Until such time that there is a more accurate dating of this event that demonstrates it did occur 14,675 just as the π formula indicates, it will leave the window open for detractors to say the formula is not accurate and false, because it was off by 1,175 years, while ignoring the nine other times it has been fairly precise.

That is to be expected because it will always be difficult for some people to accept that God exists no matter how much proof you provide them. In fact the only reason I included the last item regarding the agricultural revolution was because of the removal of man from the Garden of Eden, which represented the end of mankind's days of living much like the animals he hunted, while gathering whatever fruits and berries were available on the trees in the forests they passed through. Man was entering a phase of civilization where he would be living in larger social groups, growing his food and domesticating animals to provide for his needs and the needs of others. So I do believe that it was the intention of the π formula to take us to this time point because of its correlation with Genesis.

There will be further discussion on human evolution in the chapter on Darwinism because there is still a lot more to be said about how God left his fingerprints all over the evolution theory but especially when it came to the evolution of mankind. Without the **GodSpark**, it would be doubtful if any of us would be here today. There was no guarantee it would be a process with a successful outcome. In fact, looking at the historical record, more species ended up extinct rather than successfully making it through to modern day. Man's early ancestors were neither the fastest, biggest, heartiest, strongest etc. Members of the animal kingdom, yet they managed to survive while those more adapted to their environments perished. We will see how Charles Darwin deals with that very valid conundrum that flies in the face of his theory.

Chapter 9: The Miller-Urey and Fox Experiments

It should be no surprise by now, that science feels compelled to show the world that whatever God can do, they can do better. Or so they try to say, but the success rate or lack of it speaks for itself. Since the 1960s, students in Grade 9 or 10 biology class are taught that life is nothing special since it can be created in a test tube by teachers that don't really understand what they're talking about but its in that year's teaching portfolio, so it's a requirement to conduct the lesson. But that particular lesson isn't about education, it's about indoctrination. It is a blatant attempt by those in charge of your child's curriculum to free them from the notion that life is sacred and a gift from God. As the students are only thirteen or fourteen years of age, it proves to be quite effective in altering their thinking about the process of life. These are young men and women at an age where they are easily influenced and they don't yet have the educational background to even challenge the lesson that they're being told is one of the most important events ever to take place in a biochemistry laboratory. Had they had any prior knowledge of biochemistry, they probably would have asked some pretty basic questions that would of had their teacher tongue tied in search of answers he or she didn't have. Some of you may actually remember having taken this class because it did what it was intended to; leave you with a life-long impression that the creation of life was nothing out of the ordinary since it could be done in a test tube. That was one of the biggest lies they told you in school but nevertheless you believed it because you were never given the tools to challenge it with as I will do now.

Both The Miller–Urey experiments were chemical experiments that simulated the conditions thought to be present on Earth one and a half billion years ago. and then tested for chemical origins of life under those conditions. The principle and hypothesis was quite simple. That given the conditions on Earth at the time, they would have promoted chemical reactions that synthesized more complex organic compounds from simpler inorganic precursors. The experiment was performed in 1952 by Stanley Miller and supervised by Harold Urey at the University of Chicago.

The experiment used water (H_2O), methane (CH_4), ammonia (NH_3), and hydrogen (H_2) to recreate conditions on primitive Earth. The chemicals were all sealed inside a sterile 5-liter glass flask connected to a 500 ml flask half-full of water. The water in the smaller flask was heated to induce evaporation, and the water vapour was allowed to enter the larger flask. Continuous electrical sparks were fired between electrodes to simulate lightning in the water vapour and gaseous mixture, and then the simulated atmosphere was cooled again so that the water condensed and trickled into a U-shaped trap at the bottom of the apparatus.

After a day, the solution that had been collected had turned pink in colour, and after a week of continuous operation the solution was deep red and turbid. The boiling flask was then removed, and mercuric chloride was added to prevent microbial contamination. The reaction was stopped by adding barium hydroxide and sulfuric acid, and evaporated to remove impurities. Using paper chromatography, Miller identified five amino acids were present in the solution: glycine, α-alanine and β-alanine were positively identified, while aspartic acid and α-aminobutyric acid were less certain but recorded as being present.

At that point the teachers turn to their students and inform them that Miller had definitely created the building blocks of life and all the students are astounded because it certainly sounds impressive but was it really. The first question that needed to be asked was , "What are amino acids and what are their roles?" The definition is that they are a class of nitrogenous organic compounds that are essential components of proteins. They are not proteins by themselves, nor are they capable by themselves of controlling any function of a living organism. In other words, they are a byproduct of a chemical process and nothing more. A compounding of individual atoms into a molecule with a carbon chain and hydroxy unit, accompanied by a color change, but definitely not life. To describe it as such was misleading and a failure of our educational system to present the actual facts.

With the death of Miller in 2007, his original vials were made available to scientists to reexamine the results of his original experiments. Amazingly, they were able to confirm that there were actually well over 20 different amino acids produced in Miller's original experiments. They then went on to say that these were more than the 20 that naturally occur in the makeup of the genetic code. This in itself was a misleading statement because it masks the fact that they did not find the 20 that make up the genetic code. The reality is that the Volcanic Spark test of 2008 only found 22 amino acids, hardly enough to state there were 'well over' twenty different, and unless 20 of those 22 were identical to those that make up the genetic code, which they weren't, then that statement was patently false as well. Subsequently, in the hydrogen sulphide test of 2010, the same vials only produced nineteen amino acids. But that's only part of the story. The more important qualifier that they never talk about in the school lesson concerns how many of those amino acids that are produced are actually proteinogenic or even capable of producing the building blocks of life. Of the five that Miller identified in his original experiment, only three had that capability of being used to build proteins. Of the ones identified in the 2008 experiment, only seven were proteinogenic, which is only 35% of the number of amino acids that naturally occur to make up the genetic code. That is far from the number suggested by their statement which implied falsely that they had identified all twenty. As for the 2010 experiment, there were only eleven of the twenty identified and five of these were only the result of changing the gaseous atmosphere from the prior two experiments. Eight of the amino acids produced in the 2008 experiment didn't get manufactured in the 2010 experiment. I have included the testing results below in Table 10 so that everyone can verify these results for themselves and see how science is capable of distorting the facts when you don't know the questions to ask.

| | | Produced in experiment | | |
Amino acid	Miller – Urey (1952)	Volcanic spark discharge (2008)	H₂S–rich spark discharge (2010)	Proteinogenic
Glycine	✓	✓	✓	Yes
α –Alanine	✓	✓	✓	Yes
β –Alanine	✓	✓	✓	No
Aspartic acid	✓	✓	✓	Yes
α –Aminobutyric acid	✓	✓	✓	No
Serine	✗	✓	✓	Yes
Isoserine	✗	✓	✓	No
α –Aminoisobutyric acid	✗	✓	✓	No
β –Aminoisobutyric acid	✗	✓	✓	No
β –Aminobutyric acid	✗	✓	✓	No
γ –Aminobutyric acid	✗	✓	✓	No
Valine	✗	✓	✓	Yes
Isovaline	✗	✓	✓	No
Glutamic acid	✗	✓	✓	Yes
Norvaline	✗	✓	✗	No

Produced in experiment

Amino acid	Miller–Urey (1952)	Volcanic spark discharge (2008)	H$_2$S-rich spark discharge (2010)	Proteinogenic
α–Aminoadipic acid	✗	✓	✗	No
Homoserine	✗	✓	✗	No
2-Methylserine	✗	✓	✗	No
β–Hydroxyaspartic acid	✗	✓	✗	No
Ornithine	✗	✓	✗	No
2-Methylglutamic acid	✗	✓	✗	No
Phenylalanine	✗	✓	✗	Yes
Homocysteic acid	✗	✗	✓	No
S-Methylcysteine	✗	✗	✓	No
Methionine	✗	✗	✓	Yes
Methionine sulfoxide	✗	✗	✓	No
Methionine sulfone	✗	✗	✓	No
Isoleucine	✗	✗	✓	Yes
Leucine	✗	✗	✓	Yes
Ethionine	✗	✗	✓	No
Cysteine	✗	✗	✗	Yes
Histidine	✗	✗	✗	Yes
Lysine	✗	✗	✗	Yes
Asparagine	✗	✗	✗	Yes
Pyrrolysine	✗	✗	✗	Yes
Proline	✗	✗	✓	Yes
Glutamine	✗	✗	✗	Yes
Arginine	✗	✗	✗	Yes
Threonine	✗	✗	✓	Yes
Selenocysteine	✗	✗	✗	Yes

141

Amino acid	Produced in experiment			Proteinogenic
	Miller-Urey (1952)	Volcanic spark discharge (2008)	H₂S-rich spark discharge (2010)	
Tryptophan	✗	✗	✗	Yes
Tyrosine	✗	✗	✗	Yes

Table 10

What should be evident from the results of Table 10 is that the lessons we were taught in high school were not only misleading but that they were intentionally manipulated to provide a false narrative then as well as in 2008 and 2010. Life had not been created and at best, they could only produce just over half of the necessary amino acids to build proteins that would be the basic component of cellular life. There is still more to this story that needed correction but was never discussed in biology class. This concerns the atmosphere that was used in the experiments, which we now suspect was predominantly methane and nitrogen gas, four billion years ago, with the addition of carbon dioxide to a lesser degree. The success of Miller's experiments relied on not using the actual atmospheric condition as is evident by other research conducted at the same time. For example, the work of William Wollman and M. MacNevin at Ohio State University, published in 1953 showed that when you pass 100,000 volt sparks through methane and water vapour, all that results is a 'resinous solid' that was too complex for analysis. Because of selectivity in the school system, we never were taught the results of this other experiment.

Then there was the work of K.A. Wilde, who published in the same journal as Miller but did so two months before Miller even submitted his paper. Wilde used voltages up to only 600V on a mixture of only carbon dioxide (CO_2) and water in a flow system. In his conclusions, he observed only small amounts of carbon dioxide reduction to carbon monoxide, and no other significant reduction products or newly formed carbon compounds. Clearly it is the availability of nitrogen that is essential to producing the nitrogen based amino acids and Miller proved this but his use of NH_3 rather than N_2 meant that the conditions had been altered to favour the release of nitrogen and hydrogen from the molecules by sourcing it from ammonia.

In the Miller experiments the following formulas were used to produce a series of one-step reactions:

$$CO_2 \rightarrow CO + [O]$$ (atomic oxygen)

$$CH_4 + 2[O] \rightarrow CH_2O + H_2O$$
$$CO + NH_3 \rightarrow HCN + H_2O$$
$$CH_4 + NH_3 \rightarrow HCN + 3H_2$$

The formaldehyde, ammonia, and HCN then reacted by Strecker synthesis to form amino acids and other biomolecules:

$$CH_2O + HCN + NH_3 \rightarrow NH_2\text{-}CH_2\text{-}CN + H_2O$$
$$NH_2\text{-}CH_2\text{-}CN + 2H_2O \rightarrow NH_3 + NH_2\text{-}CH_2\text{-}COOH \text{ (\underline{glycine})}$$

This particular experiment demonstrated that simple organic compounds could be made that would be the building blocks of proteins could be formed from gases with the addition of energy. But on closer examination we see that the initial steps involved the breaking of bonds from Carbon Dioxide (CO_2) to produce the free oxygen radicals. But as we saw in an earlier chapter, the availability of CO_2 in the atmosphere in large quantities did not occur until the photosynthesis process was well established by the blue-green one-cell algae floating on top of the primordial seas. This meant that CO_2 was only available in limited quantities and the nitrogen was available as nitrogen gas and not as ammonia. So the question remains, "What would happen if the atmosphere used in the Miller experiments was closer to the actual conditions of early Earth?" In recent experiments by chemists Jeffrey Bada, Miller's graduate student, using methods similar to those performed by Miller, Bada found that in an atmosphere of low carbon dioxide and nitrogen gas, the reaction would create nitrites, which destroy any amino acids produced as fast as they formed. It wasn't until Bada repeated the experiment with the addition of iron and carbonate minerals into the mixture, that the outcome was a solution rich in amino acids. But since we know that the mineral enrichment of the Earth required the oxides derived from large quantities of oxygen, this didn't happen until life had already been established on Earth. What Bada did prove is that under the original atmospheric conditions of pre-life Earth, there wouldn't even be the few amino acids that Miller found.

Arguments still rage over the early Earth atmospheric conditions with some insisting that there was sufficiently high levels of CO_2 available as a result of volcanic eruptions, and this would be sufficient as long as the oxygen and the hydrogen atoms came from water vapour but admit it would not successfully produce natural amino acids if the atmosphere was rich in hydrogen gas. Others claim that the presence of hydrogen gas in large quantities is an absolute must to mimic early Earth conditions This ongoing argument managed to keep the Miller experiments alive until the University of Waterloo and University of Colorado conducted simulations in 2005 that indicated that the early atmosphere of Earth likely contained up to 40 percent hydrogen gas based on the escape of hydrogen from the atmosphere into space, occurring at only one percent of the rate previously believed. But their conclusion was that this excess hydrogen in the form of gas made the formation of amino acids much easier in direct contrast to the statement by Bada. Whereas Bada actually did the experiment and proved that was not the case, then one would think that Bada should have the final word.

Jim Kasting, an atmospheric scientist commented in response to the revival of the Miller experiments, "I am underwhelmed by it." He further commented, "The main problem with the study was that Miller was probably wrong about the conditions on early Earth. Analysis of ancient rocks indicate that the Earth was never blanketed by hydrogen-rich gases like methane, hydrogen sulphide or hydrogen itself, which further argues against the required availability of hydrogen atoms. Those scientists that have repeated Miller's basic experiment with a more realistic attempt to reproduce the early atmosphere have had a difficult time finding any amino acids in the resulting solution. Kasting's closing comment was, "Even then the reduced gases would not be as concentrated as they are in this experiment."

The reality is that none of these scientists really know the constituents of the early Earth's atmosphere and are shooting in the dark in every direction. But the one thing they can say with confidence is that it wasn't the atmosphere used in the Miller experiments. But bearing that in mind, science has a contingency plan as usual, or better to use the word 'excuse' for that option as well. Knowing that the conditions of the Miller experiments do exist in other regions of our solar system, some are once again proposing that the building blocks of life rode here on meteorites. This hypothesis they say is supported by the Murchison meteorite that fell near Murchison, Victoria, Australia in 1969 in which it was found to contain over 90 different amino acids. Since the early Earth was showered by meteorites, they believe the origins of life was extra-terrestrial. Of course what isn't explained is even if the first amino acids rode here on a meteorite, how did they manage to be reproduced now that they were in a less hospitable environment with an atmosphere deficient in what was needed? They want to ignore that question.

In spite of all these hypothesis and attempts to produce amino acids, it is not these amino acids which represent the emergence of life on Earth, but the actual combination of these amino acids into proteins or some similar bioproduct. Since John Desmond Bernal's suggestion that clay surfaces could have played a role in abiogenesis, there have been numerous attempts to achieve clay-mediated peptide bond formation. The few peptides formed remained over-protected and showed no evidence of inheritance or metabolism. Without these latter properties, there is no point in even producing the peptide. Others like Nick Lane have also noticed the repeated failures to actually produce anything constructive to demonstrate the appearance of life on the planet. Lane pointed out that it's not difficult to create amino acids like Miller did but the real challenge is to create nucleic acids. Those are the real building blocks of molecules like RNA and DNA. Until such time that you can produce these "replicator", molecules that can make copies of themselves, nothing thus far has provided any evidence on the origin of life. Lane says, "Even if you can make amino acids (and nucleic acids) under soup conditions, it has little if any bearing on the origin of life."

Lane actually begins to sound like he has much in common with my own personal views when he comments that replicators don't spontaneously emerge from a mixture of building blocks, just as you wouldn't hope to build a car by throwing some parts into a swimming pool. "Nucleic acids need to be strong-armed into forming more complex acid molecules, and it's unlikely that the odd bolt of lightning would have been enough. The molecules must have been concentrated in the same place, with a constant supply of energy and catalysts to speed things up. "Without that lot, life will never get started, and a soup can't provide much if any of that," he says. Without his actually saying it, because as I mentioned most scientists would sooner jump into a black hole than admit it, you know he's conceding that another **GodSpark** is needed to set the wheels in motion.

Hopefully, what has been discussed thus far will arm a new generation of students with enough information that when being taught all about the Miller experiments, as has been the core curriculum for close to seventy years now, some bright student will stand up and challenge the teacher to reproduce the experiment in class using the correct atmospheric conditions or else don't even bother wasting their time with bad information that serves only one purpose, and that is to achieve the goal of presenting a Godless world. Miller failed, end of story!

One can't simply talk about the Miller-Urey experiments without discussing the work done by Sydney Fox and Kaoru Harada in 1964 using the Miller experiment as his baseline. Fox explored the synthesis of amino acids from inorganic molecules just as Miller did but was also focused on the synthesis of proteinaceous amino acids and amino acid polymers which he named proteinoids. He created what he called "the world's first protocell using his proteinoids and water. These protocell globules were referred to as "microspheres". Fox believed that his experiments reproduced the conditions that existed on primordial Earth but as we saw in the case of Miller, this was not correct. In his lab, he did manage to create protein-like structures from inorganic molecules and the application of thermal energy, as well as microspheres that did resemble bacterial cells. Fox concluded that these microspheres could be similar to the earliest forms of life which he referred to as protocells.

The Fox and Harada experiment flowed methane through a concentrated solution of ammonium hydroxide and then into a hot tube containing silica sand at about 1000°C. The silica sand represented volcanic lava. The gas was then absorbed into cold, aqueous ammonia. The result was twelve protein-like amino acids: aspartic acid, glutamic acid, glycine, alanine, valine, leucine, isoleucine, serine, threonine, proline, tyrosine, and phenylalanine. Having produced the amino acids, the next step would be the formation of proteinoids through a process called Thermal Co-polymerization. The experiment began with L-glutamic acid heated in an oil bath. DL-aspartic acid and an amino acid mixture were added to the L-glutamic acid and heated for three hours in the oil bath under a layer of CO_2. The solution was cooled and the glass container it was in was rubbed with 20 mL of water and sat overnight. The result was a grainy precipitate. The next day, 10 mL of water and 10 mL of ethanol were added to the precipitate and filtered. The solid left over from filtering was put in cellophane dialysis tubing and left in a water bath for four days. The dialysis involved the use of sodium chloride or salt in order to complete the process. When the inside of the tubes were observed and chromatograms were taken, it showed the presence of polypeptide chains. Fox called these protein-like structures "proteinoids." The polypeptide chains were composed of glutamic acid, aspartic acid, and amino acids and the percentages of each suggested that the arrangement of the constituents were non-random.

On closer examination we can see that the experiment did not prove that proteins were formed on primordial earth using primarily heat and the naturally found substances available in the primordial seas. In fact Fox's could only make his experiment work under conditions that would resemble volcanic pools and thermal spas. His additions of ethanol and in some cases phosphoric acid meant using chemical reagents that weren't even part of the primordial Earth substrates. Fox explained the phosphoric acid would act as a catalyst for the formation of peptide bonds. A catalyst that was not available naturally. For the work by Fox to have been plausible he actually needed to simulate prebiotic Earth conditions without the addition of chemicals that weren't available in order to make his reactions work. He also needed high concentrations of the lysine, glutamic acid, and aspartic acid in order for his experiment to succeed. Therefore, not only was it unlikely that primordial Earth would have had large distributions of these amino acids available sitting on its surface, he completely overlooks the fact that life began in the seas and not in these hot spa pools located on the land masses.

It is important to have knowledge of the inability of these famous scientists to produce life of any sorts, because that has not been how their research has been presented to the billions of students that have undergone the indoctrination in our high school systems that fill young minds with incorrect information. They will tout the successes and the irrefutable nature of these experiments without ever being challenged as to identifying what are the actual milestones that are being presented. Since most of today's scientists view the work of Miller and Fox as nothing more than interesting historical episodes on how science had it's own 'the Earth is Flat' moments, it is difficult to understand why no one has challenged why this misinformation is still being taught. If there is one conclusion that can be taken away from all this research, it is the non-verbalized comment by Nick Lane, that is hidden behind the comments he did make; there has to be something more; there has to be someone more, for these reactions to actually be successful. By now we should all realize that the **GodSpark** not only was necessary to birth a universe, but it was also the essential catalyst to starting life on Earth as well. Science has provided you with a false narrative because it served the anti-Creationist doctrine and it is time that the record is set straight.

Chapter 10: The Virus Enigma

With the coming and passing of the year 2020, there probably isn't a human on this planet that doesn't have a little understanding regarding viruses. But most of that understanding is based on the destructive nature of a virus, especially one that results in a pandemic. A virus is actually far more than just a conveyor of disease and it is vital that we have an understanding of the virus in order to have an appreciation of the full apparatus that was instituted by God. Simply stated, a virus is a small collection of genetic coding, either DNA or RNA, surrounded by a protein coat. By definition it is not alive, it cannot replicate on its own and it cannot survive on its own. The first and last point would almost appear to be in direct conflict, because if something is not alive, why would it need to survive, and that is probably the most fascinating facet in studying viruses, in that you have something which is not alive but it will do everything possible not to die.

Viruses must infect living cells and use their components in order to make copies of themselves. In many cases, they will kill the host cell in the process, and cause serious damage to the host organism. Viruses are found in every possible Earth environment and it is estimated that they outnumber bacteria by ten times. They are submicroscopic, so they cannot even be viewed under a normal optical microscope. Structurally, they have only two or three components. A nucleic acid core, which can be either single or double stranded RNA or DNA, a protein coat that's in the form of capsid, and some viruses will also have a surrounding envelope which they obtain as they emerge from a cell.

Viruses can only survive inside a living cell, which suggests the first virus must have either originated within a cell or else at one time they were free-living organisms that lost the ability to live on their own and became cellular parasites. Generally, there are certain characteristics that are common to all viruses. First, they can only replicate within a host cell, and if there were any free-living viruses, they don't exist any longer. Second, they all have a size diameter of less than 200 nanometers. If we think of a millimeter marking on a ruler as being 10^{-3} meters, then imagine how small 10^{-9} will be for a single nanometer. Third, no known virus contains ribosomes, which is the essential cellular component to read the nucleic acid and then tell a cell how to make a certain protein. For that reason, a virus must take over the cell's own machinery. And lastly, there are both good and bad viruses which probably surprises a lot of people. At a later point in this chapter I will focus on the good viruses that actually reside within our bodies and are important for our survival. The play a specific role in our fertility and that too will be discussed in respect of the decreasing fertility rate that is now plaguing mankind. As pharmaceutical companies created new anti-viral compounds, fertility has decreased worldwide. There must may be a correlation.

The first issue we need to tackle is the concept of life and why we can make the claim that viruses aren't alive. Biologists generally agree that all living organisms exhibit several key properties, which include growth, reproduction, maintaining internal homeostasis, response to stimuli, and the carrying out of various metabolic processes. In can be argued that viruses do reproduce, even though they have to hi-jack other cells to do so. But one thing they cannot do is carry out metabolic processes. The cannot generate ATP and they don't have ribosomes to do translation of genetic material and therefore cannot independently produce proteins.

Because of these limitations, viruses can replicate only within a living host cell. Therefore, viruses are referred to as obligate intracellular parasites and therefore, according to the stringent definition of life, they are nonliving. There are viruses for practically every ecosystem; animals, plants, fungi, and bacteria. The same virus may cause an effect on one type of organism, but a completely different or even no effect on another. Although the term virus is all encompassing, viruses actually vary in complexity. The capsid can be a coat of protein or glycoprotein and some viruses will have a lipid envelope around the protein coat when exterior to a cell. Once entered into the cell, the virus will insert its genetic material into the cell's nucleus and take over that host cell's functions. The host cell may still continue to produce its own material but at the same time is producing more of the viral protein and viral genetic material. There are a variety of shapes and sizes to viruses as seen in Figure 19, which include:

- Icosahedral, near-spherical viruses: Most animal viruses are like this.

- Envelope: Some viruses take a section of the cell membrane and create a protective lipid envelope like the influenza virus and HIV.

- Other shapes are possible, including combinations of the above such as both helical and icosahedral forms.

- Helical: The tobacco mosaic virus is an example.

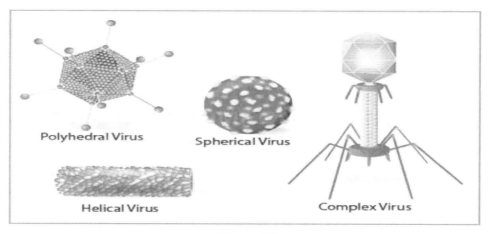

Figure 19

The manner in which viruses replicate is also very diverse, and they have an enormous growth potential, capable of releasing thousands of new virus particles through just one virus hijacking a single cell in a short amount of time. With both double stranded DNA and double stranded RNA virus types, they have the possibilities for nucleic acid inheritance. Furthermore, the single stranded forms can make use of transposition of nucleic acids within the host genome. Basically, viruses can exploit all theoretically conceivable strategies of genome replication and expression, making them the perfect genetic modifier. To gain a perspective on how many viruses there are in our world, Dr. Paul Turner at Yale University gave us this sobering comparison, "Virus genes, when unraveled and laid end-to-end, would extend 250 million light years from Earth. This would reach into the Perseus Cluster, a cluster of galaxies in the constellation Perseus." The success of viruses lies in their mutation rate which is very rapid, permitting them to avoid inhospitable scenarios very quickly.

Turbo Plus Code Writing

That being the case, what is their real purpose? To think that something reproduces itself for the sole purpose of destroying its host makes no sense at all. It would be a self-defeating cycle where eventually it would kill off the last host and would no longer be able to reproduce, effectively committing suicide if the virus had been alive in the first place. The concept of existing only for the sake of dying goes against every conceivable notion in either science or religion. There is no point for an organism or similar to come into existence if its continuance is not at least expected to be guaranteed, unless that organism is nothing more than a means to an end, a tool in a toolbox so to speak. It is my contention that viruses are those tools that are intended for a variety of purposes and have in numerous instances been responsible for many a **GodSpark** in the evolutionary process. I need you to imagine that we and every other living thing on this planet are nothing more than sophisticated computers that have specific programs that not only tell us who and what we are, they also inform us of our capabilities, behaviors and bodily functions. And like any computer, over time we require upgrades to our software and our hardware. In order to do so, a programmer has to write a bit of code that is then inserted into our program to overwrite the old code, thus replacing it. Ideally, the new code will enhance our functional capabilities and overall, we will have better performance. The same is true for any accessory devices because their performance is determined by the drivers that have been entered into our data banks. From time to time, those drivers also have to be upgraded to the latest version in order that those connected devices such as microphones, video devices, recording devices, all perform optimally. Sometimes the upgrade to our own files renders the old drivers incompatible and our attached devices are no longer functional. Other times our driver upgrades interfere with other devices and everything crashes. For those of you that have experienced the journey from Windows 3.1 to Windows 10, you know exactly how much fun that has been over the years. Truth is that in many ways, like Windows 8, it has been a nightmare and in some cases those computers ended up permanently blue screening, never to be used again. The same is true for the data storage and entry over the years. From doing programming with punch cards to data tape and six inch floppies, only to see the 3.5 shield disk last until CD ROMs took over, then DVDs and finally wireless inputs downloaded by blue tooth or the web, it has certainly been a roller coaster of computer accessory extinction. Look in anyone's closet and there's probably piles of useless, obsolete computer items just sitting there that we still can't bring ourselves to throw them into the trash.

Viruses are no different than all those written upgrades and version replacements we experienced with our computers, except that they're upgrading the genetic coding of living animals and plants. Though it is the intention to discuss Darwin's theory of evolution later in this book, for the purpose of this chapter, let it just be said that Darwin's Theory doesn't account for the shear numbers within a species that all needed to be upgraded in a very short time period due to environmental pressures, which require an immediate response. For example, the need for a heavier hair coat in order to survive an approaching ice age meant that those animals that happened to already have a heavier coat even though they were living in a warm temperate climate, perhaps even a subtropical climate, would have been the key to the survival of their species. First, keep in mind they were not the fittest of their species, since they were not ideally suited to their current environment, and in fact probably suffered for their heavier hair coat. So to be more correct, they were more like the weirdest rather than the fittest among their kind, and second, not being the norm they would have been few in number. What Darwin's Theory definitely does not account for is that these animals on the fringe of their society, would have required an opportunity to mate with hundreds if not thousands of their kind in order to account for the rapid turnover in genes within a species. Considering the slow pace of Darwin's evolutionary process, it cannot account for the incredibly rapid changes noted in the fossil records. Obviously, there had to be another stimulus involved to account for the rapid spread of physical and physiological changes within the species.

The Nutcracker Man

To understand what I have just stated, let's look at mankind's evolution as an example. We know from the fossil records that Australopithecine hominids were not much different from their close cousins, the chimpanzee. They would have shared a common environment, both on land and in the trees, competed for many of the same food types and other than the differing skull features, their body shape and bone structure were very similar. Bow legged, long armed and more of a knuckle walker than a bipedal animal, Australopithecus, as in Figure 20, would probably be even mistaken for a chimpanzee if we saw one today, other than being slightly larger than its chimpanzee cousins. I will talk more about this relationship to chimpanzees in a later chapter on human evolution.

But one day something strange and unaccounted for occurs in one of the troops of Australopithecus primates that are spread out over the eastern horn of Africa according to Darwinism; a baby is born with slightly longer and straighter legs, narrower pelvis, with the pelvic bones set to a sharper angle when walking.

Figure 20

As the infant grows, he or she tends to spend more time walking in a bipedal fashion than his troop mates, which would have raised a few eyebrows if they had any. This child is better balanced and faster but neither of these are necessarily seen as advantages by any of the fellow troop members. It will only be seen as an improvement once the species has evolved into hunters, needing to carry their spears and clubs in their hands, and to move quickly in pursuit of their prey but that's not going to be necessary for millions of years into the future. Currently, the Australopithecus is primarily a vegetarian, eating the occasional Colobus monkey, much as modern day Chimpanzees do. By all evidence of primate behavior, the differences exhibited would have probably caused this 'freak' to be shunned by many of the others, and certainly wouldn't have merited any advantage in mating rights over all the other individuals in the troop. In reality, if a male, he wouldn't probably have been given the chance to mate and therefore this progenitor of humankind wouldn't have passed on his special genes to any offspring. But obviously if we adhere to Darwinism, not only did he reproduce but he did so at such a phenomenal rate that the fossil record doesn't ever record an equilibrium point where there would be the fossil remains of two different species co-existing within the same troop, For example, Australopithecus and Homo Rudolfensis co-existing as one colony because at some point they would be at equal numbers within their own family groupings and its very unlikely their social behaviors would be so different from the present that they would have forced themselves to physically separate purely on the basis of phenotype. That is a key point which Darwinian evolution doesn't make any attempt to account for. We can excuse it when Darwin talks about birds and tortoises in total isolation, but when it comes to human evolution, the rapid transitions cannot be explained through the slow and gradual natural process that he described. Human evolution as all the evidence shows us, is rapid, amazingly fast, especially over the past half a million years and it occurs in complete pockets of transition, even though by this time the numbers of mankind's ancestors are in tens of thousands and physically separated by thousands of miles. What was required to make this happen was a rapid transformation mechanism and a vector. Exactly what a virus is designed to do.

I know that it will be difficult to accept that we may actually be the byproduct of a viral infection. That it took a virus to alter our genome and infect entire populations at the same time in order to evolve our chimp-like ancestor into the human species, but that is exactly what we do when we vaccinate against a new disease. A year ago, the major proportion of the world's populations would have been exposed and succumbed to CoVid19. Perhaps by the end of it all, 100 million people would have died. Only those with natural immunity would have survived and they would passe it on to the next generation rendering them CoVid resistant. By rapidly creating the vaccine, we have preserved a population that will always be susceptible to the virus in the future, except that they will be able to purchase and vaccinate if they are threatened by the disease. But at least we can see how a virus can effect human evolution in a very short time and if we can do that artificially, then why would it be impossible to do so naturally. I expect the scientists in the readership will now jump from their seats and object to this point strenuously, saying that, "We can do that deliberately because it is our intent to work with the virus and we do so with intent and purpose, utilizing the knowledge we possess," implying that if the virus was going to be used in the manner to alter human development, then that wasn't possible because it didn't have a designing hand behind its creation. And that's where I step in to say it may not have had a human designer at that time, but that is not to say that if the virus resulted in a positive change in human morphology or physiology, it didn't have a designer, a manipulator or a creator. Let's assume over the next few paragraphs I will demonstrate how it had all of those and that the ultimate intent and purpose was well known before the virus was released, will that alter their objections? Probably not, as science is determined to prove the non-existence of God, but I believe we can successfully argue this case in point and overcome their bias.

The explanation begins with a review of the evolutionary lines of human development as presented in Figure 18. As we can see there, the evolution of Homo Rudolfensis from Australopithecus may not have been as smooth a transition as we think. While waiting for Rudolfensis to become the predominant hominid, it would appear that evolution, within its normal incremental boundaries was experimenting with other species such as Paranthropus and Homo Habilis. Both of these other species were still more ape-like in appearance with smaller craniums as evident from the low and sloping foreheads and jawlines that were more protruding and more heavily muscled. In fact, the first specimen of *Paranthropus boisei* (Figure 21), was called Nutcracker Man, by Mary and Louis Leakey in 1959 when they discovered him in the Olduvai Gorge, Tanzania. He earned the name from his massive jaw structure, which implied he could exert tremendous bite pressure and therefore crack even the heaviest shelled nuts with his teeth. Some of the features that define modern man from our ancestors is the fact that we have upright postures, larger brains, and noticeably smaller teeth. Our jaw muscles are small and weak in comparison to other species and we've compensated for our weaker bites by possessing very thick tooth enamel, providing us with a little more protection. Because of our lack of a heavily muscular jaw structure, our skulls no longer require a cranial crest for anchoring the masseter muscles, permitting a lighter boned structure that can carry a larger brain. We have sacrificed size for efficiency and intelligence, but the emergence of Paranthropus and Homo Habilis would suggest that the change did not necessarily occur as nature's first choice.

Our close relatives, existing today, still produce significantly more bite pressure than we do, which makes us less capable of consuming anything that might be tougher in nature, such as bamboo, and which requires us to chew for extended periods of time. Our jaw muscles tire and become sore quite rapidly. Considering this evolution towards smaller jaw muscles meant that our ancestors were forced to forage for softer foods, and were suddenly in need of cooking our meals in order to make them softer, as well as use tools to break down dense matter before eating it. But at the time of our ancestor's physical change, none of these required changes appears to have been directly associated with tool making and the use of fire, so the changes occurring to the anatomy are taking place millions of years prior to the actual factors that would push evolution in that direction. That being the case, Paranthropus and Homo Habilis appear to have been better equipped to be the role models for the slower evolution paradigm. The fact that they were bypassed means that something else, something most likely entirely unexpected, forced the change.

Figure 21

Referring to the inferior strength of the human bite and the lack of muscle mass, the question must be raised as to just how weak is it? In a direct comparison of bite pressures in pounds per square inch (PSI), the human bite on average is only 162 PSI, placing us almost at the bottom of the scale for mammals. A look at our gorilla cousins with an ability to bite with the strength of 1,300 PSI and we can see just how far we have fallen down on the evolutionary ladder. Whereas, the jaws of the gorilla have adapted to chewing tough plants, enabling them with very thick and strong neck muscles, as a species we have lost those traits and for the longest time were probably not only known as being the 'naked ape' but also the ape with the least ability to protect and defend itself. If we compare these bite forces with other animals found roaming the central jungles and savanna of Africa and likely hunting our ancestors, then we have the spotted hyena with a bite of about 1100 PSI. This provides the hyena with enough force to crush the leg bones of a giraffe in order to remove the marrow from the core. By comparison, the big cats of Africa have bites that aren't as powerful, such as 1050 PSI for the tiger and 691 for the lion but still well beyond our pale human capability. Considering these animals usually bring down their prey by biting into the throats, it wasn't as essential for them that they exert massive bite pressure into this soft flesh.

For a further comparison, we can look at other animals that we don't usually associate with Africa but our ancestors would have encountered in the European environment such as bears with 975 PSI and the wolf with 406 PSI. Now it could be argued that as carnivores, it is not unreasonable that all these animals have bite pressures that are anywhere from three to seven times that of humans, excluding the gorilla of course, but nature also took into consideration that herbivores may be the ones that require the greater ability to protect themselves against predators and that would explain why the hippopotamus can bite with an incredible pressure of 1825 PSI. The bottom line is that the human skull, with its deficiency in jaw muscles, reduced size of teeth, and lack of thick neck muscles wasn't designed for tearing its food or protection and in many ways must be considered an inferior in structural anatomy, making it hard to explain how mankind could be an evolutionary milestone on that basis. Therefore, it is necessary that we have to look deeper into this mystery, because obviously, even with the notable shortcomings, there was a reason for our development in this direction. Rather than look externally, perhaps we need to look internally for the explanation and justification of our evolutionary inferiority.

Probably the most startling aspect of what may be behind this down-grading of mastication muscles may be related to the mysterious hyoid bone. It is the hyoid bone which anchors the tongue and allows a wide variety of movements of the larynx. It is the only bone in the body that is not connected to any other bone and is believed to be the singular item that made speech possible in both Homo Sapiens and Neanderthals. That is not to say that you can't find a hyoid bone in other animals, because all mammals have one, but it is only in man that it is in the right position to work in unison with the tongue and larynx to produce speech. Had that unique change not occurred, we would still be garbling and hooting similar to a chimpanzee. But it was not only the position of the hyoid that made speech possible but also the requirement for the larynx to literally drop into a position that made this amazing feat happen. Like most other animals, the human infant has its larynx sitting slightly higher within the nasal cavity, permitting it to suckle and breath at the same time, similar to an obligate nasal breather. But at around three months of age, the larynx descends into the throat region, through a slackening of the musculature, making speech possible but the infant can no longer drink and breathe simultaneously. No other animal has its larynx positioned low enough to make it possible to produce speech. The higher position of the larynx is actually a preferred safety feature. It is why your dog can seemingly begin to swallow an enormously long and large piece of meat, without encountering any choking and placing its life in peril as we humans would experience. In the case of quadrupeds, placement of the larynx at an elevated position, separate from the entry to the oesophagus eliminates the total reliance on the epiglottis, as is the case in humans because of our upright posture, to close the trachea when eating or drinking.

Furthermore, the need to swivel our heads to look right or left as compared to simply flexing our muscles right or left as quadrupeds do, necessitated the heavy musculature and ligamentum nuchae of the neck to be done away with, providing more rotational access to the atlanto-axial and atlanto-occipital joints. In sacrificing muscle strength for rotational capability, evolution created a physical weakness in the overall support and protection mechanism of the human head. But at the same time, this weakness provided the flexibility of the hyoid's relocation, thereby providing hominins eventually with the unique ability to speak.

The hyoid bone, as mentioned previously, is the only bone in the body that does not articulate with another bone. Instead, it is suspended from the tips of the styloid processes of the temporal bones by what are called the stylohyoid ligaments. The U-shaped hyoid provides attachment points to a number of muscles and ligaments that connect it to the cranium, mandible, tongue, larynx, pharynx, sternum, and shoulder girdle. Its shape can be highly variable and it consists of three major parts that are variably fused. The main part known as the body straddles the midline of the neck. It is a very thin, concavely curved bone that is either articulating or fused at its lateral ends to the horns. The two greater horns are long, thin bones that form the posterior sides of the hyoid. The tips of these horns are rounded into balls so that the lateral thyrohyoid ligaments can be attached. The lessor horns are small, conical shaped protuberances located where the body and greater horns meet. They provide attachments for the stylohyoid ligaments. The entire structure of the hyoid is suspended by the muscles and ligaments which attach it to the base of the skull and mandible from above and to the larynx and sternum from below. Attached to the hyoid itself are the muscles of the tongue, the pharyngeal wall and anterior neck muscles.

In a comparison of primate species, humans have a significantly wider hyoid, cercopithecines, such as Rhesus monkeys have the narrowest hyoids, and the flatter faced monkeys and apes have intermediate widths. Proportions of the hyoid body showed substantial variation and non-significant differences among all the different groups, so there is no hard fast rule on dimensions and shape for humans. The hyoid of the Neanderthal was almost identical to that of *Homo sapiens* and therefore, it is likely that he was capable of complex language skills similar to our own. But for both Neanderthals and *Homo sapiens* to share this unique particular trait would suggest it must have been present in *Homo heidelbergensis*, the progenitor for both species, yet, the skeletons from this early hominid do not show any evidence of the hyoid being as developed or in the necessary position for speech to occur. For this to have been the case, then these events must have occurred almost at the end of Heidelbergensis' reign on the planet, but by that time, early man had separated and dispersed himself over two continents with Sapiens in Africa and Neanderthals in Europe. This raises the question as to how two independent species, geographically separated and with little chance of encountering due to the migrations out of Africa being almost twenty thousand years apart due to repeated climate changes as discussed in a previous chapter, could possibly develop speech capabilities simultaneously and independently. The odds of doing so would be highly improbable if solely relying on an evolutionary process.

To find a possible answer it is necessary to examine the fossil records further back in time. Millions of years ago, an early ancestor of modern mammals, looking very similar to the rat, had a tiny, saddle-shaped bony structure connected to the jaw. Today, that set of bones, which we call the hyoid, makes it possible for all mammals to chew and swallow. The movement of the food in the mouth and the swallowing of the food once chewed is all controlled by muscles attached to this highly mobile bone. Early mammals in the late Permian and Triassic periods, before the Jurassic, are known to have had a rigid hyoid structure. Therefore, like lizards, they may have swallowed their food whole. It wasn't until the Cenozoic Era approximately 65 million years ago that mammals possessed a mobile hyoid.

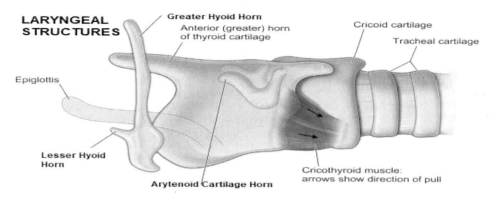

Greater Hyoid Horn

Anterior (greater) horn of thyroid cartilage

Cricoid cartilage

Tracheal cartilage

Epiglottis

Lesser Hyoid Horn

Arytenoid Cartilage Horn

Cricothyroid muscle: arrows show direction of pull

Figure 22

Since the earliest mammalian ancestor resembled a rat, it therefore makes sense to look at the rat today as a possible model of the initial hyoid structures. The epiglottis in the rat is attached to the inner surface of the inverted arch of the thyroid cartilage, and lies in line with the bottom aspect of the larynx. Whereas in man, during the swallowing process, the epiglottis does not fold back, but is squeezed between the base of the tongue and the upper end of the larynx. Food and liquids then pass over the back of the tongue and the posterior surface of the epiglottis. In this position, the inlet of the larynx is tightly closed. In animals such as the rat, the epiglottis is inserted into the posterior opening of the naso-pharyngeal duct, and thus allows breathing and olfaction at the same time while eating and swallowing, which also explains why your dog does not choke in the aforementioned example. In the case of these mammals, food and liquids flow around the epiglottis, because the food channels are laterally placed, and thus around the tightly closed inlet of the larynx. If the rat is an example of our earliest mammalian ancestors then the structure although at first appearing to be an advantage against suffocation while eating also made the rat an obligate nose breather and if the nasal airway should become blocked, then it will suffocate. More advanced mammals like the dog can breathe through the mouth as well, just as we humans do. The obvious question is then, why humans don't have their epiglottis and larynx structured in the same fashion as these other mammals. In 1928, anatomist Negus commented that the human epiglottis is unnecessary for safe swallowing, and presented his argument that it may actually be a degenerate structure of little functional importance. That comment may be somewhat extreme as the epiglottis is obviously functionally important in humans since we have no other way to avoid solids and fluids from entering our trachea simply because of gravity as a result of the lower placement of the larynx. The fact that the lowering of the larynx to a location in the throat to a position where there is a greater risk of suffocation from the mere act of eating hardly appears to be an anatomical improvement should draw every evolutionist's attention. That being the case, there are several questions that result from these previous statements.

The first one being, why did our laryngeal structures evolve differently from other mammals, since we all began on the same evolutionary pathway. Yes, we are the only ones that adopted a permanent standing posture on our hind limbs but that would be all the more reason to keep the larynx at a higher position in the nasal pharynx. At the time, there does not appear to be any justification for this to occur as a result of environmental pressures.

The second question that must be asked is if our capacity to speak is reliant on this different structure. If so, then how is it that anatomically we were already changing long before we had any such capacity and essentially man was no different from any of our primate relatives. The need did not exist at that time, therefore, was this all preplanned?

The third question to ask is why were we losing the heavy jaw and temporal musculature in one Australopithecus offshoot while at the same time preserving it in another. Why would their be evolution in two entirely different directions from a single ancestral form. It would almost appear as if some great designer was hedging his bets and trying out different designs.

And lastly, the fourth question as to whether this was all just a fortunate and serendipitous accident resulting in an unexpected but highly beneficial outcome or perhaps this was more importantly a means to an end by an unseen controlling hand?

Vector Neuroinvasion

The seeming improbability of speech to arise, as detailed over the prior paragraphs, only serves to make it possible to theorize that an initiator to both the physical and neurological changes occurred in a vectorized format that spread globally so that exposure to two different human species, even though separated by thousands of miles was no longer a complicating factor but in fact a shared and inevitable outcome. Similarly, all the changes that resulted in the modification to the musculature and laryngeal regions could also be attributed to this single intervening vector. As strange as this hypothesis may first appear, the best vector for accomplishing this feat would be a virus, and in particular an RNA virus that has the ability to transcribe the host's own DNA genomic structure, leaving behind its personal signature to be carried on through the subsequent generations. What at first might appear as dystrophic to the cranial-mandibular musculature may in fact have been another **God-Spark** to make it possible for an ape like creature to not only expand its cranial capacity but to actually modify normal mammalian physical structures in the throat to eventually acquire the unique ability to speak.

As to why our Australopithecine ancestors didn't become directly infected by this invasive organism, and it was only the later hominins that became exposed most likely has to do with habitat. Similar to their chimpanzee cousins, the Australopithecus probably lived most of their time in the open, with activities performed either in clearings or the jungle, while sleeping in the trees at night. As a non-tool user, it would not have built any type of domicile, other than perhaps binding leaves and branches into a nesting box in which it slept, nestled comfortably between the bifurcating branches of the trees. It wasn't until much later, once the hominids had lost their arboreal lifestyle that they became actual hominins or cavemen, searching for crevices and hollows in the rocks where they could find shelter and protection from the elements. But this adaptation to their habitat did not come without obvious risks. To believe that they would be the only occupants of these caves would have been naive at best. The one creature in particular that would have been sharing this particular domicile would be the bat. The co-relationship between early humans and bats needs to be explored further in order to establish any link that may have impacted directly on human evolution.

The bat's evolution, like that of man's, is not only fascinating but also a mystery as it does not correlate to the Darwinian Theory of evolution that is presented. The earliest fossil remains of the bat are 52 million years old and were only discovered in 2003. Based on the evidence from these fossils, the impression is given that bats have always been able to fly, even since the dawn of the first mammals. This is in defiance of the multiple theories that bats actually evolved from land based animals. Those theories of a slow evolution from land to the air cannot be supported by any of the fossil evidence and whereas the evolution of flying reptiles into birds took place over hundreds of millions of years with a well defined fossil record, there is no such corresponding record for the bat. In fact the exchange of walking front limbs to webbed wings appears to have happened instantaneously, once again providing its own set of questions as to how this was possible. Bats clearly do not support Darwin's theories. Like all mammalian ancestors, the early bat fossils show that early bats had five claws on each limb, which only reduced to two or three much later in their historical record. The once long hind limbs became shortened, while their front limbs extended, giving them a much greater wingspan, thereby improving both maneuverability and speed. The shorter wings of these early bats meant they probably didn't fly as far either, choosing to remain close to their home habitats.

In 2020, probably every human being on the planet became aware that bats can transmit diseases to humans, and in fact many research laboratories keep colonies of bats in order to conduct such virus research. What many may not be aware of is that bats are a primary reservoir for the rabies virus, although there are very few reported cases of rabies transmission from bats to humans. Though most transmissions of the virus are through bites, the fact is that the virus can also be acquired by contamination of the mucous membranes of the nose and mouth from bat secretions, floating as droplets in the air. Therefore, our ancestors who were sharing their caves with these prehistoric bats would have had a high incidence of exposure to rabies, simply by breathing the air within the cave. As to why we didn't have population extinctions as a result of these exposures is the most fascinating part of this scenario but it is not the only puzzling issue when it comes to rabies. The entire process of infection from this particular virus is riddled with questions as it behaves very differently from most other viruses. The incubation period has extremes of variability, ranging from fourteen days to sometimes over a year. In one report, the incubation took 38 months to exhibit itself, making this virus extremely different from any other organism that causes acute infectious disease. It was also shown by Paltauf that of the numbers of people bitten by rabid animals, only a small number actually develop the disease. A few individuals have survived the actual onset of the disease but in almost all cases, once the disease manifests itself, death is inevitable. What we can interpret from these findings is that even though our cave dwelling ancestors would have had exposure to the virus, simply from inhaling the air within the cave, the majority of them were not likely to manifest full blown rabies and the odd individual that did, would most likely die without infecting any others The virus would attempt to reproduce within its new host, ultimately being unsuccessful, but during the long period of its incubation, it would have managed to alter the cellular DNA of its human host to a degree, and it would be highly likely that these alterations would exhibit themselves through physical manifestations in the recovered hominin.

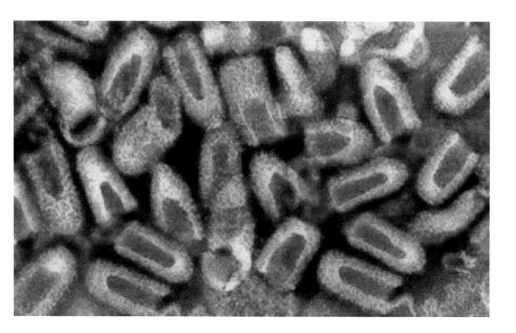

Figure 23

The above postulations are supported by the work published by Angus Munro at the Institute for Research and Advanced Studies at the University of Cambodia. Munro agrees that bats appear to be the reservoir for many, if not all the other members of the genus *Lyssavirus,* which includes rabies, in the Old World. Only on rare occasions would the virus spill over into human populations. The original virus is assumed to have been derived from an insect virus, which later transferred and infected insectivorous bats, but exactly how an insect virus was able to establish such a highly derived cycle of infection in mammals is a complete unknown. The rhabdovirids, as the family of viruses including rabies is known, have a single stranded negative-sense RNA genetic material. They apparently affect a wide diversity of genera which includes arthropods, plants and vertebrates. But the *Lyssaviruses* are now considered to be almost exclusively enzootic to mammals.

The single strand of RNA is enclosed within a proteinaceous capsid which is in turn enveloped by a membrane (derived from the host cell) that incorporates a viral glycoprotein that mediates the infection of the next target cell after the virion has been shed by the initial infected cell. The nucleocapsid provides RNA-dependent RNA polymerase molecules, which are responsible for the initial transcription of a positive RNA strand once the host cell has been compromised. This process is prone to multiple errors due to the lack of any proof-reading activity of the transcribed genome. The frequent mutations raise the possibility of altered host genomes in animals surviving the infection.

Lyssaviruses are now believed to have originated in African bats and spread to Europe, (Rupprecht *et al.*, 2017), though there are others arguing it took place in Eurasia and only later spilled over into Africa, but either scenario supports the contention that a vector could be responsible for changes that both Neanderthals and *Homo sapiens* underwent at approximately the same time. In this manner, the virus easily could have been in both locations, thousands of miles apart and ultimately affecting two different hominin populations. Historically, there is a point of interest in that a book, **Susrutasamhita,** in India from the 1st Century CE reports that in dogs, jackals, hyenas and tigers the clinical signs that were evident were that the tail, jaw and shoulders drooped, and the animals drank much more than usual. The muscle weakness has been noted elsewhere but the report of excessive drinking as compared to the more recent day reports of hydrophobia appear to be directly opposed, suggesting that over time, the clinical signs of the disease have mutated significantly.

It has been suggested that repeated infection of a species other that that which was the reservoir for the given virus biotype may result in the emergence of a new biotype as a result of serial passage in the new host species. But it was also noted that the emergence of a new biotype may either be delayed or not occur at all as a result of antibodies preset in the host as a result of being exposed to non-fatal infections from the original biotype. Therefore, it is believed that it is possible that the virus may act as its own vaccine when first exposed to a new species. How bats maintain their status as a reservoir is not fully understood but it is known that the virus has been discovered in over fifty species of non-blood sucking type bats (i.e.. non-Vampire bats), including some fish eating bats. How the transmission occurs between these bats is still to be determined. The net result of these statements is that the shared domicile within the cave may have exposed early man to the virus but because man was a new biotype that the virus had not encountered previously, then it is very likely that this attenuated the virus, rendering it non-lethal but still capable of establishing a low-level infection that possibly resulted in modification of the human genome. Just as a virus from a bat has played a major and significant role in human history in 2020, it may have done so a well, between fifty and a hundred thousand years ago.

When infected with rabies, bats experience constant vocalization and frequent echolocation in their densely packed colonies, which produces a large emission volume of aerosol from the oral and nasal mucosa of the infected bats, which is then inhaled by any other inhabitants within the cave, such as early humans. According to the work by Rudd, Schmidt-French and Trimarchi, the vocalization by rabid bats is not only incessant but the sounds are completely abnormal. This is a similar finding to that of cats with rabies, which also manifest increased vocalization but the pitch changes dramatically and is no longer cat-like. Dogs with rabies have been described as having an unusual bark and that the change in vocalization in dogs is the most consistent finding in canine rabies infection. It is evident that rabies directly affects the centers of the brain responsible for vocalization and even though early man would not have been able to speak at this particular time, those centers of the brain responsible for speech would have been affected. Between the stimulated brain center, the slackening of the jaw and neck muscles due to a partial paralysis caused by the virus, the increased flaccidity of muscle tone would have permitted the larynx to drop into a lower position. Those humans that recovered from the virus would have discovered they were now suddenly gifted with an amazing ability to create sounds through air movement and tongue control that they had never possessed prior to infection. What had begun as an illness was suddenly a miraculous and practically spontaneous advancement in human achievement. The alterations to the genome would eventually be incorporated into all cells of the body, including the gametes, so that succeeding generations would have the ability to speak without having to experience the infection by the *lyssavirus*. It would not be long until they began to standardize this range of sounds they could express into a common language to be shared by their small community. So that at one time, but much earlier than that suggested by the building of the tower of Babel, the ancestors did speak with a single voice, a common language of hoots and calls much like the other apes, but then they became afflicted by the hand of God, who brought them crashing down to the brink of death, only to find then when they rose to their feet once more, they were suddenly speaking a multitude of languages and could not understand one another any longer. That biblical story may be giving us the a modified version of what actually happened.

As the story of Nimrod and the tower of Babel indicates, mankind reestablished itself in small group or settlements, each having its own language that it shared among its own community. The biblical story is merely a fanciful tale designed to describe the dawn of speech and the many languages spoken by mankind. It is presented in a negative fashion, as if the ability to speak was the result of a punishment, that man had to suffer in order inherit this ability. It is possible that it represents one of the few early memories that our primitive ancestors recall; their having to suffer disease and possibly death, only to find that afterwards they could speak.

Aside from the fact that the virus causes this abnormal vocalization in all species, even cattle which begin to bellow strangely, the virus possesses unique mechanisms that help it remain undetected in the body for long periods of time. It begins its attack within the muscle cells, so that it can avoid the host's immune system, then actively seeks out the nerves that penetrate the muscles, binding itself to the neuronal cells, specifically to the acetylcholine receptors of these neurons. After binding at the neuromuscular junction, the virus transports itself backwards through the nervous system, traveling along the axons until it reaches the central nervous system, where it replicates in motor neurons and then quickly travels to the brain. From the brain, it travels to peripheral and autonomic nervous system. Rabies causes inflammation and swelling of the brain, but in particular that part of the brain which controls swallowing. Involuntary neck contractions when the host tries to swallow water can be seen at early stages of the disease. In humans, even the thought of a glass of water may start the patient to contract their neck muscles, preventing the swallowing action to take place, hence the characteristic of the disease being called hydrophobia or the fear of water. But obviously it was not always producing this condition as was noted from the Indian writing of *Susrutasamhita*. Clearly the virus has changed its mode of action regarding the constriction of the throat muscles as this would not have been the case during the dawn of the disease. As the hydrophobia is associated with the form of infection referred to as 'furious' rabies, it is likely that early hominids experienced only the 'dumb' or 'paralytic' rabies when infected from the bats. This latter form of rabies is slow to progress, and tends to paralyze all of the musculature rather than cause any constrictions. According to the WHO, paralytic rabies only accounts for 30% of cases now but in all likelihood, it was probably the original form of rabies, causing a dysfunctional autonomic nervous system rather than hyper-stimulating the throats skeletal musculature, as is the case in 'furious' rabies.

Taking a look retrospectively at what was necessary in order for one of the mammalian species to acquire the ability for speech, then it was a matter of several factors all taking place in a relatively short time span. There would need to be a stimulation of the vocal control centers of the brain, in fact an incredible stimulus to make a wide range of sound over different octaves, while at the same time relaxing the muscles of the jaws and throat, so not only can the larynx drop into a position where it is unhampered by any of the other structures in the naso-pharyngeal cavity but the tongue gains extreme freedom of movement. While this is all happening, it is also occurring in small pockets of population separated by large distances simultaneously, and incredibly affecting two hominin species that are separated by thousands of miles. To complicate matters further, the changes are being incorporated into the genetic coding of the cells of these two species and especially in the genetic material of the gametes so that it can be passed down vertically through any offspring born. If that isn't enough to be classified as a miraculous event requiring a **GodSpark**, I don't know how else it could be labeled. Of course, scientists working with viral and embryonic genetics would say that they can do this too through genetic modification and current technologies and there's no denying that they could, though there would probably be a few accidents along the way that could be near extinction events or simply another pandemic if it escaped from their laboratory, but it could be done. But they are missing the point when they say this. What they are admitting to, is that through vial vector intervention, and intentional genetic manipulation they could make this happen in today's world, which only confirms that somewhere around a hundred thousand years ago, there was a similar intervention and manipulation through almost identical means, with an intended purpose and it certainly wasn't by our modern day scientists.

Viral Genetic Regulation

Thus far, it has been suggested that mankind's ability to speak was the result of a viral infection. My theory is not as radical or extreme as one might think. In fact, in two separate papers, scientists working on a similar theory of how viruses can affect the evolutionary process published two distinct and fundamental processes underlying germline transcriptomes. In these papers, they provide evidence that species-specific transcriptomes are fine-tuned by endogenous retroviruses in the mammalian germline. In other words, our own genetics have been and are being adjusted by viruses on a constant basis.

Germline transcriptomes are inclusive of the mRNA present in our reproductive cells, such as sperm or ova, which contain either the male or female half of the chromosomes respectively that will constitute the full set of chromosomes of the offspring. Upon fertilization, these two halves come together to produce the double stranded helix structure Thus, the germline transcriptomes define the unique character of both sperm and egg , preparing them to produce the next generation of life.

In the study by Sakashita and Namekawa, the work revolves around the potential for endogenous retroviruses to act as gene regulatory elements in the genome. This helps fine tune species-specific transcriptomes in mammals. Endogenous retroviruses (ERVs) that are an inherent part of mammalian biology, can dramatically influence gene expression. These investigators report. ERVs are molecular remnants of retroviruses that infected the ancestral host body and over time became incorporate into the genome. Exactly as I have described our ancestor's exposure to prehistoric rabies virus.

In his own words, "What we learn from our study is that, in general, viruses have major roles in driving evolution," Namekawa explained. "In the long-term, viruses have positive impacts to our genome and shape evolution."

In another study, Maezawa and Sakashita et al., combined biological testing of mouse models and human germline cells with computational biology, including genome-wide profiling of gene regulatory elements in germline cells. That's a mouthful in science-speak, in which he was simply saying their tests revealed that the entire genome can be reorganized through these viral vectors that are referred to as super-enhancers. The virus causes bursts of germline gene expression after the germ cells enter meiosis, a specialized form of cell division that produces the haploid genome of germ cells. Their study further demonstrated the molecular process by which the viral genetic material switching takes place in these germ cells. Their so-called super-enhancers are regulated by two molecules that act as gene-burst control switches. These two molecules are identified as transcription factor A-MYB and SCML2. I know in this day of CoVid 19 it is hard to envision viruses being called super-enhancers, as if they are gifted with super powers but this is exactly what their research has proven. That during the cell division phase of sperm cells and ova cells, the genetic material is highly prone to being swapped in and out, which these viruses can take advantage of.

Should there be other genetic material readily available from another source, such as these endogenous retroviruses, then they provide transposable elements (TEs), or in other words, mobile genetic elements, that can be easily swapped in via this super-enhancer switching phase. Here's the amazing part; they estimate that this switching can account for approximately 40-50 percent of a given mammalian genome. You will also encounter these TEs referred to as "jumping genes and for a long time they have been considered as genetic threats because transposition can be harmful if genes that interfere with normal processes should be switched in and turned on. But the opposite is true too, in which they can enhance the genetic material of a species by introducing functions and mechanisms that would not have developed naturally, proving my theory is not only possible but highly probable.

Thus far, we've talked about genetic modification via viruses as a natural occurrence that has taken place as soon as their were host cells to be infected and viruses to infect them. But we live in an age now where the use of viruses to genetically engineer host cells is essentially common practice. Genetic engineering is a fully recognized branch of science that intentionally develops a trait or set of traits within an organism by inserting, or incorporating, the specific sequence of genetic code for that trait. By manipulating viruses and using their ability to attach to and invade specific cells, in order to incorporate the DNA or RNA they are carrying into the host cell, which will then recombine with the host cell's DNA, it is possible to change the host both physiologically and physically. It is this unique invasive quality of viruses that has given scientists the tool with which to open the door to the DNA of a cell and modify it to meet their intended purpose. It is a tool that can accomplish great things but it can also be the greatest single threat to the survival of mankind through intentional misuse or by accident.

The reality is that gene therapy products have been commercially marketed in this rapidly growing field with over 350 clinical trials that began in 2019. The use of biologicals, such as viral vectors, is one of the fastest growing sectors of the pharmaceutical market. Since it is now clear that many diseases have genetic origins, then it only makes sense that through genetic engineering, these conditions can possibly be eliminated. Simply stated, gene therapy uses nucleic acids as the mechanism of treatment delivered by a vector, which is typically a recombinant, replication of a virus that has had its infectious elements removed. This virus then delivers its payload of gene-encoding DNA to the genetically defective cells. These cells then use their own expression machinery and the newly delivered DNA template to express the missing protein or proteins and restore the cells to normal function. The advantage of genetic therapies is that treated cells will continue to express the introduced gene years later, thereby effectively providing in theory, a permanent cure. The concept is not new and has been in use for thirty years already when it was first successfully demonstrated back in 1991, when two patients suffering from an inherited immunodeficiency known as ADA-SCID, were successfully treated through restoration of their immune function. Since then and following the release of Glybera, the first gene therapy to achieve market approval, there have been numerous new products entering the market.

Since much of my professional work career involves vaccine development, I might as well take this opportunity to give a brief overview of what is occurring within the industry. One of the main viral vectors used for in-vivo gene therapy is the adeno-associated virus (AAV), which is approximately 20nm in diameter and comprises the outer capsid of the virus, consisting of three proteins. It is used to deliver the single-stranded DNA into the cell. AAV is known as an opportunistic parasite and thus far, no human complications from infection have been identified as a result of injection. The virus replicates inside the host cell, which provides all the production and replication functions required by the virus There are other viral vectors used for gene therapy, but AAV is less immunogenic and therefore provides a safer vector for products.

In 2018, the market value of gene therapy was $1 billion USD with a forecast compound annual growth rate of 36.5 percent, By the year 2025 it is anticipated that the market value will be $9 billion USD. In all likelihood, everyone will be receiving some sort of genetically engineered product in the next few decades as it become more and more commonplace. Just think of it, instantaneous genetic modification through an injection. It is a wonderful scientific achievement when used correctly but it is up to us to safeguard it only for the elimination of genetically associated disease. But as usual, there is already evidence of misuse of this technology and rumors of its use to produce what we identify from the comic book world as the 'super soldier.' It won't be too much of a surprise if this story should turn out to be true as the value of virus delivered genetic material to accelerate human evolution is too great a temptation for science to ignore.

It is one thing for mankind to have gained the ability to speak through a viral infection and the curing of genetic diseases through a similar process is a great achievement. What we do now is with purpose and intent, and I would suggest our acquisition of speech was with no less purpose and intent by the Creator. The appearance of what we should consider as a miracle cannot be chance and the fact that we can do similar things in a laboratory now should not in any way diminish the appearance of the miraculous event. We are only learning to master the technique now, but for a development such as speech to have occurred in the necessary sequence as I have outlined also needed to be a controlled experiment. Which only again emphasizes the fact that God is the ultimate scientist. But the Almighty new when to stop the experiment and be satisfied with His achievements. My fear is that our scientists lack the same intelligence to know when to stop.

The Origin of Viruses

The actual question that everyone should be asking at this point is why do viruses exist at all. How is it that an organism, that isn't actually alive since it does not have its own energy units such as ribosomes, and can't reproduce on its own, even exist? To be honest, there is much debate among virologists about this very question. In an effort to find an answer they have arrived at three main hypotheses. The first is the progressive, or escape, hypothesis, which states that viruses arose from genetic elements that somehow gained the ability to move between cells. The second theory is known as the regressive, or reduction hypothesis, which speculates that viruses are remnants of cellular organisms that simply refused to die. And the third theory is known as the virus-first hypothesis, which states that viruses predate or co-evolved with their current cellular hosts. In other words, for every living organism, there is a corresponding virus that came into existence at the same time.

Looking at the Progressive Hypothesis, which proposes they are escaped genetic elements, it proposes that pieces of genetic material gained the ability to move within the genome and this mobility eventually provided them with the ability to move from one cell to another. The process is very similar to how retroviruses behave now, reproducing themselves by taking over the host cell's mechanisms where they become copied through the use of the viral enzyme, reverse transcriptase, which converts the single RNA virus strand into double stranded DNA and then this DNA enters the nucleus of the cell where another enzyme, integrase, inserts this viral DNA into the host cell's genome, so that the viral genes get copied and reproduced by the cell's polymerase, producing more virus particles that then assemble and exit the cell to find a new cell to infect. For the Progressive Hypothesis to work, it only required some rogue strands of RNA to form, which would have been easy enough to originate from errors created by the retrotransposons in the cell. Acquisition of a few structural proteins and a means to exit and enter other cells and you have your first RNA virus. That being the case, then it could not have been the intent of these first viruses to kill their host, otherwise they would have ceased to exist as well. They were essentially nothing more than a programmed material that had a job to do, which was build strands of genetic material but when they failed to behave properly, there was no off switch. The major issue with this hypothesis is that it doesn't explain the structures that are unique to viruses and were therefore not borrowed from the cells, such as the complex viral capsids.

The second hypothesis mentioned was the Regressive Hypothesis which suggests that viruses may have originated via a regressive, or reductive process. When examining certain bacterial species that are considered obligate intracellular parasites, such as *Chlamydia* or *Rickettsia* species, they most likely evolved from what would have been free-living ancestors. That being the case that bacteria can lose functionality over time, then it would be possible that viruses may have been fully functional freeliving organisms that also lost functionality over time until they became entirely parasitic as they lost their genetic information to the point they couldn't even replicate on their own. Scientists point to the large DNA viruses as possible proof of this hypothesis and in particular the largest of all viruses, the Mimivirus,which has a total diamter of about 750 nm, or essentially ten times larger than the influenza virus. Mimivirus has a genome of 1.2 million base pairs as compared to the poliovirus which only has a genome of 7,500 nucleotides in total. The Mimivirus exhibits greater complexity than other viruses and is less dependent on its host for replication than other viruses. The size and complexity would suggest that at one time Mimivirus was a free living orgainism. As such, it may have lived in a symbiotic relationship with another organism, each providing benefits to the other but over time, the relationship became parasitic with one organism taking far more than it was giving. As the paraistism increased, those genes that were no longer required as the organism took what it needed from the other organism were evetually lost, until eventually the parasitic organism became totaly reliant on the other, even for the purposes of replication. Analysis of the giant Mimivirus provides support to this hypothesis as the virus contains a large number of genes associated with translation that it has no use for.

The first two hypotheses both suppose that cells existed long before there were viruses. The thid hypothesis supposes exactly the opposite, theorizing that perhaps viruses cames first as in they were the first attempts to create cellular life and that originally they could replicate as proposed by Koonin and Martin. Only later did they become more complex, manufacturing their own membranes and cell walls and eventually becoming one celled organisms. Of course the argument that naturally results would be if they had the ability at first to replicate, then why would they devolve into a parasitic organism that could neither survive or replicate on its own. It certainly couldn't be considered a case of evolving into a better life form if some did and others did the exact opposite with no other purpose than to destroy and eliminate the higher life form.

The fact is that no single hypothesis may be correct and there's the possibility that not all virues came in to existence through the same pathway. One can argue that most retroviruses arose through a progressive process, while the large DNA viruse came into being through the regressive process. Though the virus first hypothesis would be an interesting phenomena, it is the least supported by the evidence but there's always the possibility there is a fourth means by which viruse arose but we haven't discovered or thought of it as yet. But no matter what may be the actual origin of viruses, the question as to why they still exist needs to be answered. If their soul purpose is to take over host cells and eventually kill the host ogranism, then that would be a self defeating puprose that would eventually lead to the extinction of the virus itself. Since the general rule of all organisms on this planet appears to be to propogate and avoid extinction, this would not make any sense unless it was not the intial function or purpose of viuses but instead an unexpected or unantici-pated outcome of something that went wrong. In the same manner that we worry that some laboratory working with viruses in order to produce vaccines accidentally creates a virulent virus strain that escapes from the lab, what is there to stop such an occurence in nature's laboratory. Whereas the original virus format would be simi-lar in concept to the ERVs that Namekawa spoke of, a means by which to accelerate species evolution, an infinitely small percentage of these are incorrectly assembled and intead of being enhancers, they are in fact destroyers. But no matter what the case might be, there can only be one answer as to who might be in charge of nature's laboratory to make all this happen even if it can be viewed as a double-edgd sword. Considering that science is in agreement that about 8 percent of the human genome contains sequences that originally came from viruses, it would suggest that our evo-lution as a species owes a great debt to the changes within us that were a direct result of these virus infections. The benefits certainly outweigh the deficits. One may still think of viruses as terrible blights upon the world, but with 7 billion people now in existence, we must view them in their proper context. As the most successful or-ganism that has ever walked this planet, and thus far, the impact of viruses when we refere to them in a negative or disease promulgating perspective has been nothing more than a drop in the ocean compared to the positive results they may have achieved.

Chapter 11: Genetic Engineering

Even before Mendel was playing with his peas in order to determine how basic genetics worked, the Old Testament had already forbidden us from cross pollinating between certain species. To do so would be in defiance of what was ordained during the creation where God said each animal species and plant would procreate each to his own kind. It was as if the Almighty knew that at some time in the future mankind would no longer feel restrained by this command and would actively seek to break the genetic barriers. Suddenly viruses would not be the determining factors of rapid evolution but instead the natural order would be replaced with the test tube. The holy ban on mixing the species, referred to as כִּלְאַיִם; kilayim, is mentioned twice in the Old Testament. The first time is in Leviticus 19:19, where it states, "Ye shall keep my statutes. Thou shalt not let thy cattle gender with a diverse kind; thou shalt not sow thy field with two kinds of seed; neither shall there come upon thee a garment of two kinds of stuff mingled together." It can also be found in Deuteronomy 22:9–11 where it is written, "Thou shalt not sow thy vineyard with two kinds of seed; lest the fullness of the seed which thou hast sown be forfeited together with the increase of the vineyard. Thou shalt not plow with an ox and an ass together. Thou shalt not wear a mingled stuff, wool and linen together."

The translation of together did not actually refer to sowing the fields with two different crops as that would be normal farm practice but instead was a warning against using a seed derived from two different plants. We learned the danger of that when Monsanto grafted its 'suicide gene' into the seeds so that farmers would be unable to replant the following year from seed gathered in that year. This was their way to ensure that farmers had to come back every year and purchase new seed from Monsanto. What they hadn't taken into account was that neighbouring farms would be pollinated by the plants grown from their suicide seeds and now entire regions were unable to grow the next year's crops, even if they had never purchased the Monsanto seeds. The seeds didn't only represent greed and ill intent by Monsanto, it was a direct warning of the potential failure of future crops an the onset of starvation around the world. God's warning regarding hybridization was never more ominous than when Monsanto was finally brought to court and had to confess to their actions but who's to say what else they may be doing in their laboratories that defies the natural order.

So when examined closely as to what was being written over three thousand years ago it constituted a prohibition that applied to the genetically combining together of two kinds of grains if they are regarded as belonging to different species, or of grain with a vegetable, or any non-natural combination of plants. Of course early man didn't fully understand this warning and still thought it was a literal reference to having two different plants in the same garden, so that early religious leaders came out and declared that it was only permitted to sow five different species of plants as long as there were specified distances between them of no less than one cubit square. While they argued about the exact distances between crops, these religious leaders had absolutely no idea what modern man would be capable of when it came to genetic modification. Although they may not have understood during their time frame, we most certainly understand it today.

It is interesting how ancient societies interpreted the forbiddance of crossing animal species. According to Jewish leaders, they determined that you could own and rear such animals as long as you weren't the one guilty of the breeding. As their preferred mode of transportation was the mule, a cross between horse and donkey, it was alright to purchase a mule from someone else that bred it.

But when it came to the forbiddance of plowing a field with an ox and an ass, that matter confused them as it wasn't even common practice to do so. Everyone knew that to successfully plow a field you required a team of oxen, or a team of donkeys or even mules because the difference in sizes, strength, length of stride would make ploughing practically impossible. The rabbis, most of them not being farmers themselves by the time they tried to explain this ruling in the Talmud written over a thousand years after God rendered this edict assumed it must have been the way people did it in the past and accepted it at face value. Of course, they never expected or could even imagine two thousand years later scientists would be experimenting with hybrids and chimeras where they have combined the genetic material of two or more species of animals together. A dangerous practice which God obviously foresaw but since when does mankind ever pay attention.

But one thing the ancients did recognize was that these unnatural combinations had a hereditary impact that they assumed was the punishment for undertaking such activities. Naḥmanides commented that by crossbreeding a horse and an ass in order to produce a mule, what one actually gets is s a miserable creature that cannot produce any of its own progeny." Maimonides wrote in his **Guide For the Perplexed,** that the man who couples creatures of different species defies the laws of nature and of ethics, and similarly is guilty of doing so when grafting and mixing plants species. The historian Josephus wrote in **Antiquities., 4:229** that "nature delighteth not in the conjunction of things dissimilar."

As mankind experimented with the mating of lions and tigers to obtain ligers and tigons, only to find that they were infertile as well, you would have thought science would have taken the hint that the crossing of species was a bad idea. A number of theories have been offered by the scientific community to explain why hybrids tend to be less viable and generally infertile. In regards to the decreased viability the best explanation is that during the process of hybridization there are random combinations of genetic programs, which when they interact, they do so in an inharmonious way. Our cellular and body processes can only move in one direction and if simultaneously there are two very different commands for that process then like any mechanism, the process simply shuts down. The combination in a single organism of two genomes that are separately functional for the same activity will most likely have an adverse interaction. As genes are paired, to function properly they must be compatible in order to work. But the issue of hybrid infertility is a completely different matter. In these hybrids there occurs a reduction in the quality and number of gametes produced and the theory is that in some way the hybrid recognizes that it is a product of reverse evolution. Whereas, the two species may have had a common ancestor a long time ago, the reproductive apparatus is no longer willing to accept a reversal to this ancestral state. Some have described this as natural selection involving itself directly in order to increase reproductive isolation. The reinforcement of this isolation supposedly occurs when two differentiated but related species come back into contact. In order to complete its mission of reproductive isolation, the natural selection process renders the hybrids less viable and infertile.

Not everyone accepts this theory but many do accept the Dobzhansky-Muller model even though this model has some serious flaws such as the concept of their theory which simply put is "it happens." In their theory, the hybrid might actually have an advantage over the independent species of either parent. If that is the case, then the hybrid is a threat to the existence of both species and natural selection must remove it from the gene pool before it can do any damage. So much for survival of the fittest and the advancement of the superior species according to Darwin. The D-M theory fails to explain how the genetic superiority would result in the production of sterile offspring with disrupted meiosis and few viable gametes. The fact is that the theory doesn't hold water but scientist will cling to it because they have nothing else. At least the theory of gene competition causing confusion for the same function provides us with something to think about. A better causal explanation for the DM theorists is not that 'it happens' but 'God makes it happen', which makes far more sense than what they have to offer.

It is interesting when Darwin was challenged to explain how hybrids fit into his theory of evolution, he was stumped. Instead he spoke of "physiological species" in an effort to isolate those forms that were unable to interbreed due to physiological incompatibility from his theory of evolution. This conundrum weighed heavily on Darwin and in a letter dated May 17, 1891, written by his friend Thomas Huxley it said, "I insisted on the necessity of obtaining experimental proof of the possibility of obtaining virtually infertile breeds from a common stock in 1860 ... From the first I told Darwin this was the weak point of his case from the point of view of scientific logic. But, in this matter, we are just where we were thirty years ago."

This dilemma of not having an answer only led Darwin to write, "After mature reflection that natural selection could not account for the evolution of the 'physiological species'. The sterility of first crosses and of their hybrid progeny has not been acquired through natural selection."

This failure of his theory to account for the infertility of hybrids culminated in the response by Wallace who wrote, "I will say no more, but leave the problem as insoluble, only fearing that it will become a formidable weapon in the hands of the enemies of Natural Selection." Whether it was unsolvable as Wallace wanted to claim, or a reluctance to admit that perhaps there is the hand of God involved in matters of this world, Darwin eventually came to refer to it as an unknown force. He even refers to this mystery factor in his book, *The Descent of Man* (1871: vol. I, 222–223, footnote), where he writes, "The sterility of crossed species has not been acquired through natural selection: we can see that when two forms have already been rendered very sterile, it is scarcely possible that their sterility should be augmented by the preservation or survival of the more and more sterile individuals; for, as the sterility increases, fewer and fewer offspring will be produced from which to breed, and at last only single individuals will be produced at the rarest intervals. But there is even a higher grade of sterility than this. ... in genera of plants including numerous species, a series can be formed from species which, when crossed, yield fewer and fewer seeds, to species which never produce a single seed, but yet are affected by the pollen of the other species, as shewn by the swelling of the germen. It is here manifestly impossible to select the more sterile individuals, which have already ceased to yield seeds; so that the acme of sterility, when the germen alone is affected, cannot be gained through selection. This acme, and no doubt the other grades of sterility, are the incidental results of certain unknown differences in the constitution of the reproductive system of the species which are crossed." It takes a wise man to admit that he does not know the answer but even a wiser man to admit that there are unknown forces in this universe that cannot be accounted for through science.

Of course there is a reason for my raising this issue of hybrid infertility and decreased viability well beyond the fact that science still cannot offer any precise reason for its occurrence, though the theory of competing genes that don't match identically is one which does have some validity and should not be dismissed. Because the truth is we need science to have a valid theory that is applicable across the board that clearly proves the production of all hybrids results in these diminished capabilities. That what is true for the mule, the liger and all the hybrid plant species will hold true for every other hybrid attempted because that is a general rule of nature; 'the law of hybridization'. Because only then it can be pointed out that the law would appear to be universal except in one particular case and that in turn requires explanation as to how that was even possible. As we have explored all available reasons as to why hybrid offspring tend to be infertile and incapable of propagating a new species, then it is necessary to challenge all that by reminding everyone, that according to a new DNA study, as detailed in National Geographic, most humans have a degree of genetic material from Neanderthals in their makeup, anywhere from 1 to 4 percent. The study provided solid genetic evidence that *Homo sapiens* interbred with those Neanderthals that they may have encountered. They can even identify where this mating took place, pinpointing it to the Middle East during the migrations alluded to earlier in this book, as *Homo sapiens* left Africa.

Ed Green of the University of California stated it this way, "We can now say that, in all probability, there was gene flow from Neanderthals to modern humans." This statement and the evidence vindicates an anthropologist Erik Trinkhaus, who made earlier claims based on skeletal evidence that Neanderthal-*Homo sapien* interbreeding took place, only to be contradicted by early DNA evidence that suggested that did not happen because of the lack of Neanderthal genes identified. Trinkhaus goes further by saying, "That most living humans probably have much more Neanderthal DNA than the new study suggests.

The conclusions of this study were made after comparing the genomes of five modern day humans from China, France, Papua New Guinea, southern Africa, and western Africa, against the assembled Neanderthal genome. The results demonstrated that Neanderthal DNA was approximately 99 percent identical to modern human DNA. It was shown that all modern ethnic groups, other than Africans, carry traces of Neanderthal DNA in their genomes, which is not surprising because there is no fossil evidence of Neanderthal's presence in Africa. What it also suggests is that the evolved origins of Neanderthals from *Homo heidelbergensis* took place somewhere else other than the African continent.

Based on this finding, the first opportunity for *Homo sapiens* to encounter their more primitive cousins would have been about 60,000 years ago in Middle Eastern lands when sapiens first left Africa and where archaeological evidence suggests the two species overlapped for a period of time. Genetic anthropologist Jeffrey Long, similarly co-authored a new study that found DNA evidence of inter-breeding between early modern humans and an "archaic human" species, which he presented at a meeting of the American Association of Physical Anthropologists in Albuquerque, New Mexico.

We can excuse Darwin for not knowing that modern humans and Neander-thals would have fallen into his web of 'physiological species' in which he en-trapped himself, because during his time, Neanderthal was believed to be an ances-tor of early man and not a separate competitive species. For the sake of argument, let us examine the fact that the genome of Neanderthal and *Homo sapien* are very similar with less than a percent difference and that might be close enough for some scientists to argue that the 'physiological species' argument does not apply because they are 'almost' the same species. So on that basis I will dismiss tigers from lions and panthers in a direct comparison, because in the wild, these three species will likely never mate. Nor would a horse and donkey or a zebra, These matings are forced upon them by human interference. But that is not the case when we examine llamas and alpacas in their natural habitat. Here are two animals that like Nean-derthal and *Homo sapien* are 'almost' the same species, so much so, that unless one is familiar with llamas and alpacas, one cannot tell the difference except for the size. But in the wild, these two species will naturally mate to produce a 'huarizo', the product of a male llama and a female alpaca, and this offspring is sterile. Alt-hough recently researchers at the University of Minnesota have claimed they can perform a minimal genetic modification and thereby preserve the fertility. But 60,000 years ago, there weren't any university researchers around to do the same for the two human species. They mated naturally, without any 'scientific' inter-vention and they produced sterile offspring, an event which according to everything we have looked at shouldn't have happened but it did. If ever there was an occa-sion that required a '**GodSpark**' this was it because what shouldn't have happened did, and we now have undeniable proof now that it did occur.

Section Three: Darwinian Evolution

Chapter 12: Survival of the Fittest?

The Year was 1859 and Charles Darwin had just published his ***On The Origin of Species***. Science heralded it as the year that finally put an end to religious dogma but what most people aren't even aware of is that Charles Darwin wrote in his book, that not only did he think evolution required something like the power of the Creator in order to breathe life into the start of the entire process but also commented that even though a species might evolve it appeared to be a selective process, where some life forms did and others did not. He had no explanation for this selectivity. The real question that everyone should have been asking at the time when they read his book was who might he have been inferring made the selection.

Darwin was aware that the scantiness of the fossil record failed to demonstrate an evolutionary progression for all species. In fact, some ancestors of certain species looked exactly the same from the fossil record as their modern day progeny did. Whereas, other species, such as the evolution from ape to human demonstrated tremendous change over a brief interval of time as compared to the entire record of cosmic time. Hence his comment that there was a selection process and that evolution was not a naturally occurring process but in some way that he had not determined, a controlled process. Darwin's failure to identify the key did not stop his colleague Thomas Huxley declaring the book of Genesis to be nothing more than a fable designed to appeal to the myths of pagans. It was a bold declaration that immediately set religion and science in opposition and destroyed any bridges that could have been built to find a reasonable solution that would satisfy both groups.

Whereas Darwin recognized his theory resulted in numerous dead ends, where certain species appeared to meet an evolutionary dead end, or perhaps completely disappeared rather than evolve, even though by all accounts they were a dominant and fit species that met his definition of 'survival of the fittest.' On the other hand, Huxley refused to admit that evolution was an inherently faulty process that didn't always achieve its goal and became the chief proponent for a smooth evolutionary process, even if it meant supporting a blatantly false fossil record purporting to outline the transition of Eohippus to modern day horse. The obvious error by both these gentlemen is their belief that evolution is a slow transitional process, a gradual transformation up the evolutionary ladder but this is certainly not the case when looking at the evolutionary development of man. The thirteen million years to transition from a gibbon like ape into Australopithecus, only to see the first of the pre-hominins like Ramapithecus develop two million years later, and then the appearance of *Homo erectus* a mere few hundred thousand years later is a clear indication that evolution makes tremendous leaps with each change when the rule of 'π' is involved. Furthermore, once a species is on that evolutionary ladder, each subsequent jump occurs over an equally shortened time period as demonstrated in an earlier chapter. There is no natural or physical law that can explain the dramatic change or the acceleration that occurs with each evolutionary leap unless one accepts the rule of 'π' as being one such rule. With each step on that ladder it is almost as if you can visualize that unseen hand, redesigning the previous model, with little intention to build on the earlier design but instead making a full restyling as we look at the progression of features in Figure 18.

Darwin would have done himself a favour if he had added the phrase, evolution only occurs within the limits of 'intelligent design.' What do I mean by this? When you look at all life on earth, there appears to be only a few design patterns that are followed. Vegetative life has its own design on how it is to look, behave, function and grow. Fish in the sea have their design concept that they all seem to follow. Insects will look, behave and develop as insects always have, and so on and so on. Even after several mass extinctions that have occurred during the earth's timeline, a perfect opportunity for new lifeforms to develop with uncharacteristic designs from the prior inhabitants of the earth, none the less these new species follow the same design pattern that was in use before. Mammals still have four legs, one head, one tail and so on, even though these would have been perfect opportunities for new life forms to develop. If our genetic code, which one hundred years after Darwin was shown to be a double helix DNA construct, is capable of mutation and tremendous and rapid change, then why did it revert to the same standard pattern that has always been in use since life forms began on earth. This would suggest that although evolution is capable of change, it has limitations and limits were also encoded into our genetic material by some unexplained process according to science, but easily explained by religion if we accept there is a superior intelligence guiding the process.

The degree of control is conclusive though science is not prepared to admit it. Even though all phyla, referring to invertebrates and vertebrates and all their subsequent genera and species developed independently, the fact that the same genes for visual apparatus are responsible for sight in all of them should be scientifically impossible if we adhere to the concept of random genetic mutation and modification. Once again it would appear that there was only a single design pattern and however that design came into existence, it was inserted into all life forms no matter how different they might be. As humans we may be unique but these instances of common genetic structures remind us that we are not as different as we may think.

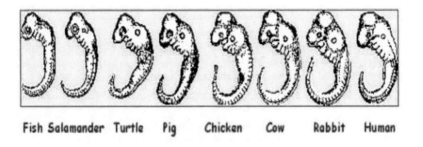

Fish Salamander Turtle Pig Chicken Cow Rabbit Human

Figure 24

A quick look at embryological development from fish to humans as in Figure 24, once again show the commonality of our original designs, looking almost identical in the early stages as we transition through the developmental stages to reach the endpoint. As we watch the disappearance of the gill slits, the tail, etc. from the developing human embryo, we cannot help but recognize that we are nothing more than a developmental process that was written in to an immutable genetic code. 'How can that be' if all genetic material is predisposed to mutation and exchange of nucleotides? How is it that certain segments of our DNA are safeguarded from any such occurrence? Certainly we have numerous defects where normal development did not occur, but in many cases these were the result of the introduction of chemicals during pregnancy that altered development at a cellular level such as the effects of Thalidomide in the late 1950s and early 1960s. In most cases, where genetic defects are involved, the offspring do not survive to a reproductive age, but still they exhibit a general structure, both anatomically and physiologically, that follows the original design concept. The safeguards that have been 'locked' in to our genetic coding are no different than us passwording certain material on our hard-drive, ensuring that it cannot be erased, overwritten or altered by anyone else but ourselves. If we use this as an analogous metaphor, then who was it that passworded our DNA? It obviously appears to have been done intentionally.

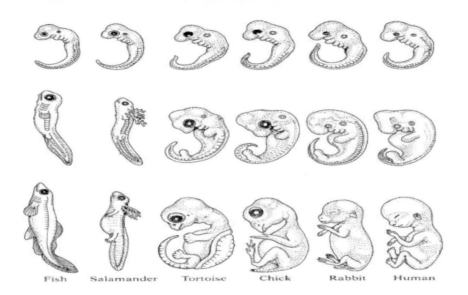

Fish   Salamander   Tortoise   Chick   Rabbit   Human

Figure 25

Those that wish to argue against this intentional intervention such as Nobel laureate Weinberg, resort to a dismissive attitude when he tries to explain life in the universe by stating that the universe is pointless and life is nothing more than a farcical universal joke.   Hard to believe that one of the smartest men in the world would provide a summation of our existence as nothing more than a cosmic error without rhyme or reason.   But scientists often become facetious, dismissive and sarcastic when faced with questions they cannot or will not answer because to do so would force them to admit that there may be something 'more'.

The biggest argument against Darwinism came in 1992 when analysis of the Walcott fossil samples were completed. Walcott was in charge of the Smithsonian Institute at the turn of the twentieth century and he was what you would call an avid fossil collector. Whereas others would have a vacation suntanning on a beach in the Caribbean, Walcott could be found digging his way through layers of rock. Having come upon a huge source of fossils in the Canadian Rockies, he was faced with a conundrum. The rock in which the fossils were embedded was known to date back to the pre Cambrian era, over five hundred million years ago. But the fossils discovered represented a huge range of plant species and animal species. There were crustaceans, mollusks, insects, worms, sponges and fish. All animals that shouldn't have existed at the time of the dating of the rocks. Walcott knew that his discovery radically veered from everything Darwin had suggested regarding evolution. So his solution was to lock away his findings, only to have them rediscovered 80 years later when the Smithsonian was clearing out his boxes. Scientific American reported the finding, questioning whether the theory of evolution was no longer suitable to explain the latest findings. Then came similar articles in National Geographic and the New York Times, each questioning if Darwin's theories had finally met their match. It was time to recognize that evolution was not necessarily a gradual process but could make leaps and bounds under what they termed as "still undefined circumstances".

That, as you have seen is the scientific community's way of handling anything that is not congruent with their own theories. From the astrophysical data discussed at the beginning of the book, to the failure to produce the necessary building blocks of life, and on to the huge gaps in the evolutionary profile, it's always been a game to them to kick the can further down the road with the hope that some new evidence will turn up to save them from having to admit that there is enough evidence to suggest that the only way our world and our existence could have come into being was by their being a cosmic intelligence, who would be the Creator.

Chapter 13: Selective Evolution

One of the chief arguments presented by evolutionists is that given the same conditions, identical circumstances, similar environmental pressures and repetitions of social frameworks, the evolutionary process will intercede in the same manner as it has done before. In other words, the conditions that invite evolution may be random but evolution itself is not and it will occur when it is faced with the same opportunity. We need not look any further than the work of paleontologist Elso Barghoorn who discovered micro-fossils of bacteria and algae in rocks that were dated to be 3.5 billion years old. Three hundred million years earlier, there were deposits of organic carbon found and that is about the same time that water as a liquid appeared on the surface of the earth. Throw in the right temperature, proportion of gases in the atmosphere, electrostatic discharges as lightning, and the correct amount of UV radiation from the sun and 'voila', you have life. There was nothing random about it. As soon as the right conditions were available, the natural processes to evolve life on earth began. Yes, it was a miracle, but the miracle being that it was that easy and that's all it took for the Creator, but as soon as science tried to reproduce the event, they failed.

The problem with Darwin's theories is that he viewed everything as a gradual, slow progression, yet the fossil record proves him to be very wrong on that account. As mentioned earlier, the sudden burst of life forms during the Cambrian Explosion, where one celled organisms are suddenly replaced by a multitude of multicellular life not only in sheer numbers but in the variety of life forms they assumed, is not only astounding, but it is Un-Darwinian. Suddenly there were creatures with internal structures and appendages, optical receptors and breathing apparatus, as if they appeared overnight. Of the thirty-four animal phyla in existence today, one can find in the fossil record of just over half a billion years ago representatives of each one of those phyla, all appearing in a single burst of life. When calculations from the dating of the Cambrian rock layers came back that this all occurred in a span of five million years, and from the beginning of that period to the end there was little change in these life forms, the Darwin advocates were faced with a serious dilemma. Where were the step-wise life forms throughout this period, where were the common ancestors, An entire layer of fossil forms was missing from the record and the hard core Darwinists excused away the entire matter by suggesting the precursors were only soft tissue organisms that left behind no fossil trail, ignoring the fact that there were already fossil records for soft-bodied creatures and one-celled organisms that proved this line of thinking to be false. So instead they insisted on a gap in the fossil record of perhaps up to two hundred million years that was missing and when that was found it would explain this spectacular surge in lifeforms in the Cambrian age.

Of course, contrary to their expectations, there is no missing layer in the fossil record. What has been found thus far is exactly what happened, as difficult as that might be for some to accept. Just in the same manner 3.5 billion years ago the right conditions sprang into being for the release of one celled organisms, so to did these conditions around 550 million years ago come together in such a manner that the development of complex life forms had any shackles removed, permitting it to become be not only divergent and complex but unrestrained in how quickly it could reproduce. That is the true nature of evolution in the sense of, 'if it can happen, then it will happen and it will do so quickly.' Which of course led to the next excuse by the Darwinists, who insisted , 'yes, that might be the case and if it happens so quickly, then the transitional animals never had the length of time to leave behind a legacy of fossils, or that they transitioned into their final forms so quickly they became an inferior competitor for their higher level progeny, who in turn saw to their early exist from the earth timeline. But then, even considering a rapid disappearance as a possibility, how could there be absolutely no record of the existence of these transitional organisms. With 34 phyla and millions of fossil samples collected from all over the world, it would be impossible not to have encountered even a single transitional sample in all that time. No, it must be definitively stated that by the end of the Cambrian period, there was a sudden burst of multicellular life forms all at once without any evolutionary trace,

Certainly, this does not mean that there are no transitional animals as part of normal evolution. We can look at the Eohippus, probably no bigger than a cat, with its multi-toed feet and see its fossil record as it transitioned into the modern day horse. We can do that with lots of animals once they had become complex in their morphology, seeing how some species lost appendages in order to adapt to their habitat or even gain features, much as we discussed the change of the position of the larynx in order to acquire speech. But the Cambrian explosion is something different. Its as if nature had let its imagination run wild all at once and instead of demonstrating the patience over time that Darwin had preached, it threw all its toys on to the mat all at once. The only time we see something similar but still not to the same degree is following the Earth's several near extinction events, see Figure 26, where a majority of life forms are wiped out and shortly afterwards, short in earth timeline terms, the planet is once again teeming with new life forms. We see this occur after a mass extinction around 439 million years ago when 86% of life on Earth disappeared and then again 364 million years ago when 75% of species became extinct. The worst mass extinction event occurred 251 million years ago when 96% of species were lost and then another around 200 million years ago, which saw the balance of lifeforms swing back to the dinosaurs after mammals had actually overtaken them. But of course the one we are most familiar with is the extinction event of 65 million years ago which saw the end of the age of dinosaurs, and in fact, the loss of 76% of life on Earth. If we had relied on the slow pace of the evolutionary process, we most likely would have never recovered from these five events, as just when a life form was about to reach its pinnacle, it was hit with another disaster that erased its existence from the planet. In order for life to have succeeded and reestablish itself, it needed to recover and diversify rapidly after each event, making leaps and jumps that have no correlation to the evolutionary process as described by Darwin.

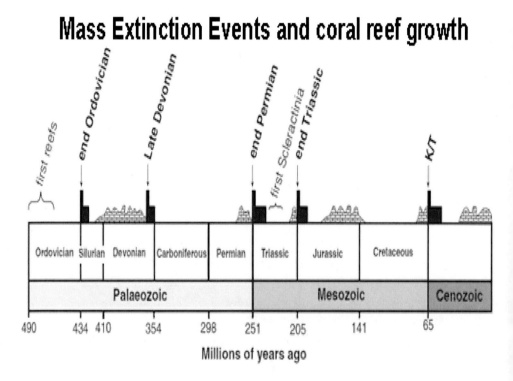

Figure 26

These sudden explosions of life that have occurred at least seven times in Earth's history, beginning with the one-celled organisms three and a half billion years ago, defy scientific theory, yet there can be no denying that they happened. Extreme jumps from practically nothing to everything, each one in a very short time that don't appear to have allowed the expected sequential transitions to reach the end product. It simply was there, without any fossil record to explain how. Evolution as a natural law is there to fill a void and it most certainly did that when it came to these seven events. But the fact that it occurred each time when necessary and did so at an accelerated rate when required should make it clearly evident to everyone that there is nothing random about evolution. It has nothing to do with 'survival of the fittest' because in the five extinction cases cited, it was most likely the fittest that disappeared completely, leaving behind those that had some peculiarity that permitted them to survive. It was survival of those on the fringe, the ones that could adapt to a less hospitable world because they were never fully adapted to the world that had just been destroyed. But how these leftover weak links in the chain could suddenly become masters of their new environment, reproduce at a phenomenal rate and mutate into a variety of lifeforms that rivaled the numbers that had been lost during the extinction event is still a mystery from the perspective of science but certainly not a mystery to those that can see the **GodSpark** that would have made it all possible.

Rather than being a universal process that allowed everything to adapt, mutate and evolve at a steady but slow rate to reach the pinnacle of their existence, as would be expected with normal Darwinian Theory, instead it would appear that we have a highly selective process, that identifies those species that it will advance, while at the same time deciding that other species will remain essentially as they have always been, with very little change over millions of years. Natural selection says that the competitive nature between species would be the determining factor of which will become the dominant species, and as it evolves it will expand its capabilities at the same time it expands its domain. For example an animal that eats at the vegetation at the roots of the trees will eventually reduce that source of nourishment and look upward at the leaves and the fruit hanging from the branches of the trees and will have options of learning to climb, or growing taller, or even having an extended neck in order to reach those leaves. They are afforded this luxury of time to adapt and evolve because they were dominant according to Darwin's theories and the continuous evolution permitted them to hold on to that position. Extinction events change that picture dramatically. They necessitate adaption, mutation, and behaviors to change all at once in order to survive. These changes must be immediate or else they become just one more species that ceases to exist. Man can wear another animals skin when it becomes too cold, or light a fire when the sun is no longer visible, or store his food for long periods by hanging it to dry out from a tree so that it is still edible weeks later, but we're not talking about anything walking the Earth at that time with that level of intelligence. Yet, there is no denying that somehow animals managed to survive the climatic changes, the atmosphere becoming thick with ash and dust that blackened the skies, and the lack of photosynthesis that obliterated the vegetation from a blade of grass to the tallest trees. Then when the worst of the catastrophic event was finally over, after thousands of years, the world was practically back to normal according to the fossil records, with dozens of scores of species swimming in the oceans and walking across the terrain or flying in the skies. Going from the chaos of a near extinction event to suddenly having an orderly world cannot depend on the randomness of natural evolution. And yet, to generate meaningful order out of chaos five times by the laws of natural selection would be an impossibility. There are approximately thirty million species of animal life existent in the world today. It would be hard to believe that there would have been more than that prior to each of the extinction events. But if there were, what would that mean? If the last event that wiped out the dinosaurs and in the process three quarters of the life on Earth, does that mean there were close to 120 million different species of animal life before that time and we just happen to be part of the fortunate 30 million to survive. I doubt very much there were that many species that survived. The numbers of different species were probably in the thousands, not the millions. For those thousands to branch out and evolve into thirty million would require a new species to arise every two or three years. As much as someone wishes to believe in the evolutionary process, that's not going to happen unless something else is accelerating the rate and making it happen.

Darwin was wrong! He said there would be no sudden appearances of a new species. In fact, the opposite seems to be true where sudden appearances is the natural order of the world, especially after a catastrophe. The reality is that nature most often functions in ways that are unnatural! It is as if it is being directed on how to behave, when it must accelerate and when it needs to slow down. When it needs to branch out and create new species, and when it needs to stop because there are once again enough.

The Lizard Man

One of the greatest riddles of evolution centers around the absence of the lizard man. When asked if I think there's a missing link in the evolution of mankind, my response is that there most certainly is. *Homo reptilius* is missing! It is hard to believe that the strongest proponents of evolution don't believe that natural selection and survival of the fittest should have also extended and applied to the reptilian world as well. Perhaps this is due to some innate herpetophobia by us as a mammalian species but there is no reason why the same evolutionary pressures exerted on mammals should not have been forcibly present in the lizard world as well. The absence of any such development in the reptilian world definitely warrants investigation because according to our modern theories the failure in the development of anything close to the Lizard Man doesn't make sense.

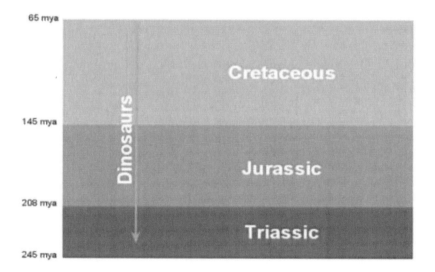

Figure 27

For approximately 180 million years, as seen in Figure 27, dinosaurs dominated this planet. That is three times longer than the time period of mammalian domination. And during the mammalian age, it took approximately 35 million years for the first apelike creature to evolve, and then a further fifteen million years for the first ape-men to be present. Yet, dinosaurs, having been the dominant species for a period six times longer than it took for a primitive mammal to become an ape, could never progress further in all that time to being anything more than just a giant lizard. That certainly defies how evolution is supposed to work. In fact, in all that time, the best the dinosaur world could produce were creatures with about as much intelligence as a chicken. The velociraptor, with its almost wolf-pack mentality as portrayed by Hollywood, is nothing more than movie industry fiction. They may have hunted in a pack but there was nothing strategic in either their planning or methodology. They simply tracked and killed.

But there is one dinosaur that has raised a few eyebrows because of statements made regarding its potential intelligence and that is the Troodon, better known as the Stenonychosaurus. According to researchers like Dale Russel, it was among a limited number of dinosaurs in the process of developing higher cognitive reasoning and intelligence. Though this small dinosaur is not well known, it was likely the main predator of mammals during the Cretaceous period. To have that capability, then it had to be more intelligent than the mammals it hunted. For that reason alone, it had to have a larger brain than most other dinosaurs. Now, others will argue that wouldn't be that difficult, since the average brain size of the larger dinosaurs was about that of a walnut but that ignores the fact that in order to catch a mouse you needed a better mouse trap. Or in other words, Troodon could have only caught his prey if his brain to body mass was a comparative ratio to that of mammals and not that of other dinosaurs.

What we do know bout Troodon is that it appeared on Earth approximately 76 million years ago, or 11 million years before the extinction event. As small dinosaurs go, it stood about 11 feet tall and weighed approximately 50 kilograms. Like other dinosaurs, it was an egg-layer, but its outstanding feature was it had a very large brain relative to its size. By comparison, larger than any brain to body mass ratio of reptiles living today, suggesting it had an intelligence at minimum which rivaled that of birds. Troodon isn't by any means a modern discovery. A single tooth was discovered by Joseph Leidy in 1856 but he did not classify it as a dinosaur, but rather as a small lizard. But in the 1930s fragments of Troodon's feet, hands and tail were discovered and there was suddenly a bigger picture available of this small dinosaur. Egg clutches were discovered by Jack Horner in Montana that have been attributed to Troodon, showing that the female laid two eggs per day for around ten days, resulting in clutches that contained anywhere from 16 to 24 eggs.

Though not well known, Troodons were actually a large family of theropods spread across multiple continents but all sharing that single most significant characteristic, the large brain. Troodon also had larger eyes than other theropods, suggesting that it may have possessed night vision. Greater visual acuity also implies that it had centers of the brain that were well developed. But along with this greater acuity, there is speculation that it may have had binocular vision as well because the eyes are set towards the front of the head rather than on the sides. Considering stereoscopic or binocular vision is a trait of humans, the question that needs to be answered is just how intelligent was Troodon? With its eyes that were closer to human quality, brain that was larger than its prey, hands that were capable of grasping objects, it is evident that this dinosaur should have been on the pathway to *Homo reptilian* status. But there in lies the enigma of evolution. With eleven million years ahead of it before extinction, why didn't it evolve further? Where was so-called natural selection when you needed it?

Figure 28

We can look at all the standard arguments that are made as to why Troodon, seen in Figure 28 could not advance further up the evolutionary ladder. The first being that there was not enough time before the extinction event of 65 million years ago occurred. Considering the extinction event at the end of the Triassic period happened approximately 205 year ago, and the appearance of Troodon was 130 million years later, that was twice as long as it took for the mammalian survivors of the K/T extinction event to transform into an apelike creature that eventually spawned humans. As for the time from ape to ape-man, the eleven million years that Troodon did have on the planet was more than enough to make similar advances if evolution acted as a natural law and with the same time clock for mutational events to occur. No, time was not an issue. There was more than enough time for their to be an evolutionary pathway that would be clearly identified in the fossil record. The fact that no such record exists suggests that further evolution of Troodon had been stopped.

As to the argument that besides the enlarged brain, the advancement of humans required our primitive ancestors to be bipedal also does not seem to apply as Troodon was bipedal when it came to locomotion. The shorter arms would indicate they were not used for running and may have only been used for standing and short distance crouching during a hunt, but that would be all. The larger eyes and binocular vision meant that Troodon would have spent long periods of time standing erect searching for prey. Troodon had the freedom of its front limb to grasp and although it did not have opposable thumbs in the sense that primates have, it did have a manual dexterity that permitted its three fingers to come together in a claw like action. Greater definition of its hand should have been realized over time if evolution was in play, much in the same way our earliest mammalian ancestors had to evolve from a paw to a primate hand. But once again, the further evolution of this simple appendage of the Troodon appears to have been stopped and it made no further advancement even though it already possessed the basic structures to make it possible.

It requires a social structure in order to evolve is the next argument those defending Darwinian rules of evolution will make next, even though such a rule is not actually applicable to evolution, which should occur no matter what the social status of the animal is, but may be applicable to the development of humans. So we need to look carefully at that aspect as well and by all the scientific insights to date, Troodon was a pack animal. The close proximity of egg clutches from different females meant they spent long periods of time in close proximity. The suggestion that even males would sit on the clutches meant that the normal territorial aggression displayed by males of other species had been eliminated as well. Therefore, as a social pack animal, means of communication also had to development, accounting even more for the animal's larger brain.

Other arguments might claim that as an egg layer, there is an arrested development as compared to mammals that can have long gestation periods, which permits advanced development of the offspring. The correlation to gestation period to evolutionary advancement and intelligence might seem like a good argument at first but then we simply need to look at gestation periods among different species and realize that the correlation doesn't really exist. We merely need to look at these gestation times to realize there does not seem to be a guiding principle that governs why some are short and others long. From the platypus which does lay eggs that hatch in 7 to 10 days, to the African elephant that has a pregnancy of 645 days, the gestation periods make very little sense. Mice, rats and shrews can vary from 21 to 28 days but an Eastern American mole, which would not appear to be any more advanced than these others will take 42 days. Yet 42 days is the same time frame for most varieties of kangaroos. As for bats, these can vary from 35 days for the Brown Bat to 180 days for the Fruit Bat. That is even longer than some primates, such as the lemur at 146 days or the slender Loris at 174 days. Our human gestation of 270 days is nothing compared to the sperm whale's 535 days or the Walrus's 456 days. Even a donkey is longer than the human gestation at 365 days. The cow's 286 days is comparable, but to suggest that those extra 16 days has made the calf more developed than the human infant would be a ridiculous statement, unless one wants to argue that the calf or foal is up and about, walking around shortly after birth, whereas the human infant will take another nine or so months. Once again that argument is faulty because a pup or kitten born around 62 days of gestation are up and running around after a few weeks of being born.

The one argument that could provide any justification for the failure of a dinosaur to advance and evolve to a human-like level that might have made any sense was the cold-blooded argument. Since our modern day reptiles are not homeothermic, they have no way of self-regulating body temperature, and thereby are subject to the environment in order to gain heat to carry out metabolic functions. In the absence of heat, they become dormant, practically a state of hibernation until such time they can absorb the necessary heat from the surrounding environment. This reliance on external temperatures in order to regulate body temperature certainly could be an impediment to development. But the assumption that dinosaurs were all cold-blooded is based on our knowledge of modern day reptiles and since we know the ancestors of both mammals and birds, both being warm-blooded, was a lizard, then it only stands to reason that some dinosaurs therefore also had to be warm-blooded. Although it had always been conjectured that this must be the case, it wasn't until 2014 that there was scientific proof that warm-blooded dinosaurs did exist. The 2014 study published in Science suggested that dinosaurs were neither warm nor cold-blooded, but rather "somewhere in the middle." By testing fossilized eggshells from the omnivorous Troodon, a herbivore

Maiasaura and from a Megaloolithus, they were able to calculate the temperatures of these eggshells at 100.4, 80.6 and 82.4 degrees Fahrenheit for the Troodon; 111.2 degrees Fahrenheit for the Maiasaura; and 96.8 degrees for the Megaloolithus. Using a process known as "clumped isotope paleothermometry" they arrived at their findings.   By performing the same test on eggs from cold-blooded invertebrate shells found in the same area, the scientists were able to eliminate the environmental factors as external temperatures would have had the same effect on all the egg shells tested. The Troodon samples were 50 degrees Fahrenheit warmer, the Maiasaura was 59 degrees Fahrenheit warmer and the Megaloolithus were between 37.4 and 42.8 degrees Fahrenheit warmer than the invertebrate eggs. For these findings to occur then it was necessary for those dinosaurs tested to metabolically raise their temperatures well above the environmental temperature.

Having looked at all the arguments available as to why this particular dinosaur should not have evolved at the same rate, or at least at a comparable rate to our primitive ape like ancestors, it would appear that there is no justification for it not happening. In fact, with the much longer time periods that dinosaurs ruled the earth, the real quandary is to why it didn't happen several times over during the intervening periods between extinction events.

Figure 29
As an interesting footnote to *Homo reptilius*, the discovery of lizard like figurines from the ancient Pre-Mesopotamia's Ubaid Civilization adds a layer of

intrigue to the question as to why they didn't evolve as it would appear that this ancient civilization for some reason was asking the very same question. But it wasn't just this one civilization but others as well that felt somehow there was this 'missing link' from evolutionary history as seen from Figure 29, which was carved in Sierra Leone. It is of keen interest because it does portray an accurate depiction of what *Homo reptilius* would have probably looked like had he existed. Why so many cultures would have thought that a lizard man should have been a naturally occurring species had evolution been allowed to function as it was intended to do, will always be a mystery. But no great a mystery as to what stopped it from happening. It is hard to dispute the natural conclusion that in someway there was an intervention that stopped Troodon from developing any further. This is not a reference to the K/T extermination event but instead a reference to a species that was showing clear evidence of evolving naturally and by all rights should have continued at a pace no differently from that exhibited in the evolution of mankind, yet it reached a point where it appears it could go no further. It was a bipedal, intelligent, socialized and moderately warm-blooded creature, that already exhibited advanced ocular specialization, manual dexterity and what must have been extraordinary hand eye coordination, but it simply stops progressing for eleven million years until it is wiped from the face of the earth by an asteroid impact. Whereas in every other chapter we spoke of the **GodSpark**, here is a clear cut example of what can only be termed as the God Stop! There is no other way to describe it other than a supernatural force intervening and overriding the natural laws of selection and evolution.

Chapter14: Devolution

The simple fact is that Darwin had it wrong! A strong statement from someone who firmly believes in the evolutionary process and sees it as the best tool God has in his tool kit, but still, an unavoidable reality that must be accepted if there is to be a meaningful dialogue regarding evolution. Often people will simply state 'Darwin' without having any appreciable knowledge of what he even wrote. It is fashionable in today's age for one to claim they follow the 'science' even though they don't have a scientific bone in their body. But as soon as you try to engage them in a discussion, they accuse you of being anti-science and practically every other conceivable derogatory adjective they can muster. I can only laugh, because my entire life has been devoted to science and most of them probably don't even realize they're alive and well from the work I've done for the past forty years in both the biological industries as well as universities. The reality is that the lay public doesn't really have a clue about science. They swallow what they're told by media talking heads that don't understand what they're saying and by teachers who teach, because as we you used to say, "those who can do, and those who can't teach." It is not meant to be offensive but only a reference that many teachers can only parrot what they have in the school curriculum without necessarily understanding what they're teaching. Unfortunately the solution to that deficit has been Google and Wikipedia and that is hardly an improvement when the blind start leading the blind. But I will talk more about that later. First we must look at what Darwin actually had to say.

Published in 1859, the theory as expressed in his book, ***On the Origin of Species*** was popular in a world where the industrial revolution was taking place and capitalism was quickly becoming the new way of life where people no longer had to rely on prayer to lift them out of poverty, they now had the opportunity for factory work to do that. We must take a look at Darwin's primary statement in which he said, "As many more individuals of each species are born than can possibly survive; and as, consequently, there is a frequently recurring struggle for existence, it follows that any being, if it vary however slightly in any manner profitable to itself, under the complex and sometimes varying conditions of life, will have a better chance of surviving, and thus be naturally selected. From the strong principle of inheritance, any selected variety will tend to propagate its new and modified form." Translated into the modern day vernaculum, Darwin was simply saying the better lifeform will survive because it will eliminate its weaker competitors. It was this same credo that fueled both capitalism and colonialism because the smarter, more civilized society, i.e.. Britain at that time, had the right to invade other lands and subjugate or eliminate the native population because they were inferior. Taken to the extreme, it is the same logic which fueled the race hatreds and genocides perpetrated by the Nazis in World War II. Darwin had essentially given free reign to the superior population to eliminate by any means whomever and whatever they considered to be the inferior population or species. Of course if we look at this as a spectator from another planet, we would not necessarily see the strongest, or the most beautiful perpetuating its species at the expense of weaker, uglier species. In situations where territorial habitats cross paths by accident, the inferior species will often gain the upper hand simply because of random opportunity. For example, if a massive flock of wild goats or sheep were crossing a plain, only to be followed by a herd of wild buffalo, would the fact that the buffalo might all die from starvation be an indication that the goats or sheep were the superior species? Because of their split lip, sheep and goats can graze down to ground level and often pull grass and other plants out by the roots so that there is no regrowth. When the buffalo come through, a herbivorous species with thick lips, restricting it to eat longer blades of grass, was it their inferiority due to their lips that made them the weaker species? Were these sheep and goats actually superior because they could graze down to the very roots of the plants? The answer is no, as neither species is inferior or superior. Had the buffalo roamed through the plain first, it would have been very likely that both species would have survived without any losses, but random events made that impossible and the opportunity was lost.

We can look at another example where it cannot be said one species is superior or inferior to the other. If we look at the lemur of Madagascar with its dietary intake of nectar and pollen from the trees in its environment and somehow the wild scutellata bee migrated from the Sahara and became even more ferocious through mating with local honey bees so that it was competing with the lemur for the pollens and in so doing it caused the extinction of the lemur, did that mean it was the superior species or just an unfortunate set of circumstances that couldn't be prevented. The assumption by Darwin's theory that extinctions were all the result of a struggle for existence where the environment could not sustain the growing populations of either species and therefore the superior species wins, is clearly not the case and misses the point that survival is often based on random events and opportunities, having nothing to do with the superiority of the species. I can extend Darwin the benefit of the doubt that he was unaware of all the extinction events that occurred, rendering survival of the fittest meaningless, because it was the exact opposite which occurred, with survival dependent on having characteristics that were of practically no use or actually detrimental to what had been the normal environment. For example, the animal that possessed night vision had survived only by scavenging at night for leftovers by the superior species, but now with clouds of dust and ash blocking out the sun, it suddenly had an advantage. Or the animal that had developed a hair coat and suffered terribly due to the tropical environment, suddenly benefited when an unexpected blizzard came out of nowhere and summoned in an ice age. The point being, Darwin seemed to miss that interspecies survival was dependent on unexpected circumstance and opportunity, whereas intraspecies or closely related species survival was dependent on aggression.

Darwin's next error occurred when he made the statement, "There is grandeur in this view of life, with its several powers, having been originally breathed into a few forms or into one; and that, whilst this planet has gone cycling on according to the fixed law of gravity, from so simple a beginning endless forms most beautiful and most wonderful have been, and are being, evolved." Well the Cambrian Explosion of life has certainly proven this statement to be wrong. There was no such thing as a few forms of life arising and then this limited number branched out like a tree, each division of the branch increasing the number of life forms exponentially. The Cambrian Explosion was more like a light switch that the moment it was turned on, the Earth was teeming with thousands upon thousands of different life forms. This wasn't a tree, it was an overgrown thorn bush.

Despite these errors, which universally in our present time we are well aware of, Darwin's theories are still expounded as if they are the laws of the universe engraved in stone. In his next book, *The Descent of Man, and Selection in Relation to Sex*, published in 1871, he extended his theories to account for human evolution through natural selection. Considering that the in his theory it was the great hunter, the muscular, athletic and smarter than the average bear type that got all the woman and filled the world through his procreation only, it is surprising how small a percentage of the human race actually shares these characteristics. No matter which race you examine, the 'ubermensch' or superman that Darwin predicted would be the one to spread his genes and generate the human race doesn't seem to have had much success in establishing those genes through the subsequent generations.

Darwinists, or as they are called now, Neo-Darwinists, defend their arguments by stating that the evolution process in a slow moving mechanism taking millions of years and therefore, we cannot identify it or see it in real time. The only way it can be studied is through the fossil record. But it was Darwin that claimed evolution is in a state of constant motion towards better change then that would mean there must constantly be examples even in the present of real change or transitional forms between evolving species. For example, our pet dogs should be very different from the dogs that sat around our campfires fifteen thousand years ago. They have been domesticated, educated, taught to understand language and to live with and along side our technological achievements. But the reality is that dogs today, other than having a variety of breeds that we purposely bred, are no different from their ancestors that we first encountered. With all the exposure they've had and all the pressures of an advancing environment, why are they still lying at our feet and chasing sticks when we throw them. Even with my own dog which I know perfectly understands how the elevator works in our apartment building, she makes no effort to press any of the buttons to operate the elevator herself. Her failure to evolve any further than what her ancestor 7,000 generations ago (assuming two years for each generation of a litter of puppies) may have been like, is certainly a criticism of Darwin's claim of constant evolution.

Even the reliance on the fossil record by Darwinists presents a problem because there are so few transitional life forms in the fossil record. Darwin admitted that this was a problem, but excused the absence by suggesting more transitional life forms would be discovered after his death. He expressed this excuse when he said, "I believe, in the extreme imperfection of the geological record," and it was accepted without question by all those that supported his theories, he was forgiven for this oversight and failure to find in the fossil record his indisputable evidence. Since Darwin's death, hundreds of thousands of fossils have been found but still the gap of transitional life forms exists. What it has shown with the five mass extinction events that occurred is the exact opposite of transitional forms. Instead there are sudden bursts of life forms that suddenly appear, demonstrating extremes of diversity and complexity. These near extinction events actually create more gaps that the Darwinists can't seem to fill so they merely gloss over them as if they were immaterial.

Paying respects to his father, who was a medical doctor and in particular an ophthalmologist, Darwin wrote in his ***On The Origin of Species***, "To suppose that the eye with all its inimitable contrivances for adjusting …focus …admitting different amounts of light… correction of …aberration, could have been formed by natural selection, seems, I freely confess, absurd in the highest degree…" It would almost appear to be a confession on his part that he knew that this theory didn't make much sense when it came to complex structures which weren't inherent to only one species but in fact were shared by every living creature. The eye in particular he understood to be a problem. But Darwin couldn't even imagine how much of a problem the eye was going to be when espousing his theories. Random mutations in a species was how Darwin described the advantage of one species over another. There was no protocol or formula to follow; it simply happened and when that mutation turned out to be a benefit to the species it occurred in, then it was passed down into successive generations. Science has come a long way since the days of Darwin, especially when it comes to the issue of gene identification. The loci for the Pax-6 genes is a key regulator for eye development in vertebrates. But a similar gene, an analog, has been found to control the eye development of everything else as well, including insects, mollusks, nematodes, and other worms. Of those phyla that all have visual systems, there is this common gene group between all of them. If one was to compare the amino acid composition of the human gene to that of the zebra fish, there is a 97% correlation. To the common house fly, it is 94%. For Darwin's theory to be correct, all these different life forms, whose phyla came into existence over 500 million years ago, just all happened to develop similar visual structures purely by chance. If one was to do the math, then of the slightly over 100 amino acids that makes up the gene in any organism, in any phyla, with a possibility of one of twenty different amino acids to line up in the identical sequence for the gene in each species of those different phyla, the odds would be astronomical. Just imagine the incredible odds for the first two amino acids of the gene in each phyla to match. A one in twenty chance that that amino acid 'X' will be in slot number one. But for that same amino acid to be in that first slot for a completely different phylum would b 1/20 X 1/20, or a one in four hundred chance. For a third phylum to match would suddenly jump the odds to one in 8,000. A fourth phyla and its one in 160,000. And for that fifth phyla it is an impressive one in 3.2 million. But that's only for the one amino acid in that first slot. In order to have that same incredible event happen in the second slot would be one chance in 10.2 million. Extend that out for well over one hundred amino acids, in fact 130, and the resultant odds against it ever happening is well beyond imagination. And yet that is what happened according to those firmly entrenched in Darwinism. They want you to believe that all this happened by random chance and that each phylum developed the identical gene independently. You don't need anyone else to tell you that just isn't going to happen, no matter how firmly you want to hold on to your evolutionist beliefs. The only way it would have been possible was if the gene was present in whatever could have been a common ancestor to fish and insects, and arachnids and worms, and everything else that had need of a visual apparatus. But what would that common ancestor even be? A one celled organism? A sponge? Whichever it may have been, that organism didn't even have eyes, so why would it have even bothered to manufacture a gene that it didn't require nor had the sentience that it would recognize it might need such a gene millions of years into the future? Therein lies the problem and Darwin knew it. Rather than someone else raise the issue, he raises it himself as if to say, "I know it can't be explained now, but perhaps in the future it can be, so don't attack my theories simply because it all falls apart when we talk about eyes."

It reminds me of a saying I was once told that is analogous to what we have just discussed. It was one of those pearls of wisdom you never forget but you never know when you're going to be able to use it. "The pot and the stove did not make the meal." Certainly they were necessary to hold all the ingredients in the pot while the stove heated them all to cook before the meal could be served but neither of them were anything but tools or intermediates in the process. Someone actually had to select the ingredients, stir them in the pot and set the temperature on the stove correctly. They weren't going to cook themselves. This certainly is the case with the visual apparatus. The genetic code had to be designed, assembled, tested and uniformly distributed among all the phyla and that wasn't going to happen by itself. Darwin couldn't say the words that were necessary because his career depended on his continuation of being funded by the university and scientific community. So to admit that his own theories could not dispel the fact that there was a universal designer, a template that was being guided by forces that he either couldn't identify or didn't want to identify, would have spelled the end to his illustrious career. Darwin had seen from his own investigations the **GodSpark** and it frightened him.

Voices of Science

It is not easy for any scientist to speak out negatively on Darwinism. For some it has actually been career suicide. It is common knowledge within the scientific community that if we do not agree with the mob mentality then there exists a high probability that we will be ostracized, penalized, demoralized and even some cases criminalized by being accused of breaking corporate or university policy. The paradox is that Darwinism has become the new religion and any of us that dare to speak out against it are heretics. Nevertheless, there are still a few brave enough to weather the storm and let their voices be heard. I will now take the opportunity to quote the statements of some of these courageous individuals in the past and present.

Michael Behe, PhD from the University of Pennsylvania in biological sciences said, "Molecular evolution is not based on scientific authority. There is no publication in the scientific literature--in prestigious journals, specialty journals, or books--that describes how molecular evolution of any real, complex, biochemical system either did occur or even might have occurred."

Paleontologist Niles Eldredge is quoted as saying, "No wonder paleontologists shied away from evolution for so long. It never seems to happen. ... Evolution cannot forever be going on somewhere else."

Geneticist John Endler stated, "Although much is known about mutation, it is still largely a 'black box' relative to evolution. Novel biochemical functions seem to be rare in evolution, and the basis for their origin is virtually unknown."

In 1999, Professor of Anthropology, Jeffrey Schwartz stated, "…with the exception of Dobzhansky's claim about a new species of fruit fly, the formation of a new species, by any mechanism, has never been observed…"

Professor of Biochemistry, Klaus Dose is recorded as saying "More than 30 years of experimentation on the origin of life in the fields of chemical and molecular evolution have led to a better perception of the immensity of the problem of the origin of life on Earth rather than to its solution. At present all discussions on principal theories and experiments in the field either end in stalemate or in a confession of ignorance."

Max-Planck Institute Scientist, Wolf-Ekkehard Lonnig was quoted in the paper in 2014 as saying, "A scientific hypothesis should be potentially falsifiable....the idea of slow evolution by 'infinitesimally small inherited variations' etc. has been falsified by the findings of palaeontology... as well [as] genetics. Yet its adherents principally reject any scientific proof against Neo-Darwinism. So that, in fact, their theory has become a non-falsifiable worldview, to which people stick in spite of all contrary evidence." Lonnig continues with a warning that these Darwinists are actually a threat and danger to scientific investigation when he says, "According to Neo-Darwinism, all important problems of the origin of species are, at least in principle, solved. Further questions on the validity of evolutionary theory are thus basically superfluous. However, such a dogmatic attitude stops further investigations and hinders fruitful research in science."

Perhaps mathematician I. L. Cohen summed it up best when he said, "Micro mutations do occur, but the theory that these alone can account for evolutionary change is either falsified or else it is an unfalsifiable, hence metaphysical, theory. I suppose that nobody will deny that it is a great misfortune if an entire branch of science becomes addicted to a false theory. But this is what happened in biology ... I believe that one day the Darwinian myth will be ranked the greatest deceit in the history of science"

Professor of Physics, Paul Davies at Arizona State University was not afraid to make the following statements which he included in his many articles and books, "There is for me powerful evidence that there is something going on behind it all. It seems as though somebody has fine-tuned nature's numbers to make the Universe. ... The impression of design is overwhelming."

It would be unforgivable if I overlooked my fellow Kiwi, Michael Denton, a Senior Research Fellow in molecular biology at the University of Otago in New Zealand, who wrote in his book, *In Evolution: A Theory in Crisis*, "It is the sheer universality of perfection, the fact that everywhere we look, to whatever depth we look, we find an elegance and ingenuity of an absolutely transcending quality, which so mitigates against the idea of chance. Alongside the level of ingenuity and complexity exhibited by the molecular machinery of life, even our most advanced artifacts appear clumsy. ... It would be an illusion to think that what we are aware of at present is any more than a fraction of the full extent of biological design. In practically every field of fundamental biological research ever-increasing levels of design and complexity are being revealed at an ever-accelerating rate." It wasn't that Michael Denton was an anti-evolutionist, because like myself he believed whole-heartedly in evolution, just not the evolution of Darwin. He made this abundantly clear in 1995 when he said, "I think the current Darwinian picture is insufficient. I don't think it gives a credible and comprehensive explanation of how the pattern of life on earth emerged. ... The theory of evolution permeates much of our thinking now in the Western world. I think there are problems with the current Darwinian world, and they should be discussed. ... My fundamental problem with the theory is that there are so many highly complicated organs, systems and structures, from the nature of the lung of a bird, to the eye of the rock lobster, for which I cannot conceive of how these things have come about in terms of a gradual accumulation of random changes. It strikes me as being a flagrant denial of common sense to swallow that all these things were built up by accumulative small random changes. This is simply a nonsensical claim, especially for the great majority of cases, where nobody can think of any credible explanation of how it came about. And this is a very profound question which everybody skirts, everybody brushes over, everybody tries to sweep under the carpet"

Yale Computer Science Professor David Gelernter revealed his view of Darwinism in an essay, writing, "Perhaps the biggest flaw with Darwinism is how hard it would be to randomly make new functional proteins. Darwinian evolution depends on a huge number of them. Our understanding of molecular biology developed after Darwin. His theory doesn't fit well with this new understanding. Immense is so big, and tiny is so small, that neo-Darwinian evolution is — so far — a dead loss. Try to mutate your way from 150 links of gibberish to a working, useful protein and you are guaranteed to fail. Try it with ten mutations, a thousand, a million — you fail. The odds bury you. It can't be done." Gelernter went on to say that it wasn't the math that stifles Darwinism, it is his belief that Darwin didn't even understand the biology, having no knowledge of molecular structure. Intelligent design is an absolutely serious argument. It's the 'first, and obviously most intuitive one that comes to mind.' It's got to be dealt with intellectually. It can't be dismissed with anti-religious bigotry."
Gelertners's view has not been met kindly by others in the scientific fields. He describes the reactions as follows. "You take your life into your hands to challenge it intellectually. They will destroy you."

Swedish biologist and author wrote the following, "The reasons for rejecting Darwin's proposal were many, but first of all that many innovations cannot possibly come into existence through accumulation of many small steps, and even if they can, natural selection cannot accomplish it, because incipient and intermediate stages are not advantageous."

Most of us are aware of Edwin Hubble, for whom the Hubble telescope was named but it is unlikely we are familiar with this graduate student, Allan Sandage. But Sandage was an astronomer in his own right and received the National Medal of Science and the Craford Prize in astronomy. Having a view and perspective of the universe few of us would ever have, Sandage said, "I find it quite improbable that such order came out of chaos. There has to be some organizing principle. God to me is a mystery but is the explanation for the miracle of existence, why there is something instead of nothing. The world is too complicated in all its parts and interconnections to be due to chance alone. I am convinced that the existence of life with all its order in each of its organisms is simply too well put together. Each part of a living thing depends on all its other parts to function. How does each part know? How is each part specified at conception? The more one learns of biochemistry the more unbelievable it becomes unless there is some type of organizing principle--an architect"

A Canadian Entomologist and former Director of the Commonwealth Institute of Biological Control in Ottawa wrote, "It does appear to me, in the first place, that Darwin in the Origin was not able to produce paleontological evidence sufficient to prove his views but that the evidence he did produce was adverse to them; and I may note that the position is not notably different today. The modern Darwinian paleontologists are obliged, just like their predecessors and like Darwin, to water down the facts with subsidiary hypotheses which, however plausible, are in the nature of things unverifiable. As we know, there is a great divergence of opinion among biologists, not only about the causes of evolution but even about the actual process. This divergence exists because the evidence is unsatisfactory and does not permit any certain conclusion. It is therefore right and proper to draw the attention of the non-scientific public to the disagreements about evolution. But some recent remarks of evolutionists show that they think this unreasonable. This situation, where scientific men rally to the defense of a doctrine they are unable to define scientifically, much less demonstrate with scientific rigour, attempting to maintain its credit with the public by the suppression of criticism and the elimination of difficulties, is abnormal and undesirable in science."

Wernher von Braun, the German rocket scientist, is probably best remembered for being the man to convince John F. Kennedy that the US could beat the Russians in the race to the moon. He is probably overlooked for being the scientist that invented the rockets that bombed London during World War II. So it might surprise people to hear him in his own words when he said, "We in NASA were often asked what the real reason was for the amazing string of successes we had with our Apollo flights to the Moon. I think the only honest answer we could give was that we tried to never overlook anything. It is in that same sense of scientific honesty that I endorse the presentation of alternative theories for the origin of the universe, life and man in the science classroom. It would be an error to overlook the possibility that the universe was planned rather than happened by chance."

At the core of all these statements from the plethora of brilliant scientists presented is the argument for intelligent design. It is not that any one of them is suggesting evolution is a hoax, that is not the case at all. What is being said is that evolution cannot be solely responsible for everything on Earth by its own accord and through pure random accumulated occurrences. For evolution to be successful it needs to be repeatedly reliant on the **GodSpark,** though only a handful will actually identify that being God. It is not surprising since even after the Neo-Darwinists have shamed and denigrated some of these free thinking scientists, they then begin to attack their entire belief system, daring to expose them as having religious inclinations. On a purely scientific level, the discourse can remain somewhat cordial but as soon as the 'R' word, religion, is mentioned, the attacks become rabid, practically maniacal from the evolutionist crowd. That's why you will have seen most statements carefully skirt around saying God specifically and referring to him in vague terms.

But it is important to highlight the main arguments these anti-Darwin scientists have raised because they still need to be addressed by the Neo-Darwinist movement with answers that are scientifically valid. Thus far their tactic of avoidance seems to be the only one they are practicing. As already mentioned, the fossil record is highly imperfect and it can no longer be blamed on the slow pace and lack of sites for digs, as there are more happening around the world now than ever before, but instead it is time to face the reality that the slow evolutionary transitional stages required by the theory did not happen. Paleontologists have tried to say this for almost a hundred years, and even though they are the undisputed experts in the field, the Darwinists refuse to listen to them. Instead they scream out to dig deeper, look harder and don't tell us they're not there!

At the beginning of this book, the immutable laws of the universe were presented because no matter what some scientists might insist, these rules of nature cannot be overruled. Buried in these rules it the main scientific reason why there is no evidence for the Darwinian view of evolution. The second law of thermodynamics is the very antithesis of Darwinism. Whereas Charles Darwin wanted to convince everyone that minute mutations occurring by the thousands will accumulate until an organism evolves into a superior form from its previous state, the second law states explicitly, that everything will break down due to increasing entropy. There is no denying this law which stipulates that all systems in our reality will breakdown. Organisms will not become more complex but will actually become more disorganized. This is what I refer to as **Devolution** rather than Evolution. The law of entropy is well proven, well known, and universally accepted, yet when it comes to Darwin's theories, all supporters of Darwinian theory want to deny it even exists. It is a fact that no exception to the second law of thermodynamics has ever been identified. All biological processes are subject to the laws of physics and chemistry and must operate in accordance with the second law of thermodynamics.

No scientist worth his salt will deny the laws of thermodynamics. So when the Neo-Darwinists try to argue that these fundamental laws only apply to a closed system and they see the world as an open system where energy can be drawn on from other sources to override the entropy. They want you to believe that an organism with a set amount of energy in its body can tap into another sources of energy at times it wants to evolve. The 'Force' may be with the Jedi but it certainly doesn't play a role in evolutionary processes. All joking aside, the source of energy they point to is the sun, suggesting that at beneficial mutational events, solar radiation powers the process making it possible. They ignore the fact that most of the Sun's radiation comes into contact with life forms as ultraviolet radiation, generating heat and light at the same time. Ultraviolet radiation is often used for sterilization because it doesn't stimulate organisms, it actually destroys them. Anyone that had skin cancer as a result of the Sun's radiation will tell you that the mutation that occurred in their cells was not beneficial.

To even suggest that mutations are a mechanism of 'order' is naive. Mutations tend to disorganize, causing a breakdown of normal processes, which means they are aligned with the Law of Entropy. That being the case, then natural selection is not capable of establishing order. Until the Neo-Darwinists can demonstrate that their theories can override the natural laws of thermodynamics or even reverse them, then there still can be no proof as to the accumulation of little mutations as indicated in Darwin's theories. The lack of transitional evidence in the fossil record exists because the advancement of the species through gradual mutations does not exist. Evolution most likely exists but it is not according to the arguments they have presented thus far.

But I cannot hold this failure of his theories against Charles Darwin himself. I appreciate that the biologists of the nineteenth and early twentieth centuries were not in possession of the vast knowledge of biological and chemical processes we possess now. DNA, as the backbone of genetics wouldn't be explained for almost another hundred years after Darwin. So how could it even be expected for Darwin's theories to put together the amino acids in the proper sequence for even one gene if he didn't have a clue that they even existed. The concept, had it been revealed to him through some time travelling mechanism would have surely given him pause and caused him to reconsider his theories. Darwin would have had to admit that the complexity of biochemical systems is so great that there was absolutely no chance that it could have been produced randomly. Millions upon millions of combinations that would have needed trial and error, failing thousands of more times than succeeding before a single successful mutation would be identified. I defer to astrophysicist, Sir Fred Hoyle, who probably described it better than anyone else could have when he said there would be about as much chance of anyone assembling all the biochemical, chemical, genetic processes to produce a life form as there would be for a blind man to solve the Rubik's Cube. Always a master of the metaphor, Hoyle also said that there was as much chance for life to have evolved from nothing as there would be for a tornado to sweep through a junkyard and assemble a functioning jumbo jet plane.

It is not without lack of effort on the part of scientists to try and create a beneficial mutation in order to prove their case. Geneticists have experimented with generations of fruit flies by exposing them to extreme conditions, such as radiation, mutagenic chemicals, heat, cold, darkness, and high intensity light producing a large number of mutations but not a single one truly beneficial and in almost all cases actually deleterious, causing the premature death of the fly. They always come to the conclusion that the mutants produced either die, are sterile, or revert to wild type. They could not forcibly make them evolve.

What is the primary motivation of these Neo-Darwinists? It no longer seems to be the advancement of science because if it was, they would welcome new theories and begin exploring other avenues that could explain the advancement of life on Earth. Whether life is the result of intelligent design or not, the focus should be on identifying possibilities, not building scientific beliefs on exclusion principles, simply because the acknowledgement that there may actually be something in the universe that they can't fully explain terrifies them. Man may not be the center of the universe after all. No one ever said he was supposed to be, yet any other concept to them is intolerable. There's is a belief of all or nothing and since they are not willing to let go of their beliefs, then no matter how much evidence may be accumulated to demonstrate the inherent gaps in Darwin's theories, it only makes them clutch on tighter to those beliefs and resist harder to any challenging information. The credo of the Darwinist has become, 'Although we cannot identify ancestors or "missing links," and we cannot devise testable theories to explain how particular episodes of evolution came about, nonetheless, we know these things to be true.' That being essentially true, then Darwinian evolution has become more of a philosophy than a science.

I am an advocate for evolution because I see it as indispensable tool for intelligent design. From everything written thus far in this book, it can be seen that behind it all there was not only intelligent design but the inevitable **GodSpark** to ensure it all moved in the right direction at the right time. If the Darwinists insist that multiple micromutations in a positive direction can occur as long as there is an alternative source of energy to overcome entropy, then are they not actually admitting that a sentient being is responsible because the events they describe could not occur by unaided natural processes that we know of. Does not the obvious gaps in the fossil record, which fail to show the transitional stages in the development of a species, prove that instead of tiny, incremental advances through mutations there are these sudden, unexpected leaps? Therefore, it is time to admit that evolution is not exclusive of a supreme being, but it actually has a requirement of there being a God if it is to function at all.

Section Four: Planet of the Apes

Chapter 15: Chimpanzee Versus Australopithecus

The obvious question that needs to be asked when discussing the development of the chimpanzee and that of the human ancestor Australopithecus is a simple 'Why". It is obvious from Figure 30 that there was very little to differentiate the chimpanzee on the left and the Australopithecus on the right when they were co-existing four million years ago. Considering the DNA of modern day humans and chimpanzees only differs by 1.63%, it can be assumed that difference was even smaller when compared to Australopithecus. Phenotypically, there was very little to separate the two species. The only major separation was geography, presuming that the topography of the African continent hasn't changed too drastically over the intervening years, so that what exists today resembles the environment each species encountered when they first went their separate ways.

Figure 30

There was about as much difference anatomically, socially and behaviorally between these two African cousins as one would find between a mountain gorilla and a forest gorilla today. Yet one would continue to evolve into this highly sophisticated creature designated as man, while the other had met its evolutionary dead end. Finding the key to exactly why this happened unlocks the truth about evolution. The shared secret between the chimpanzee and Australopithecus is key to one of the greatest mysteries of all time. There was nothing natural about it at all. It was not a natural law of the universe, applied equally to all. In fact, when it came to selection, the process was obviously very restrictive and limited, with application having very little to do with survival of the fittest. Discovering the true nature of this selection process will explain exactly why we are here as the most intelligent creatures on the planet while our cousins are still sleeping in the trees of the forests and jungles of Africa.

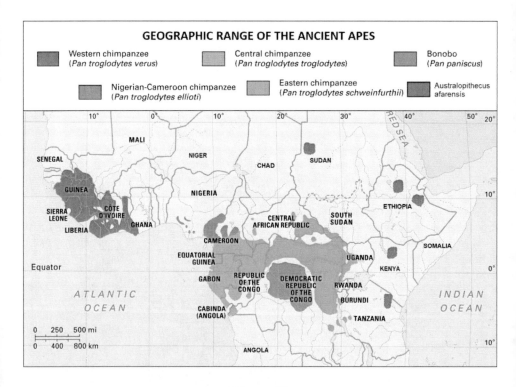

Figure 31

As can be seen in Figure 31, there was a band of activity extending from 20° North to 25° South of the Equator. Though the map does not show it, there was another hotbed of activity in South Africa, where a species identified as *Australopithecus africanus* roamed. Though the areas of finding fossils are marked in red, it can be assumed that the entire range between the finding areas could constitute the range of territorial roaming by the Australopithecus. Based on the present day topography of Africa, it would appear that the chimpanzee inhabits the predominantly rain forested areas of this central band whereas the Australopithecus became established in the Savanna areas where there were less forest and more grassland. But what should also be obvious is that the chimpanzees lived west of the rift valley that runs at the edge of the African tectonic plate and the Australopithecus inhabited the areas east of the rift valley. Currently, Africa's Great rift valley is moving at a rate of 6.5 mm a year. Not very quick but enough to suggest that the divide has been widening constantly and four million years ago the edges may have been 26 kilometers closer. Along this rift are found Africa's deepest lakes as water filled the divide as these plates separated. To the west are the large, tropical basins, the largest of which is the Congo Basin, beginning in the highlands of the rift valley and serving as the drainage area for the Congo River, which is Africa's largest river in terms of discharge volume, as well as the deepest river in the world. Africa's other major river, the Nile, flows from Lake Victoria in the rift valley northward across 11 different countries. Clearly this rift valley played a significant role in the emergence of Australopithecus but the how and the why is certainly not clear. For the answer we need to look at the geography and topography of the regions as it is now and as it may have been millions of years ago.

As far as the now, scientists at the Max Planck Institute compared the bonobo, also known as the pygmy chimpanzee, genome directly with that of chimpanzees and humans. They discovered that humans share about 1.6% of DNA with the bonobo, that is not shared with the chimpanzee. Similarly, the same amount of DNA is shared only with the chimpanzee, but not with the bonobo. This is highly significant, because it meant all three of these species originated from a common ancestor about the same time, whereas it was believed chimpanzees and bonobos had been a later divergence all of their own. To have a common ancestor from which three separate and distinct populations of apes, that being humans, chimpanzees, and bonobos meant there had to be a large and diverse gene pool available for that to happen. The scientists calculated there must have been a least 27,000 breeding individuals constituting this gene pool. At that point the diversity that was unique between humans and chimpanzees, as well as the one between humans and bonobos, remained unique because those two species remained divergent and didn't interbreed, which would have resulted in a shared difference to humans and would no longer have remained a unique difference to each species. Seven million years ago, the common ancestor of bonobos and chimps retained this diversity until their population completely split into two groups. But therein lies the mystery regarding human evolution. As three distinct subsets of this ancestral population's diverse gene pool, that could only have been maintained through physical separation, As all three species would have shared the same number of chromosomes at time of the divergence, the interbreeding needed to cease completely, until such time that humans lost a pair and reduced to 23 pairs, while chimpanzees and bonobos remained at 24 pairs. But it also meant that even though they could produce viable and somewhat fertile offspring, the chimpanzees and bonobos never did, otherwise they would not have preserved the unique differences they each have with humans genetically.

The Garden of Eden

In 2013 the geologist Mark Maslin surmised that East Africa was a hotbed of evolution, because for the past five million years, everything about the landscape in that region has changed. A year later Brian Hadwerk came to a similar conclusion of how the change in climate, resulting from the change of terrain may have played a role in the evolution of mankind. But there is a major problem with both their statements, and that is the fact that other fossil remains of much older hominid ancestral-like apes have been uncovered in the area and date to time periods far earlier than Australopithecus. Many of these early developing primates proved to be dead ends, but they were still happening with regular frequency and this was well before the five million year period being referred to. Nonetheless, it does not disprove that changes to the environment resulted in the evolving stage for hominids, only proving that these change may have been occurring much earlier than today's scientists have calculated.

The geologic and climatic alterations of five million years ago must have been tremendous, because whatever they were, they managed to physically separate these three species from their common ancestral home and prevented the cross-sexual relations that would have eliminated the resultant genetic divergence. The tectonic activity described previously is also known to have produced numerous basins suitable for lake formation as reported by As the rift extended southward causing the formation of faults and subsequent magma activity, it was also creating lake basins in the northern parts of the rift during the Miocene period which began 23 million year ago and ended 5.3 million years ago. But the lakes and basins in Kenya and Tanzania are of Early Pliocene age according to Tiercelin and Lezzar, 2002, so not as old as the ones to the north, being perhaps somewhere between 5 to 4 million years in age. They observed that the appearance of these large deep lakes across a large geographical area where sudden and synchronous at specific times and that may be the key to the divergence of the three populations. The important fact to remember being that chimpanzees don't swim. They don't even like the water. Examining figure 31, it can be imagined that there was an area of origin where this common ancestor resided around present day Rwanda and Burundi. The three populations of divergent species would have staked out their territories based on specific characteristics and dietary requirements. Bonobos furthest west, Australopithecus furthest east and the chimpanzees remained in the lands in the middle. At that time, around the end of the Miocene epoch, there was little geographically that prevented them from moving freely in this band running west to east. Topographically, there would have been little difference between the three areas that they staked out, each having laid claim to their own little paradise.

To each species, using whatever cognitive though processes they possessed at the time, they would have had their heaven on earth. The band which they inhabited would have been relatively flat, covered in forests and having a very narrow range of temperature, fluctuating no more than five degrees, with plenty of rainfall so that the trees were always full of ripening fruit and covered in thick green vegetation. Every sort of animal conceivable would have lived in the band but with their elevated social behaviour and troop mentality, they would have been able to fend off the predators that threatened them. It was existence that reminds me of what is written in **Genesis**, Chapter 2:

ח וַיִּטַּע יְהוָה אֱלֹהִים, גַּן־בְּעֵדֶן־־מִקֶּדֶם; וַיָּשֶׂם שָׁם, אֶת־הָאָדָם אֲשֶׁר יָצָר.

8 And the LORD God planted a garden eastward, in Eden; and there He put the man whom He had formed.

ט וַיַּצְמַח יְהוָה אֱלֹהִים, מִן־הָאֲדָמָה, כָּל־עֵץ נֶחְמָד לְמַרְאֶה, וְטוֹב לְמַאֲכָל־־וְעֵץ הַחַיִּים, בְּתוֹךְ הַגָּן, וְעֵץ, הַדַּעַת טוֹב וָרָע.

9 And out of the ground made the LORD God to grow every tree that is pleasant to the sight, and good for food; the tree of life also in the midst of the garden, and the tree of the knowledge of good and evil.

י וְנָהָר יֹצֵא מֵעֵדֶן, לְהַשְׁקוֹת אֶת־הַגָּן; וּמִשָּׁם, יִפָּרֵד, וְהָיָה, לְאַרְבָּעָה רָאשִׁים.

10 And a river went out of Eden to water the garden; and from thence it was parted, and became four heads.

יא שֵׁם הָאֶחָד, פִּישׁוֹן--הוּא הַסֹּבֵב, אֵת כָּל-אֶרֶץ הַחֲוִילָה, אֲשֶׁר-שָׁם, הַזָּהָב.

11 The name of the first is Pishon; that is it which compasseth the whole land of Havilah, where there is gold;

יב וּזְהַב הָאָרֶץ הַהִוא, טוֹב; שָׁם הַבְּדֹלַח, וְאֶבֶן הַשֹּׁהַם.

12 and the gold of that land is good; there is bdellium and the onyx stone.

יג וְשֵׁם-הַנָּהָר הַשֵּׁנִי, גִּיחוֹן--הוּא הַסּוֹבֵב, אֵת כָּל-אֶרֶץ כּוּשׁ.

13 And the name of the second river is Gihon; the same is it that compasseth the whole land of Cush.

יד וְשֵׁם הַנָּהָר הַשְּׁלִישִׁי חִדֶּקֶל, הוּא הַהֹלֵךְ קִדְמַת אַשּׁוּר; וְהַנָּהָר הָרְבִיעִי, הוּא פְרָת.

14 And the name of the third river is Tigris; that is it which goeth toward the east of Asshur. And the fourth river is the Euphrates.

טו וַיִּקַּח יְהוָה אֱלֹהִים, אֶת-הָאָדָם; וַיַּנִּחֵהוּ בְגַן-עֵדֶן, לְעָבְדָהּ וּלְשָׁמְרָהּ.

15 And the LORD God took the man, and put him into the garden of Eden to dress it and to keep it.

Table 11

Though the entire band across the center of Africa was lush and green, that part in the east was designated for Australopithecus. Religious leaders will argue that the stories in the **Book of Genesis** are a direct reference to man fully formed as *Homo sapien*, I would argue that God never says that. All he does say is that He breathed life into a creature that in turn is designated as man, but never made the distinction of it being man's final form. It is only us, with our homocentric thinking that said He had to be referring to our current physical state. But the man in this chapter is little more than an animal with a slightly higher level of intelligence. He exists only on the fruits and food provided by nature, having no agricultural skill of his own, no tools and as we know from the story regarding the Tree of Knowledge, he is naked just like every other animal, not possessing the self awareness to know what is his current condition. For all intent and purpose, he is nothing more than an animal.

For three thousand years man has been searching for the Garden of Eden, that place denied to man forever because of Eve's great sin of listening to the serpent. There are those that take the story literary, others that call it a myth, but I have always viewed it as something much more, a retained memory that mankind had pressed into its subconsciousness from its primitive origins to which God set it into a context that could be grasped far more easily by the Children of Israel. The deciduous forests, jungles and rain forests that created this remarkable band of incredible life across central Africa was a paradise for all the living creatures that inhabited it. Author Jodi Picoult, I think puts it into words better than anyone else could, writing, " "Africa – You can see a sunset and believe you have witnessed the Hand of God. You watch the slope lope of a lioness and forget to breathe. You marvel at the tripod of a giraffe bent to water. In Africa, there are iridescent blues on the wings of birds that you do not see anywhere else in nature. In Africa, in the midday heat, you can see blisters in the atmosphere. When you are in Africa, you feel primordial, rocked in the cradle of the world." The cradle of the world, the cradle of life is an apt description. A place that most who have visited, say they belong after they have left. How could one even think such memories could be erased from the mind after coming into being in such a place. Yes, it was the proverbial Garden of Eden but as a species we cannot go back again.

But Chapter 2 of **Genesis** provides other hints to man's African origins by discussing the rivers that flow from the basin, this cradle which rocked us into existence beginning with the tenth sentence. The first is the פישון Pishon that encompasses the land of Havilah where there is gold and precious stones. Neither the name of the river nor the land is known, its whereabouts being delivered cryptically, almost as if God wanted it to remain hidden for eternity. When we look at the rivers that have their heads originating from the basin of the great rift, as seen in Figure 32, these four can be identified. The Congo River in the West, the Nile in the East, and the Zambesi in the south. The current water course of the Niger doesn't' extend to the Congo basin and would appear to be unconnected to the boundaries of the Garden of Eden except that the geological history of the area tells us that once Lake Chad was actually a great inland sea and it would feed the Niger River as much as it now flows into the Congo. With the lake continuing to diminish in size as it has been shrinking for millions of years, the modern day solution to save the lake is to rejoin it with the Niger River. Once completed, the northern boundary of the garden will have been restored. From sentences ten to thirteen, the **Genesis** story, with its cryptic descriptions and mysterious names only manages to talk about two of the rivers. Then all of a sudden it switches direction, and in one sentence both the third and fourth river appear in the east and are not disguised but instead are well known rivers of Mesopotamia.

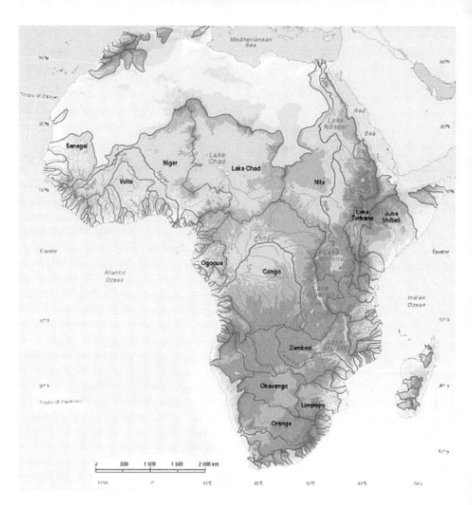

Figure 32

The fourth river in the east is called פְרָת (Phrath) and therefore easily recognized, since we know it as the Euphrates but it just doesn't happen to be on the African continent.   Yet, as seen in the upper right hand corner of Figure 32, it is not the river furthest east, that privilege belongs to the Tigris, which is mentioned in the same sentence. Clearly, this fourteenth sentence is designed as a diversion. Whereas the details of the earlier four sentences were drawing our focus to the African continent, this last sentence, short in details and making no attempt to disguise the names of the rivers takes us thousands of miles to the northeast and away from identifying the location.

But this diversion in itself is a clue, because it immediately suggest that we must be looking for a location far to the southwest, which takes us into the heart of the African continent as we search for Eden. It appears to be a game of reverse psychology, as if God realized what was being divulged would actually make the Children of Israel abandon their migration to Canaan, which was towards the Tigris and Euphrates, because they would question why bother continuing the exodus in that direction if paradise existed in the completely opposite direction. Recognizing what might result in a conflict, the names of two rivers they were familiar with were suddenly revealed and they would then be content that Moses was taking them in the right direction.

If this was the case, then that meant it was possible to decipher the concealed locations of the two rivers that had been disguised. As we look for the Pishon River, we need to remember that the Congo River was not known by that name to those that lived in the Congo. The natives referred to it as the Enzadi, or Great Gatherer because of all the tributaries and rivulets that extended from it. Ancient Hebrew defines the name Pishon as meaning the Great Diffusion. Depending how one looks at the tributaries that stem from a major river, one may see them as either stemming or diffusing from the main river, or feeding into the main river as if they're being gathered. It is also important to note that Havilah, which is encompassed by this river because of all its tributaries, is a land of massive gold and jewel reserves. The Democratic Republic of the Congo is regarded as one of the richest countries in the world in terms of its natural resources. It sits on massive deposits of iron ore, platinum, diamonds, gold and uranium. In fact, gold production has been increasing since the year 2000, where by 2016 and 2017, gold production in Congo was recorded at 37,000 kilograms. The mines of the Congo's Katanga and Kivu provinces, contain some of the world's largest reserves of cobalt, gold, copper, and diamonds, as well as tin, tungsten, and tantalum. The description in Genesis 2:12 certainly seems apt.

As for the second river is referred to as the Gihon and it encompasses the land of Cush. It is common knowledge amongst Biblical scholars that the land of Cush is the Ethiopia of today. Therefore the Gihon being referred to must be the Blue and White Nile Rivers that flow to the north and completely run the length of Ethiopia. Identification of the Gihon as the Nile River was also made by Josephus in his book Antiquities of the Jews i. 1 & 3 two thousand year ago. As the name from the Hebrew is derived from the word meaning 'burst forth' it aptly describes the Nile which will burst over its banks and inundate the land with its precious Nile mud that made agriculture and survival in Egypt possible.

Now some may argue that the name of the third river is concealed as well and therefore my assumption that it was hastily provided in order to create a diversion of the people's attention from searching for Eden in Africa is incorrect. But that argument fails because the name of the third river has always been translated as the Tigris, even though that is not what it says in the Hebrew. The river is called חִדֶּקֶל the Heddekel, in the Hebrew, which admittedly bears no resemblance to the name Tigris, but it is practically identical to the name of the river as it was called by the Akkadians before it was known as the Tigris, the Idikla. The mention that it runs east of Ashur and the fact Akkadians were a Mesopotamian people would suggest that identification as the Tigris has always been correct, the only error being that the city of Ashur actually sat on the banks of the Tigris and was not distant from the river as the sentence suggests.

It is understandable that the location of Paradise would not want to be revealed in **Genesis.** The birth of a new nation requires that the people remain united in their cause and their destination. It was already possible to begin putting together the puzzle pieces from the first four sentences where the garden was located, and that would have been disastrous if some of those journeying on the Exodus came to a realization that they were heading in the wrong direction if they were in search of paradise. It is why sentence fourteen stands our like a sore thumb, diverting anyone away from thinking too much about the chapter and returning them to the course upon which they were heading.

The Miocene Epoch

To understand the emergence of the chimpanzee, bonobo and Australopithecus, it is necessary what was occurring in the time period prior to their divergence. The Miocene Epoch existed from 23 million to 5.3 million years ago and is probably the most bountiful period for students of paleoprimatology. Not only was man's earliest ancestors experiencing dramatic changes but so to was the geomorphology, climate, and vegetation in the world. It was a time of highly active volcanic eruptions and tectonic plate movements creating mountain ranges where once flat plains stood. The vegetational changes that resulted from the formation of these mountain ranges played a major role in primate evolution. Many areas that had been thickly forested were altered into grassy knolls or else long stretches that have been identified as plains, prairies and savannas. Animals that had been arboreal, spending most of their time in trees were now faced with a new reality that they had become grounded. It was not that they couldn't find trees in which to live, it was just that the abundance of grasslands made it necessary for them to learn to travel long distances without the use of brachiation. For animals such as the primates, this transition was not too difficult, their ability for bipedal walking an asset for this new lifestyle.

As the reformation of the landscape was taking place during the Miocene Epoch, if a species was to survive it had to adapt quickly. There was not time for a slow mutational process of genes to take place. It was essentially a case of change your habits or die and this applied not only to the primates but to all the other species of animals as well. Migratory pattern, dietary requirements, even daily living habits had to alter immediately or they would not manage to survive. Many species didn't and what emerged from this epoch were the ancestors of the species we are familiar with today. But at the same time these species were learning to adapt they were also undergoing rapid morphological changes that weren't aligned with the painfully slow methodical pace of evolution as described by the Darwinists. In fact, it was almost as if an experimental laboratory had opened and was generating modifications at break-neck speed, some of them useful and others than only hastened the extinction of a species. In the case of hominid evolution, it was a time where changes seemed to be taking place with an unnatural regularity.

From material found in the Moroto District of eastern Uganda, in 1997 the description of a new genus and species, _Morotopithecus bishopi_, was announced. The 20 million year old fossil displayed the earliest traces of modern hominid skeletal characteristics. Even though the Proconsulidae were flourishing at the time with many genera and species, the apes and monkeys were emerging from this primitive ancestor as seen in Figure 19. By the mid Miocene, proconsul disappeared, and suddenly the Old World monkeys began diversifying, while the hominids remained relatively steady in their Pierolapithecus form. As seen in figure 19, the gibbons had already separated from the hominid stock which was being carried in the genes of Pierolapithecus.

Natural selection and mutational evolution certainly wasn't taking place as expected. Some genus and species were racing through a variety of forms at unheard of speed, only to suddenly crash and disappear from the fossil records. Others, by comparison were moving at a snail's pace even though experiencing the same environmental pressures, only to speed up later and then slow down again. In the Siwālik Hills of northern India and Pakistan, the remains of several species of Middle to Late Miocene Sivapithecus were discovered. In the 1970s the first facial skeleton was found, which combined primitive hominid features with derived orangutan-like characteristics. It was proof that the orangutan lineage completely separate from the rest of the hominids, which meant that the next contemporary finding in Africa should be an ancestor of the human/gorilla/chimpanzee line only. This was confirmed with the discovery of the eight million year old Samburupithecus, from northern Kenya, but was complicated by the complete cranio-dental discoveries of Graecopithecus, from several sites of a contemporaneous age in Greece. If Africa was the cradle of hominid existence, then how could there be a simultaneous presence of this hominid ancestor in Europe, across the Mediterranean? With the first flooding and then evaporation of the Mediterranean Sea approximately 5.6 million years ago when it became separated from the Atlantic, only to be refilled 5.3 million years ago when the Earth's plates shifted once again, it meant there was land route across a valley before 5.6 million year before now. For the three hundred thousand years when it evaporated and became a salt flats there was no likelihood of anything crossing it at that time. As such, the presence of Cercopithecus like monkeys in Europe meant that they had entered Europe long before the sea ever formed. Evidence of Dryopithecus in Spain would place this migration at approximately 15 million years ago. For Samburupithecus to be present in Kenya, while a European counterpart with similar features existed in Greece, would have required a migration of 4,600 kilometers or approximately one year, managing 12 to 13 kilometers a day, every day but with no apparent reason why they would have even made this migration. Animals migrate for food, water, or for protection, None of these reasons would appear to apply to the early hominids because the finding of their remains in Africa show that they were not under any threat of extinction by remaining where they were. Studies of migratory patterns of land mammals indicate that the caribou probably travels the furthest but only because of the wide fluctuations of climatic and biotic conditions. In comparison to an African counterpart, Zebras will migrate the most, completing their round trip by covering around 1600 kilometers in the process. At almost three times that distance, with an abundance of food and a stable climate in central Africa, it is highly unlikely there were any migratory patterns by early hominids between Africa and Europe.

This could only mean that simultaneous to the evolution of hominids in Africa, the identical process was taking place in Europe from an earlier species, such as the ancestors of monkeys that separated over thousands if not millions of years into their respective habitats.. For two different genetic pools, to have identical mutagenic results according to the rules of Darwinian evolution it cannot and will not happen.   What it does tell us is that the genetic codes within these two populations was already pre-programmed to respond exactly in accordance with one outcome.   That would mean that an early ancestor, such as Proconsul, had a large enough population that it spread out over vast areas of land which included both Africa and Europe, but at the same time began an evolutionary process independent of any differences of climatic, geographic, sociological, biotic, or any other pressures that may have been exerted in either of the two regions.   Proconsul was pre-programmed to produce a developing line of hominids no matter where it was located, even if its environment was perfect and there was no need to change.   If nothing else screams 'intelligent design' this is it.   The coding to respond to whatever minimal **GodSpark** may occur was already in place.   That spark only needed to trigger the mechanism and for that reason we have two identical hominids that both show they structurally were precursors for gorillas, chimpanzees and humans.

The enigma presented by early hominid fossil discoveries in Europe only serves to magnify the prior statement that animals intended to involve are already pre-programmed with the genetic code to complete that evolutionary process.   A concept which completely eradicates the notion of natural selection.   One merely has to look at the fossil remains found in a lignite mine in norther Italy back in the 1950s to appreciate the truth of that statement.   The skeleton was complete and excellently preserved but it certainly wasn't that of any miner.   It was called Oreopithecus, and it possessed several characteristics that made it definitely hominid.   Its canines were short and wide like those of humans, it had no true facial protrusion or snout, and the pelvis and spine provided evidence that it was capable of bipedal walking.   Its arms were long, hands having long curved fingers indicating that it was a brachiator, swinging from tree limb to tree limb. Recent studies have definitely confirmed *Oreopithecus bambolii* was a hominid but the dating presents a problem because it was calculated to have lived 7.5 million years ago.   By that time gorillas and chimpanzees had already separated off from the ancestors of man and here was a gibbon like ancestor that should have been long gone by that time, as his counterparts in Africa were no longer present.   This Oreopithecus was evolving at its own pace, completely independent of its African relatives, under an entirely different set of impinging factors and environmental circumstances, yet it was still following the identical pathway, albeit slower. One would say it was late to the party but it had not choice but to evolve as its programming indicated it must

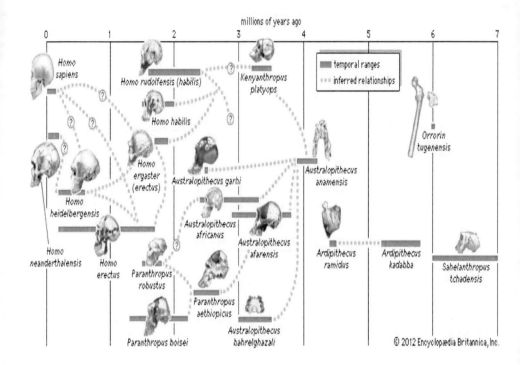

Figure 33

As evident from Figure 33, the hominid lineage was well on its way towards producing Australopithecus, with *Sahelanthropus tchadensis* occupying the Congo basin's Garden of Eden, while Oreopithecus was still hanging from a tree branch in Norther Italy. Over the past twenty years numerous other fossils from hominid species have been uncovered and they all have the same message. Evolution of humans was not linear, it was convergent, meaning that there were multiple lines of hominids evolving, each at their own pace and totally isolated from one another. Almost as if someone was conducting experiments in different laboratories spread across the globe, looking to find which one would produce the best results.

The Pliocene Epoch

The Pliocene Epoch, which followed the Miocene, extended from 5.3 million to 2.6 million years ago. Compared to the present day, the Pliocene was very similar the world today with its geographical morphology and varied climate. It would be expected that, during the Pliocene given the effectiveness that environmental selection of the African savanna played in human evolution, essentially more modernized forms of primates, excluding man would have made their appearance. Yet no fossils remains indicating attempts to modernize ape lineages can be found during the Pliocene, and the same practically holds true for monkeys, which also show so very few changes in their fossil record. What did characterize the Pliocene was the expansion and diversity in Africa of the human line, with *Ardipithecus ramidus* at 4.4 million years ago in Ethiopia and Australopithecus approximately 4 million years ago appearing all the way from the northern regions of South Africa to the southern Sudan. This arrested development in the evolution of other primates would almost suggest that they had reached the end of their programming. A chimpanzee was to be a chimpanzee and nothing further, while a gorilla would remain in its form until the end of time. Now that the hominid line was moving steadily towards its destination of *Homo sapien,* there doesn't appear to have been any further need for the other primates to carry on with the experiment.

As strange as that may sound, that is exactly how it appears and that natural selection and evolution as a continuous process as a biological truism is actually false. It only occurs within set boundaries and limitations and the how and who may be responsible for setting those boundaries is outside the scope of natural law. Now one could argue the end of the Miocene and beginning of the Pliocene Epochs was a time of tremendous upheaval that directly impacted on the Congo Basin and altered the regions inhabited by Australopithecus to such a great extent that it forced the hominid line to adapt and change far more rapidly than it ever had to prior in history. The extraordinary forces of plate tectonics and a changing climate have transformed East Africa from a relatively flat, forested region to a mountainous fragmented landscape dominated by the rapid appearance and disappearance of huge, deep-water lakes. And according to the Darwinists, this highly variable landscape forced an ape to emerge smart enough to question its own existence. But the undeniable reality is that Australopithecus was already there before the Earth was being reshaped and it was already on a rapid evolutionary track without any of these environmental pressures.

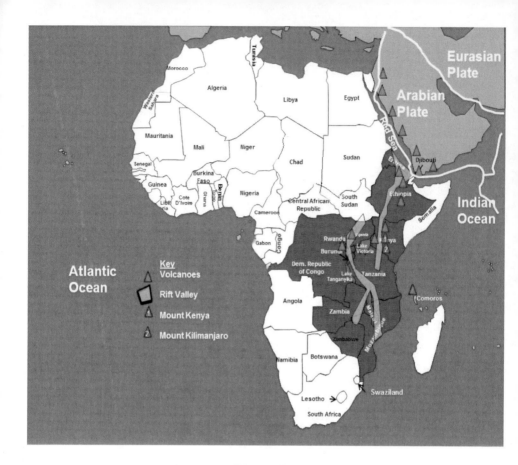

Figure 34

Approximately five million years ago, at the same time as the peaks of Himalayas were reaching skyward, the rifting process of east Africa began in Ethiopia and gradually moved south finishing in Mozambique about four million years later as can be seen in Figure 34. The East African Rift was caused by a pool of magma located under northern East Africa, which heated the earth's crust to such a degree that it split like an over ripe fruit. As a result, a deep, wide, valley half a mile above sea level was created, with mountain ranges on either side that rose to a height of two miles. And it can be said with certainty that the effects of the rift formation on the local climate was dramatic. The mountains prevented moist air from the Indian Ocean from passing over East Africa, causing the region to dry out even further, thereby changing the topography of East Africa completely. Cut off from the flat Congo basin that was richly covered in tropical forest, that area east of the rift had become a mountainous landscape with plateaus and deep valleys, where vegetation varied from forest to desert scrub.

Australopithecus had gone suddenly from the Garden of Eden to areas having only limited vegetation with much larger distances between food sources. Bipedalism was suddenly no longer a novelty but a necessity in order to reach these other areas with food. Crossing over the rift and returning to the Congo basin was a practical impossibility with the newly risen highlands forming an almost impenetrable and continuous north-south barrier extending from the Red Sea to southern Tanzania. These highlands included the Ethiopian Massif, rising up 1,500 meters, consisting of large tablelands, dissected by deep valleys. Further south lay the East African Highlands forming two mountainous arcs abutting on the eastern and the western rift valleys. The Kenyan highlands, at an average elevation of 1,500–2,500 m, were flanked to the east and south-east by Africa's two highest mountains, Mt. Kenya and Mt. Kilimanjaro. To the south, a long arc of more mountains but at a lower elevation. In the west, the western rift mountains ran from western Uganda to southern Tanzania. Between these two arcs is a large tableland, in which lay Lake Victoria, a deep and impassable body of water. For Australopithecus there was no return to the garden. Its future from then on resided in the savanna of east Africa, where the natural vegetation was dominated by wooded grassland and shrub-land. The only continuous zones of closed evergreen forests existed in southwestern Ethiopia and on the edges of the Congo Basin with some isolated patches of forest still to be found in areas of Kenya, Tanzania, and Uganda, but most often growing on steep inhospitable slopes.

But the rise of these mountainous ranges also meant changes to the west of the rift valleys. Increasing wet conditions prevailed over the Congo Basin as a result of the presence of the East African highlands. There was a local effect upon winds, temperature, and rainfall. As some of these mountains were active volcanoes, the ash they spewed into the air affected temperatures and solar radiation on either side of the rift. To assume that only Australopithecus to the east of the rift was affected would be incorrect. Its primate cousins to the west were also dramatically affected but there is no record of them undergoing any further evolutionary change.

Temperatures to the east of the rift remained steady except for the southern highlands of Tanzania and the northern part of the Sudan by the Red Sea and northern Somalia. The temperatures seasonally vary by no more than 5°C. In these regions, highest temperatures generally occur in February-March before the main rains, while lowest temperatures are found in July-August, during the relatively dry but cloudy season. It is believed these temperature ranges have been steady for millions of years and therefore, Australopithecus did not have to endure any extremes in temperatures after the rift occurred, creating the situation where Australopithecus didn't change much at all. The extremes changes to the environment didn't cause an evolutionary surge as Australopithecus adapted to its new environment. For the next two million years, Australopithecus remained genetically stable as a species.

Actually, the most profound period for human evolution didn't occur until about 2 million years ago. At that point in time, the fossil record reveals the highest diversity of hominid species ever to occur, including the appearance of *Homo rudolfensis* and Homo ergaster. It is also the time of the first major dispersal of hominins out of East Africa and into Eurasia. The reason for the migration may have been due to the freshwater lakes appearing and disappearing along the whole length of the East Africa Rift valley, which forced these new species to emerge from Africa in a search for a stable source of water and not food.

At this time there was still continuing volcanic activity that caused the basement rocks of the Ahaggar and Tibesti mountains of the central Sahara to rise. I can only imagine what our hominin ancestors thought as they finally left the African Rift region and migrated towards the Levant in Eurasia. It was a period when the great lakes of the rift could no longer be depended upon for water and every time they looked up to the mountains they'd see erupting volcanoes that showered the lands with ash. It makes me thing of what is written in **Genesis** chapter 3:

כג וַיְשַׁלְּחֵהוּ יְהוָה אֱלֹהִים, מִגַּן־עֵדֶן--לַעֲבֹד, אֶת־הָאֲדָמָה, אֲשֶׁר לֻקַּח, מִשָּׁם.

23 Therefore the LORD God sent him forth from the garden of Eden, to till the ground from whence he was taken.

כד וַיְגָרֶשׁ, אֶת־הָאָדָם; וַיַּשְׁכֵּן מִקֶּדֶם לְגַן־עֵדֶן אֶת־הַכְּרֻבִים, וְאֵת לַהַט הַחֶרֶב הַמִּתְהַפֶּכֶת, לִשְׁמֹר, אֶת־דֶּרֶךְ עֵץ הַחַיִּים. {ס}

24 So He drove out the man; and He placed at the east of the garden of Eden the cherubim, and the flaming sword which turned every way, to keep the way to the tree of life. {S}

Table 12

And the early ancestors of man were sent forth from what had been their Garden of Eden, to trod the ground from where he originated no longer. This primitive man was driven north west because the eastern passage to the Congo Basin was no longer passable, the mountains erupting with their lava, pouring down into the valleys from every direction. And the mountains stood their like giants, leviathans breathing fire, forcing this ape-man to turn away from the forests which gave him life. What I believe you read in Genesis is an apt description of the actual event. It's all a matter of interpretation and how God felt it necessary to explain the flight from paradise to a people that only had the vaguest of recollections of their primitive past.

In This Corner

The cessation of any further evolutionary development by the chimpanzee will always be a bone of contention to the primate paleontologist who insists that they just haven't found the fossil remains of any of the chimpanzee's or gorilla's ancestors yet. In most likelihood they have found the remains, but because they looked no different from the representatives of both species today, they'd rather assume it is recent remains that managed to become displaced deeper into the layers of the earth through quakes and small rifts. The alternative would be to admit they were the fossils of early ape ancestors and for some inexplicable reason, chimpanzees and gorillas look the same as they always did. Of course to admit such a thing as I mentioned would send shivers down the spines of any Neo-Darwinists because they would have to admit that evolution is not a universal principle and something is controlling the selection. That would be a bitter pill for them to swallow.

It was as if there were two contestants in the ring, battling it out for the championship. The winner gets to evolve into a more advanced species, while the loser has to remain exactly what it currently is. When both the Chimpanzee and Australopithecus arrived on the scene it was probably that close that either one could have earned the title of champion hominid to evolve. But once one did begin the process, the other was switched off, and that is an essential recognition that it is more than merely intelligent design at work, it is also a case of direct interference. A negative version of the **GodSpark** to prevent any further advancement. Though stopped in it evolutionary tracks, the wonderful opportunity presented of being able to have a window in time to actually see what our Australopithecus ancestors may have been like by examining today's chimpanzee is a gift to be treasured. Chapter 18 will do exactly that, looking at mankind's chimpanzee cousins in their wild habitat and extrapolating what they do to how once upon a time the Australopithecus had lived.

Examining the physical anatomical features between these two species, in order to make a direct comparison, provides perhaps the only clues to understanding exactly why one species was chosen over the other to become the ancestor of man. The Chimpanzee along with the bonobo, are the apes most closely related to humans. They inhabit the tropical forests and savannas of equatorial Africa from Senegal in the west to Lake Albert and northwestern Tanzania in the east. Individuals vary considerably in size and appearance, but chimpanzees stand approximately from 1 to 1.7 meters tall or 3 to 5.5 feet in height when erect with males being taller than females Weights vary between 32 to 60 kilograms or roughly 70 to 130 pounds. In comparison, Lucy, probably the most well known Australopithecus, was just 1.27 meters tall or 4 feet 2 inches tall and weighed 27 kilograms or 59 pounds. Based on fossil evidence from over 300 individuals, Australopithecus appears to have been on average for males about 1.51 meters tall or four feet eleven inches and weighing in at 42 kilograms on average or 92 pounds. Females on average were 1.05 meters tall or three feet five inches and weighed 29 kilograms or 64 pounds. Assuming that chimpanzees have most likely increased in size over the past few million years, then it is most probably that there was no difference in height and weight between these two cousins four million years ago.

Male chimpanzees tend to be larger and more robust than females and are generally covered by a coat of brown or black hair, but their faces are bare except for a short beard. Skin colour is generally white except for the face, hands, and feet, which is darker or almost black. The faces of younger chimpanzees are often pinkish or whitish. Without any physical evidence, we can only surmise that Australopithecus had the same coat and colouration but we can see that the sexual dimorphism of males being larger was true for man's ancestor as well.

The chimpanzees diet is primarily vegetarian, consisting of more than 300 different items, mostly fruits, berries, leaves, blossoms, and seeds but also bird eggs and chicks, many insects, and occasionally carrion. Chimpanzees also hunt, both alone and in groups, stalking and killing various mammals such as monkeys, duikers, bushbucks, and wild pigs. *Australopithecus afarensis* had mainly a plant-based diet, including leaves, fruit, seeds, roots, nuts, and insects…

and probably the occasional small vertebrates, like lizards. It is possible that like the chimpanzee, it would catch the occasional Colobus monkey to add red meat to the diet. Examination of the remains of their teeth using dental microwear studies indicate that generally they ate soft, sugar-rich fruits, but their tooth size and shape also suggests that they could have also eaten hard, brittle foods as well when their regular diet wasn't available due to seasonal changes. From what we can tell, the diet of the chimpanzee and that of Australopithecus bore very little difference.

The female chimpanzee bears a single baby at any time of year after a gestation period of about eight months. The newborn weighs about 1.8 kg or about 4 pounds and is almost helpless, clinging to the fur of the mother's belly as she moves. From about 6 months to 2 years, the youngster rides on the mother's back. Weaning takes place at about 5 years. Males are considered adults at 16 years of age, and females usually begin to reproduce at about 13 years. The longevity of chimps on average is 45 years in the wild and 58 in captivity but there have been examples of chimpanzees living up 80 years. Once again, there is little reason to believe that these time frames would have been any different for Australopithecus. Compared to modern humans they aren't that different, therefore we can assume our ancestors biorhythms functioned very similar to that of the chimpanzee.

Perhaps the clues to any differences lies in the size of their respective brains. The average weight of a chimpanzee brain is 384 grams. But *Australopithecus afarensis* had a slightly larger brain size with a cranial capacity of about $450cm^3.$ As the space between the brain and skull has to be accounted for, thickness of the dura, etc., then the actual size of the brain would have been about 400 grams in weight, so perhaps not that much different from the chimpanzee. By comparison, the average adult human brain today weighs in at 1300 to 1400 grams within a cranial spatial capacity of about $1,500cm^3$. From the perspective of relative intelligence, there appears to have been very little difference as well. One might argue that there is possible evidence of Australopithecus being a tool user but that doesn't matter because we know chimpanzees are rudimentary tool users as well, from using sticks to fish out insects from trees, to carrying heavy sticks on occasion to use as a club. It would also appears that chimpanzees know how to use certain plants medicinally to cure diseases and expel intestinal parasites.

All points considered, there does not appear to have been much difference between the two species to account for why one remained genetically stable, undergoing very little if any change over the past few million years, while the other made incredible leaps from approximately two million years ago to the past hundred thousand years. As far as habitat, food supply, living conditions, and social systems and behaviors were concerned, Australopithecus was in as stable an environment as was the Chimpanzee, yet despite this apparent stability and lack of pressures for change, Australopithecus seemed compelled to do so. It was almost as if Australopithecus inherited a genetic instability that caused radical changes to occur after being stable for over 1.5 million years. As can be seen in Figure 33, sometime prior to two million years ago, Australopithecus began producing a large number of Australopithecine varieties, *Paranthropus* and *Homo habilus*. This can be better seen in Figure 35, as it is actually an incredible number of genetic variances produced by a single species in a very short period of time. At the bottom of that figure it can be seen that the chimpanzee has not undergone any variations, which should be considered highly peculiar since the both came from the same genetic stock along with the gorilla.

But what we do know is somewhere along the way, the number of chromosomes between chimpanzees and Australopithecus must have undergone a change, so that chimpanzees and gorillas have 48 or 24 chromosome pairs, while the hominids only had 46 or 23 pairs. Originating from the stock species, it is a certainty that they all shared the identical number of chromosomes initially but somewhere along the way, that changed. Two options exist being that either chimpanzees and gorillas had identical chromosomal breakages resulting in the formation of a new chromosome pair, or that Australopithecus experienced fusion of two pairs of chromosomes into a single pair of longer chromosomes. The answer as to which situation occurred was published in the Procedures of the National Academy of Sciences, October 1991 by Ijdo et al. Their research shows an abundance of evidence for the fusion of two ancestral chromosomes on chromosome 2 as the result of fusing what were originally chromosomes 1 and 3.

Human chromosome 2, is still found as two smaller chromosomes in the great apes. Ijdo describes the event as follows: "Similarities in chromosome banding patterns and hybridization homologies between ape and human chromosomes suggest that human chromosome 2 arose out of the fusion of two ancestral ape chromosomes, 1 and 3. Molecular data show evidence that this event must have occurred only a few million years ago. Although the precise nature of this putative fusion is unknown, cytogenetic data point to either a centromeric or telomeric fusion in the vicinity of region 2ql. The observation that telomeric DNA is present in chromosomal band q13 suggests that telomeres, the extreme ends of chromosomes, may have been involved in this fusion. Normally, telomeres form a dynamic buffer against loss of internal sequence and prevent chromosomes from fusing. By contrast, non-telomeric DNA ends are subject to degradation by nucleases and to fusion by ligation."

In other words, this telomeric fusion that was observed was an extremely rare event since it is the job of telomere's to keep the gene sequences stable and in tact. Their study demonstrated that it was telomere-telomere fusion that occurred and was responsible for the evolution of human chromosome 2 from two ancestral ape chromosomes.

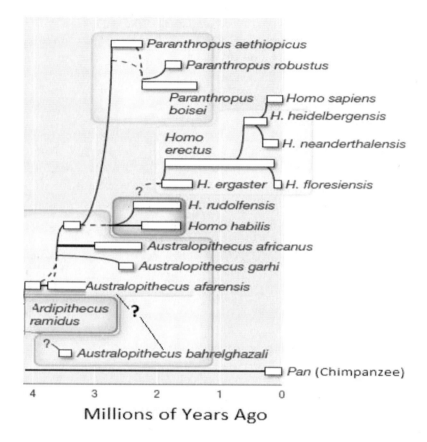

Figure 35

In an effort to describe how unexpected this type of fusion is, they said it was a is a rare occurrence in normal lymphoblasts and fibroblasts, and was more commonly observed in 20-30% of the cells of certain tumors. They suggest that this rare fusion may have destabilized the chromosomes, resulting in other fusions which accelerated the genetic modifications and triggered the rapid evolutionary response. Yet, with all these changes, there doesn't appear to have been the normally expected deleterious effect, such as cutting off the individual from sexual reproduction with the parent population that still have 48 chromosomes. In order to create a new species, a fairly large portion of the population would be required to experience this fusion simultaneously. This would have nothing to do with natural selection but would be the result of intentional genetic modification or manipulation if it actually did happen to a large number of the population all at once. But if it was only an individual or handful of hominids that experienced this fusion, then defying the usual sterility occurrence where animals of different chromosome number interbreed, these few mutated hominids would still need to interbreed with the members of their colony having 48 chromosomes and produce fertile offspring.

The situation in this case is that telomeres, that were designed as part of our cellular genetic mechanism to keep the ends of chromosomes from fraying or breaking did something that they normally don't do. They fused, thereby creating one pair of chromosomes out of two original pairs. As a result of an unknown trigger, this fusion took what had been a stable genome established on 48 chromosomes for almost two million years in the Australopithecine species and turned it into a genetic slot machine that every time the arm was pulled down, a new species was created.

What also can't be explained is how something that is a genetic aberration which should have resulted in this mutation no longer being able to mate and produce fertile offspring with its closest relatives, such as chimpanzees and gorillas, but also not being able to do so with its own parent population which still possessed 48 chromosomes. Either it was able to inexplicably overcome this expected infertility as had been pointed out a few paragraphs ago or else this fusion mutation was not unique to a mere handful but in fact one of many occurring at the time to many in the colony so that there were plenty of 46 chromosome potential mates available upon reaching maturity.

But what seems the most improbable outcome of this fusion, complicating this scenario even further, is that there must have been so many offspring experiencing the mutation simultaneously that in a very short time, being a million years or so, they were able to not only displace but replace the old 48 chromosome parent population. This scenario required that the old Australopithecus population became extinct, even though we see that comparatively there was very little difference to the chimpanzee which had no problem continuing to exist as a stable population.

As if these weren't enough highly impossible events to take place as a result of this chromosome fusion, the fact that these chromosomal mutations, reconstructions, aberrations, defects or whichever other descriptive term is chosen are usually deleterious in nature and quickly removed from the gene pool, this one not only is retained but continues to promote further fusions or aberrations as a variety of new hominin species are produced, all seemingly viable and potentially fertile, defying what were considered firm and fast rules in genetics.

If we were to string all the aforementioned events together and calculate not only the plausibility of their occurrence but also the possibility, the odds against such events having a positive and successful outcome would be nil. If ever there was a **GodSpark,** this was it, because by all rights, modern man should not exist.

Chapter 16: If Only They Could Talk

Though there has already been discussion on mankind's capability for speech and the proposal that it may have been the result of a virus, what has not been discussed is why animals, such as apes, having practically identical laryngeal and pharyngeal structures aren't able to speak. It is a question being asked concurrently by a lot of scientists around the world. Much of this recent research has focused on primates, in which acoustic investigations have been intense and a broad range of species has been studied. Focus has been on the larynx as it is the main organ of vocal production, using a combination of three-dimensional computer models built from CT scans with detailed digital measurements, using a protocol designed to characterize gross features of laryngeal morphology consistently across each species.

Each larynx was characterized by a set of 10 measurements. The most variable measurements were associated with the ventral extent of the larynx, followed by vocal fold length, and the distance between dorsal cricoid and ventral thyroid cartilages in the central plane. In comparison to other carnivore species, there appeared to be a marked difference with primates exhibiting larger larynges for the same body length. The results suggested that, for similar body lengths, the primate larynx is approximately 1.38 times larger than a carnivore species' larynx on average. This enlarged larynx as part of primate evolution needed to be explained, since if it was necessary in order for speech to be possible, then it was already in a process of enlargement before speech was even possible. And if it was enlarged in order for speech, then why does only one species actually talk, if the others possess the same structural organ.

In trying to explain the difference in size as a result of function rather than actual size of the animal or related to the need for speech, scientist explored whether the role of the larynx in protecting the respiratory system during feeding was involved. Even though it is the epiglottis that occludes the trachea during swallowing, the larynx also offers protects against aspiration of food or liquid via its reflex closure and coughing mechanism should the epiglottis be bypassed. Theories such as the threat of choking on large pieces of minimally-chewed meat would lead to evolutionary selection pressure for a smaller larynx in carnivores. A practical theory but it does not explain the overall differences in larynx size observed among primates. Not too mention that not all carnivores are obligate meat eaters, some are more omnivorous and share a diet similar to some primates and therefore this postulation does not appear to be correct.

A second possibility is that differences in relative larynx size between primates and carnivores are a result of tidal volumes of respiration, thinking that different patterns of locomotion between primates and carnivores may place different demands on oxygen metabolism. But recognizing that some carnivores are arboreal, then there was no support for this hypothesis found among these comparatively arboreal carnivores which all possessed a relatively small larynx. Furthermore no one could actually say how a relatively small versus large larynx would benefit the muscular and locomotor requirements of a terrestrial versus arboreal lifestyle.

The next hypothesis was that increased oxygen supply would be supported by a larger primate larynx and that would result in greater brain function. But again, looking at the relative intelligence of a monkey versus a dog, there wasn't enough data to support such a hypothesis.

A fourth hypothesis was the possibility that the differences in relative larynx size between primates and carnivores reflected the role of the larynx in vocal communication. The majority of primate species are found in tropical forest environments, whereas carnivores occupy a much greater diversity of habitats. Since forest environments reduce the usage of visual signals because of all the trees, but they are ideal for echoing the lower frequencies which are possible to generate by a larger larynx. This hypothesis appears compatible with the larger relative size of the primate larynx, but not its increased size variation. If variation in larynx size is contingent upon variation in habitat, then the carnivores would be predicted to exhibit greater larynx size variation, not less, as was observed.

The fifth hypothesis suggested a larger larynx was ideal for sexual selection as the lower-frequency vocalizations would deter any challenge from other apes as part of the intrasexual competition but would also be suitable for attracting suitable mates, assuming that other primates besides man find a deep, low voice sexy. However, the study failed to find a significant difference between primates and carnivores when it came to sexual mating strategies based on lower frequency vocalization.

Having exhausted all possible hypotheses, the only one that remained was that the cartilaginous structure of the larynx likely correlates with its acoustic capabilities, as seen in Figure 36, and ultimately the soft tissues of the larynx that are responsible for vocal production are increased proportionately to the size of the larynx. More soft tissue results in more differentiation in sound production and therefore, a heightened probability of being able to speak. The scientists drew the following conclusion from their studies that if the relative flexibility of the primate larynx is robust to future analyses, then it may have to do with evolutionary lineage, which in turn may in turn explain why primates have developed such diverse and complex uses of the vocal organ. In other words, the larynx was in a development phase to possibly be capable of speech at some future time, even though speech was not conceptually known to the primates in any manner other than their hoots, howls and growls and their brain centers for speech had no evidence of increasing gray matter to either develop or analyze the content of speech. It simply is a case of putting the cart in front of the horse, according to these scientists, but their supposition that the larynx was being designed for future use begs the question of who was responsible for this design. With no apparent need, societal or environmental pressures, then the restructuring of any anatomical structure without those external drivers will not occur.

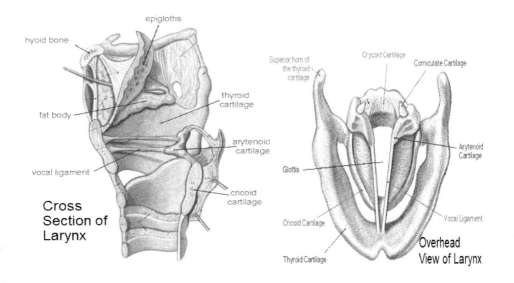

Figure 36

That being the case, how is it possible that evolution was instituting a change in morphology towards a characteristic that didn't even exist and certainly from the fact that all the other apes except for man, still managed to survive in their environments without the capacity or need to speak to survive normally. Essentially, the larynx was being engineered for future possible use, as just mentioned, which has nothing to do with natural selection and everything to do with intelligent design.

All that was missing was a stimulus to the brain to create the realization that the ape could make different sounds that it could string together as actual words because they already have the vocal ligaments in existence as seen in Figure 36. As discussed earlier, the rabies virus provides such a stimulus, promoting a wide range of vocalizations, that once recovered from infection could be harnessed into speech. But for all this to take place would imply that from the onset, the increase in the size of larynx, the increased mass of soft tissue and cartilage, the viral infection to stimulate the brain, and cause a relaxation of musculature so that the human larynx falls into a lower position in the pharyngeal cavity was all part of an elaborate and calculated plan. For the scientists to actually come to this realization that morphological change for speech was already in progress before the concept of speech even existed, is truly an example of **GodSpark.**

Chapter 17: The Ngogo Chimpanzees

To anyone that has seen the documentary The Warrior Apes it is like looking through a window into our own past as we trod the savanna with our troop of Australopithecus relatives. As far as time machines go, it is as close to perfect as it can get, and yet, there are those anthro-paleontologists that insist that there had to be more, otherwise there is no explanation as to why we continued to evolve, while the chimpanzees are caught in a time suspension of stagnation. That is where much of the confusion revolves around adaptation versus evolution. Darwin's theories automatically assumed if an animal needed to adapt, then it had to evolve, but what he failed to recognize was those higher order animals with a superior intelligence can adapt without physical change. If the climate changes, as in an ice age, a higher order animal, such as man can wear the skin from another animal, or light a fire for heat. Man does not have to evolve in order to physically meet the challenge of the changing environment, instead he can simply adapt a behavior and overcome it. The same is true with chimpanzees, but obviously to a lesser degree as they haven't nailed down the control of fire as yet, but as far as tools, hierarchies, social structuring, task designation and primitive language/communication, they have done very well in adapting their behaviors as necessary to meet their circumstances. So well in fact, that there is no need to evolve further. But that creates a serious dilemma when arguing the need for hominin species evolution. Comparatively, Australopithecus had adopted to its environment very well too. So well, in fact, that it could expand its territorial dominion over areas the chimpanzee was unable to encroach upon, such as the extensive grasslands and the mountain slopes. That being the case, there was no further need for Australopithecus to evolve further either, but regardless of that fact, it did evolve into a variety of species without the urgent need to do so. Chromosome fusion was part of the story as touched upon in a previous chapter but there also had to be something more. Something on a level that even science can't explain and possibilities will be looked at in the next chapter. For now, this chapter will focus on the chimpanzee, the living, breathing antithesis to Darwinian evolution

Chimpanzees are primarily vegetarian, the bulk of their diet consisting of fruit, leaves, flowers, and seeds. But as very graphically displayed in the documentary by David Watts and John Mitani, chimpanzees do form hunting parties from time to time and search the forest tree tops for Colobus monkeys. What is truly amazing as one watches the hunt, is that it becomes obvious that each chimpanzee in the hunting party has a different role and function. Those which are fastest and strongest brachiators are sent into the treetops to chase the prey. Those not so gifted will mark out a perimeter in the trees, where they wait in order to block off any escape routes. In the beginning, there is a series of hand signals and head movements, as they are assigned their tasks and acknowledgement that they have understood. Once deep in the forest, though the members of the hunting party can't see each other at that point in the hunt, you can tell they're following a practiced routine, so that they know exactly where every one else is at a specific time. An incredible display of cognitive spatial mapping ability of both place and time

Numerous colonies or troops of chimpanzees have been studied since Jane Goodall first provided the world with man's first close encounter of his wild cousin. And just like man, it turned out that these colonies had their cultural differences as well. In a comparison of two of these colonies, Gombe and Tai Forest one of the most striking differences was how they would eat the monkeys they had caught. Gombe chimpanzees only eat them after they are dead, whereas Tai Forest chimpanzees will eat the Colobus monkeys while still alive. Its true significance is that the Gombe chimpanzees are displaying what could be considered as ethical and empathetic characteristic. The ability to feel for another species, which might be considered in our world as being 'humane'.

The chimpanzee is both an arboreal and terrestrial mammal. Generally, chimpanzees are quadrupeds, walking on all four limbs but tending to do so on the knuckle of their hands. In addition, chimpanzees brachiate while living in the trees but on the ground they will also travel bi-pedaly for a distance, especially when they are carrying tools or food.

It has always been thought that chimpanzees have an average troop size of no more than twenty or thirty members because any more than that would require a level of organization and communication that only humans were thought to possess. The Alpha male leads the troop and the male chimpanzees are constantly playing politics either with brute force or diplomatic grooming. Females leave their natal groups when they sexually mature. Males have dominance over females although there is a dominance hierarchy within the females as well. Their society is termed fission-fusion and patrilineal multi-male, multi-female. The reality is that it follows an imperial structure with very little difference from what has been seen in human history. As emperor, the alpha-male is surrounded by a few of the most loyal males in the troop that have shown no evidence of wishing to displace him and seize his position. Others that seek favor from the alpha-male will try to ally themselves with the few males in his special support group. Having their favour usually earns them some limited trust from the alpha-male, but those wishing to eventually challenge the emperor, will attempt to make the same bonds with the closed group that directly surround him but for purposes of trying to have them betray their leader either actively, or inactively by not interfering when the attempted coup takes place. This intention demonstrates not only a high degree of forethought and planning a willingness to deceive and betray which had always been thought of as a purely human qualities. Playing politics is highly sophisticated group think.

Chimpanzees use a number of social mechanisms to communicate with each other, having two different types of displays they commonly use, The first which consists of inhaling rhythmically and loud hooting. This is used as a challenge display and communicates to the rest of the group the intentions of the their leader. When chimpanzees want to show that the are self-confident and assertive they an inflating display in which they press their lips together and hold their breath while puffing out their chests. But studies of the Ngogo chimpanzees indicated that they have far more ways of communicating, such as hand signals and eye movements. The signs have a universal nature, other chimpanzees immediately recognizing them and taking the necessary actions they have been instructed to do. Primatologists have realized long ago that the great apes have a natural ability for learning sign language, capable of learning not only hundreds but thousands of words but whereas they considered this a major breakthrough in human-ape communications, they weren't aware that the apes were using such signs at a much lower level already in their natural environment. Washoe was one of the first chimpanzees able to communicate with American Sign Language. Washoe was even able to teach some of her learned sign language to her adopted son Louis. Primatologists determined that chimpanzees have the cognitive ability to process language as well as any five year old human child. But as indicated, chimpanzees have naturally been able to communicate with each other through their facial expressions, the baring of teeth as they smile, eye movements and hand signals. The most popular hand gesture used by chimpanzees is the extended arm with open palm. It can have a variety of meanings determined by both how and when it is being used. It can beg for attention, or it can be used to signify that they are no threat. It can request an alliance, or it can ask for emotional and physical support. Teaching chimpanzees ASL doesn't mean we have taught them to be any smarter, it only means we've added to their already existing skill set.

Though much is written about the male hierarchy, the chimpanzee troops also have a female hierarchy in existence but physical strength is not the determining factor of its structure. In fact physical altercations between females is rare. The ranking female is also recognized by the males in a troop and she can remove food and items from males without any resistance. The females in the troop appear to have the ability to calm and restore peace within the troop when males become aggressive. Exactly how the females exert this power over conflict is not understood as exactly what leverage they extend is not unknown. The society still revolves around the Alpha male but it is not always about dominance through physical force but through the qualities of leadership. An Alpha male that comes to rule through violence and brute force is often dethroned not by an other male but by a group of males in the troop that remove him by the same brute force that caused his rise to power. Other Alpha males have been seen to rule by their ability to prevent conflict, distilling peace among the others, and consoling those that have been the victims of aggression. The Alpha male that can keep the peace is rewarded with respect and sexual privileges given to him as his earned right, not simply because he has managed to claim the position. His organizational abilities are put to the test when the male chimpanzees go out on patrol to protect their territory or to invade the territory of rival chimpanzee troops. The organization and militarization of these war parties is quite complex and usually intended to deliver a message rather than all out warfare.

After two males within the same troop have fought, it is the Alpha male's role to see that there is reconciliation. During this process, the two males must sit across from one another and make a large amount of direct eye contact. The Alpha male ensures that however long it takes, they will finally make eye contact and continue to do so until the reconciliation process is completed. The Alpha male plays an important role in ensuring that the males within the troop behave, even if it means they just tolerate one another as seen with the establishment of strategic coalitions and intra-troop alliances formed by some males acting together against another male. One male may refuse to accept the friendship of another male unless that male also accepts the friendship of a third male. These treaties and bargains can actually be quite complex and often when the agreements cannot be arranged, the Alpha male will beat the offending party as a public display to show what happens when reconciliation and agreement cannot be achieved.

It has been argued that the Bonobo chimpanzee evolved from the common chimpanzee via the Founder Effect. This effect refers to a small group from the original population becoming isolated from the original group and then evolving differently due to both their environment and the limited gene pool from which it can draw. The evidence that is used for this argument was that the common chimpanzees are blood types A and O whereas the Bonobo chimpanzees are only blood type A. The separation of the two species by the Congo River meant that their competition for food was different as the common chimpanzee to the north of the river has to compete with gorillas for its food. This theory worked well until DNA analysis of the common chimpanzees to humans as well as Bonobos to humans showed that humans had the same percent gene difference to each species of chimpanzee except they were two entirely different sets of genes involved, meaning that Australopithecus had to develop the pre-human difference to both chimpanzees and bonobos at the same time, indicating both species existed at the time that all the great apes separated from their common ancestor. This point is raised only to serve as an indication that originally, when the proconsul ancestor to the great apes was evolving and developed into species we recognize as gorillas, chimpanzees, bonobos and Australopithecus, there was no apparent reason why three species would stop their progression and one would carry on to eventually become human. There was obviously a selection process taking place but it wasn't natural selection. The process actually appears deliberate and that is further recognized when examining how the conditions that science had assumed spurred on human evolution are also found to exist within the chimpanzee colonies in their natural habitat, yet they did not respond to the stimulus.

What needs to be pointed out is that each of the highlighted traits in the preceding discussion of the characteristics of chimpanzees were all raised at one time as the determining factors that promoted human evolution and defined us as being human. Only humans could maintain a large social pack because of the strict requirements to maintain order over a large number of individuals. The degree of hierarchical development involving rules, enforcement, communication and cohesiveness, was beyond that of any herd or pack animal other than man and therefore it must have been man's desire to live and be interactive within a much larger community structure that forced him to evolve. Well, that certainly isn't the case when looking at the Ngogo chimpanzee. They seem very content with remaining exactly as they are despite their incredibly large troop number.

Another argument that was raised was once the brain had achieved a certain degree of intelligence, then if the diet included a high protein level that could only be attained through eating meat, then the brain would continue to increase in size and intelligence. This theory was used to explain Australopithecus's continued evolution, presuming that it had progressed from being a completely herbivorous creature to resorting to becoming a carrion eater in times when food was not readily available. It is still not uncommon to hear people refer to certain meats, such as fish as being brain food, the protein levels presumed to being utilized directly to expand gray matter. Once again, the discovery that chimpanzees add meat to their diet regularly has proven that this had nothing to do with advancing the evolution of their Australopithecus cousin.

Once animals developed a need for expanded communication, then speech would be a natural result, many of the evolutionists surmised as they tried to come to grips with the human ability to speak. But once again, the chimpanzees in the wild with their ability to communicate complex concepts on their hunting parties and when dealing punitively with one of their own troop members has shown that this hypothesis was false. Speech was not a direct result of a need to express and communicate successfully. The chimpanzees have developed their rudimentary communication system to meet their needs and there are no signs of any speech development as would be witnessed in an expanding repertoire of sounds being made over the years. The chimpanzee today, makes the identical sounds as it did millions of years ago and there is no evidence that that will change in the future.

The argument that tool use was the key that spurred on the evolution of *Homo habilus* towards further evolution towards *Homo sapiens* has been in use for a very long time and one that is generally accepted by most scientists. As long as there was no evidence of other animals utilizing tools then it was an argument that couldn't actually be challenged. But once those studying chimpanzees in the wild reported back with what they had observed, that all changed. Chimpanzees using twigs to fish out insects from rotting logs, stones to strip or cut meat from their kill on the hunts, even picking up sticks to use as clubs in the battles against neighbouring chimpanzee troops. The Tai forest Chimpanzees eat Panda nuts which they open using two stones as anvil and hammer. The rocks needed to perform this task are found far from the location of the Panda Nuts so the chimpanzees not only needed to cognitively remember how to open these nuts but to also remember where they can find the tools to do so in what has become a multi-step process. In all these examples, the fact is that tool use is a normal way of life for the chimpanzee and has been for a very long time, yet it showed no evidence of advancing along an evolutionary pathway because of it. It was just one more theory that our chimpanzee cousins managed to blast out of the water.

According to all that science has postulated and theorized regarding what are the promoting factors that encourage the evolutionary process, it is clear that what was assumed to be true for the Australopithecus, when applied to the chimpanzee does not in any way support the theories and that can only mean that the Australopithecus and all its subsequent evolutionary spawn are not the norm but exceptions that have still not been explained through any of the scientific suppositions. The only explanation that explains the selection of the one species over the other under almost identical circumstances is the **GodSpark**.

Chapter 18: The Hominin Revolution

They say you can't keep a good man down. That certainly appears to be the situation when discussing evolution of the Homo species of mankind. What began with a proliferation of various species resulting from Australopithecus's chromosomal accident, certainly did not slow down with the coming of *Homo habilis.* With the recent addition of *Homo floresiensis*, also known as the 'Hobbit' due to his halfling size similar to the hobbit description by Tolkien, it would be surprising to think we've reached the end of discovering the multitude of homo species. In just over two million years, ten different homo species, only a few of which are actually on the direct family tree from which *Homo sapiens* sprouted. It should be noted that *Homo rudolfensis* depending on which chart is being looked at is either a direct ancestor or a dead end path in human development. He would not be the only one, with *Homo antecesor, Homo georgicus, and Homo denisovans* also being similar dead ends. The multiple evolutionary lines within such a short period of time is remarkable. As I have mentioned previously, shortly after the terraform changing events 5.2 million years ago, the pressures upon Australopithecus don't appear that extreme considering there does not appear to have been any such pressures on the chimpanzees and gorillas on the other side of the rift.

Discoveries made at Aramis in Ethiopia thirty years ago, that have been dated to 4.4 million years old, reveal an intriguing and unexpected mixture of features that were used in the past to designate the hominid as being Australopithecus but were different enough to still warrant a new genus designated as *Ardipithecus ramidus*. Subsequent discoveries revealed another species of Ardipithecus, which has been called *Ardipithecus kadabba* but it and a similar fossil found at the Kenyan site of Lukeino have been dated to approximately 6 million years ago, which was even prior to the formation of the rift. Suddenly, the hypothesis suggesting that Australopithecus needed to evolve because of the changed ecosystem as a result of the formation of the Eastern African Rift is no longer supported. Fossils dated to seven million years ago were discovered at Toros-Menalla in Central Africa and these have since been assigned to another new species and genus named *Sahelanthropus tchadensis*. Being on the western side of the rift, this species did not even share a similar environment experienced by Australopithecus. It should be noted, that at one time or another, all of these different species have been proposed as a likely ancestor to the later hominins. Obviously, they all can't be direct ancestors of the human race. What needs to be accepted is that rather than being an ancestor, some of these had to belong to an archaic 'proto-hominin' species that failed to evolve further. Therefore, the questions that need to be raised once again is how the selection process was made as to which species would continue to evolve and which would become dead ends. There doesn't appear to be any protocol that provides a logical conclusion on how the selection process could occur naturally.

At this point I must explain the taxonomy that has been used thus far and what will be used hereafter when referring to the homo species. The original classification for the study of human evolution was to refer to every species that was determined to be the genus homo as being 'hominids'. But with the dawn of genetic mapping of all the species on earth, the close relationship between man and chimpanzees, including the bonobo, meant that they were hominids as well. The term hominid now includes in addition to Homo, the great apes, such as the gorilla, the Pan (chimpanzees and bonobo), as well as the Pongo clades (orangutans, lufengpithecus, meganthropus and others). The undeniable genetic similarities in coding meant that the genus pan, the Pongo clades and the gorilla are now classified as hominds (Hominidae). As a result, another name needed to be applied to the human subfamily and the one chosen was 'hominin'. Therefore, any discoveries that are made where the researcher is confident that the only living representative of that species is a modern human, then the subfamily is referred to as hominin and not hominid.

How the terminology changes in both taxonomy classifications and frequency of changes is an indication of how little we understand the ladder of successive steps. No sooner does the paleoanthropologist think that he's found that elusive missing link between two species, when someone else is finding a third species that can easily displace the others on that ladder. Not too long ago, the taxonomic classifications looked like this:

Superfamily Hominoidea (hominoids)
    Family Hylobatidae (hylobatids)
        Genus Hylobates (gibbons)
    Family Pongidae (pongids)
        Genus Pongo (orangutan)
        Genus Gorilla
        Genus Pan   (chimpanzee and bonobo)
    Family Hominidae (hominids)
        Subfamily Australopithecinae (australopithecines)
            Genus Ardipithecus
            Genus Australopithecus
            Genus Kenyanthropus

> Genus Orrorin
> Genus Paranthropus
> Genus Sahelanthropus
> **Subfamily Homininae (hominines)**
> Genus Homo

Whereas today, the new classification is as follows:

Superfamily Hominoidea (hominoids)
  Family Hylobatidae (hylobatids)
      Genus Hylobates
      Genus Symphalangus
      Genus Hoolock
      Genus Nomascus
  Family Hominidae (hominids)
   Subfamily Ponginae
      Genus Pongo (pongines)
   Subfamily Gorillinae
      Genus Gorilla (gorillines)
   Subfamily Homininae (hominines)
    Tribe Panini
      Genus Pan (panins)
    Tribe Hominini (hominins)
     Subtribe Australopithecinae
      Genus Ardipithecus
      Genus Australopithecus
      Genus Kenyanthropus
      Genus Orrorin
      Genus Paranthropus
      Genus Sahelanthropus
     Subtribe Hominina (hominans)
      Genus Homo

This new Taxonomy tree is a very telling story of exactly what has been discussed in this section of the book. Two tribes, almost identical at one point in time, living similar lifestyles and sharing almost identical habitats, until the great African rift occurred and physically separated them so that those in the west remained in a forested, tropical ecosystem, and those in the east found themselves in a lesser treed environment but more of a sprawling grasslands. Their genetic makeup was practically identical, their diet did not change tremendously, but whereas the chimpanzee still had to compete with the gorilla for territory and food, that was no longer an issue with the Australopithecines. As can be seen from the table, the Panini tribe only has the one Genus to arise from it, even though I would argue that the chimpanzee and bonobo have enough differentiation to be considered two genus. But in any case, the fact is that the Panini Tribe never underwent rapid evolution in the five million years of separation from the Hominini Tribe. On the other hand, the Hominini underwent not only rapid but multiple evolutionary differentiation because of the inherent instability of the Australopithecines, which can only be explained by the genetic instability created with the telomeric fusion of chromosomes 1 and 3. That destabilization is still apparent with the rise of the hominans just over two million years ago as seen in Figure 37. As this figure clearly indicates, these multiple species within the genus Homo overlapped each other for hundreds of thousands of years, yet even though all were equally robust to eventually become modern man, only one branch of the several managed to do so.

The first archaic hominid was not discovered in East Africa, but at the Taungs Limeworks in 1924, in what is now part of South Africa. The young child's skull from Taung was attributed to a new species and genus, *Australopithecus africanus*. More discoveries followed at Sterkfontein and Makapansgat, and eventually included within the genus and species, *Australopithecus. Africanus*. Heavier jawed fossils with slightly larger post canine teeth and flatter faces were discovered at Kromdraai and Swartkrans, and more recently in caves at Drimolen, Gondolin and Coopers. These larger toothed findings were assigned to a second genus, Paranthropus, having two recognized species, *Paranthropus robustus* and *Paranthropus crassidens*. The Paranthropus remains are sometimes referred to as the 'robust' australopithecines because of their large faces and jaws. Two skeletons found recently at a site called Malapa have been assigned to a separate species, *Australopithecus sediba*. In 1959, Mary Leakey uncovered the OH 5 cranium at Olduvai Gorge. It was first designated as being Zinjanthropus, but later was renamed *Australopithecus boisei*. Subsequent discoveries at Olduvai and other sites, notably from Shungura, Koobi Fora and West Turkana, all located in the Omo region, and from Konso in Ethiopia, have confirmed that they came form a distinct species that was even more derived than *Paranthropus robustus*. Thereafter, Zinjanthropus and his relatives got redesignated as *Paranthropus boisei*, possessing a massive, wide, flat face and a large mandible. Remains from West Turkana has been assigned to a separate species called *Paranthropus aethiopicus*.

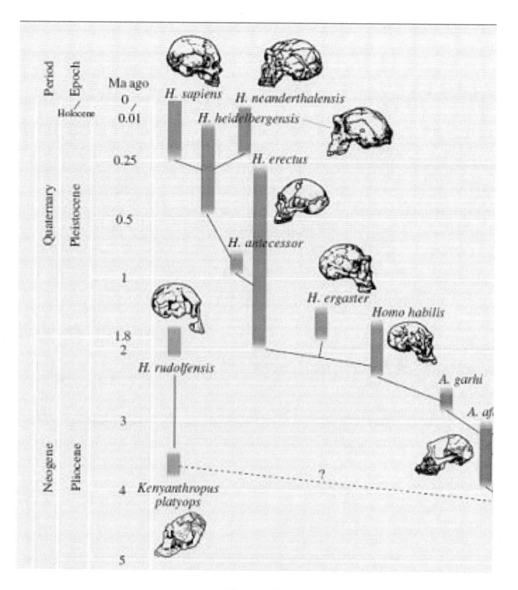

Figure 37

What needs to be taken into consideration is the number of species that have just been named under the genus Australopithecus and the genus Paranthropus because these are just the tip of the iceberg. Ardipithecus, Kenyanthropus, Selhelanthropus and Orrorin, haven't even been discussed. But furthermore, each genus then subdivides into four or five species, each possessing the potential to evolve into modern man. It is not the case of only one possible pathway, as modern anthropology presents in a nice tree that narrows down to one tree branch, but instead a bush, with multiple branches weaving in and out in multiple branches. In fact, to time travelers going back three million years ago, they would witness colonies of ape-men, numbering perhaps 30 to 40 in a clan, spotting the large canvas of grasslands in eastern Africa. And these clans would in turn be part of a larger tribe consisting of thousands of individuals. But as they approach the territory of the clans they encounter, they realize that the clan in one territory will look very different facially, in size and in build from a clan in another territory. With six genus and perhaps five species in each, the time travelers would encounter possibly thirty different looking species. In order to have become an established species would have taken thousands of individuals in the gene pool to create the definitive features that mark each species. The numbers of members of that would be involved in a distinct species are often overlooked because of the limited number of fossil finds, which leads us to think of a genus or species as being only the one or two fossil remains that are found. This mentally blocks our recognition that these one or two skeletons may actually represent ten or twenty thousand individuals that are the source from which they were derived.

Therein lies the problem in paleoanthropology. How does one explain the disappearance of thousands of individuals that belong to a particular species, even though it had the same capacity and capability to thrive no differently from the one species that eventually continued on to evolve into modern man? What could have possibly eliminated perhaps twenty-nine potential competitors from claiming that title? Or even more of a riddle, why is there only one species of man inhabiting this planet at this moment in time? If we look at the equidae, we still have the horses, with all their different subspecies, the zebra, the donkey, and the wild ass. Even something as rare as the Rhinocerotidae has the Ceratotherium, the Dicerorhinus, the Diceros and the Rhinoceros in existence. In the family Camelidae one still finds the Bactrian camel, the Dromedary, the llama and the alpaca. And the list goes on and on for practically every other family of mammal. Many of the genus from the same family competed for the same territory, the same food source, experienced the same climatic conditions, yet they are still here to this present day. We, on the other hand are all that remains from the subfamily homininae. If all those other mammals with their multiple species within the genus represent normal evolution, why are we the only species left in our genus?

In reference to Neanderthal, we can now surmise that Homo sapien interbred and absorbed that particular species into our gene pool but that can't account for the disappearance of every other hominin genus and species. The Bible appears to retain some ancient memory of the different hominin species co-existing at one time on this planet. We find that reference in Genesis Chapter 6.

1 And it came to pass, when men began to multiply on the face of the earth, and daughters were born unto them,

א וַיְהִי כִּי־הֵחֵל הָאָדָם, לָרֹב עַל־פְּנֵי הָאֲדָמָה; וּבָנוֹת, יֻלְּדוּ לָהֶם.

2 that the sons of God saw the daughters of men that they were fair; and they took them wives, whomsoever they chose.

ב וַיִּרְאוּ בְנֵי־הָאֱלֹהִים אֶת־בְּנוֹת הָאָדָם, כִּי טֹבֹת הֵנָּה; וַיִּקְחוּ לָהֶם נָשִׁים, מִכֹּל אֲשֶׁר בָּחָרוּ.

3 And the LORD said: 'My spirit shall not abide in man for ever, for that he also is flesh; therefore shall his days be a hundred and twenty years.'

ג וַיֹּאמֶר יְהוָה, לֹא־יָדוֹן רוּחִי בָאָדָם לְעֹלָם, בְּשַׁגַּם, הוּא בָשָׂר; וְהָיוּ יָמָיו, מֵאָה וְעֶשְׂרִים שָׁנָה.

4 The Nephilim were in the earth in those days, and also after that, when the sons of God came in unto the daughters of men, and they bore children to them; the same were the mighty men that were of old, the men of renown. {**P**}

ד הַנְּפִלִים הָיוּ בָאָרֶץ, בַּיָּמִים הָהֵם, וְגַם אַחֲרֵי־כֵן אֲשֶׁר יָבֹאוּ בְּנֵי הָאֱלֹהִים אֶל־בְּנוֹת הָאָדָם, וְיָלְדוּ לָהֶם: הֵמָּה הַגִּבֹּרִים אֲשֶׁר מֵעוֹלָם, אַנְשֵׁי הַשֵּׁם. {פ}

Table 13

The narrative attempts to explain a very difficult concept to a primitive society, being that there was a tremendous amount of trial and error in the evolution of man and for millions of years there were multiple species of ape-men inhabiting the earth, many of whom, though they looked very different, were still able to interbreed with the other species. To a species that stood perhaps less than five feet, when encountering another species well over seven feet tall as will be discussed later in this chapter, it would naturally appear to them as if they were in the presence of a superior race. Earlier in the book I had used this as a possible reference to how Neanderthal may have viewed Cro-Magnon or *Homo sapien* when they first encountered one another. Perhaps it was in reference to far more than just these two species. In the discussion of the cross-mating of different species, the hybrid is always different from either parent. In the case of man, it would appear that it produced an offspring referred to as the Nephilim, a term that is never explained in the Old Testament, other than saying they were mightier than a normal man in a time that had been long forgotten. But sentence 3 which seems out of place in the story, almost sounds as if God had made a conscious decision to eliminate these multiple species until there would only be one 'man' remaining. And that event too is told in the Old Testament in a manner that explains to us how he managed to eliminate these competitive species all wanting to become man as seen in Table 14. In the same chapter, just three sentences later God reveals his plan to reduce all the different species vying for the position of *Homo sapien,* by selecting one species to continue on.

ז וַיֹּאמֶר יְהוָה, אֶמְחֶה אֶת־הָאָדָם אֲשֶׁר־בָּרָאתִי מֵעַל פְּנֵי הָאֲדָמָה, מֵאָדָם עַד־בְּהֵמָה, עַד־רֶמֶשׂ וְעַד־עוֹף הַשָּׁמָיִם: כִּי נִחַמְתִּי, כִּי עֲשִׂיתִם.	**7** And the LORD said: 'I will blot out man whom I have created from the face of the earth; both man, and beast, and creeping thing, and fowl of the air; for it repenteth Me that I have made them.'
ח וְנֹחַ, מָצָא חֵן בְּעֵינֵי יְהוָה. {פ}	**8** But Noah found grace in the eyes of the LORD. {P}
ט אֵלֶּה, תּוֹלְדֹת נֹחַ--נֹחַ אִישׁ צַדִּיק תָּמִים הָיָה, בְּדֹרֹתָיו: אֶת־הָאֱלֹהִים, הִתְהַלֶּךְ־נֹחַ.	**9** These are the generations of Noah. Noah was in his generations a man righteous and whole-hearted; Noah walked with God

Table 14

Of course there is no wickedness in the beasts and other creatures of the Earth as mentioned in sentence 7 of Table 14 that God should accuse them of crimes for which they too must be punished. So what is He actually saying in this sentence? Firstly, God is not suggesting he is going to wipe out the entire human race, אֶמְחֶה אֶת־הָאָדָם, as these words indicate a process of partial removal as in trying to blot up a spilled liquid. It is a cleansing process applied generically to mankind as seen by the insertion of 'the' before mankind. The sentence should actually read, "I will blot out the man", as if to say, a particular part of man's presence rather than all of it by insertion of the definite article. It is used in the same manner that one would say, "Tomorrow we clean house," the lack of an article suggesting it will be every house in the group you are talking to, being so broad in scope, but as soon as you say "the house" then everyone knows it is only one particular house you are a referring to. The other noticeable word used is עַד , inserted prior to beast, creeping thing and fowl. Because of the use of the מ at the front of the word מֵאָדָם the implication is that עַד is translated as meaning 'up to'. So the sentence reads that the blotting procedure will be from man up to the beast, up to the creeping things and up to the fowl, implying a definite limitation. It is not suggesting that it was all inclusive, once again only a partial elimination and not total annihilation. In this context, we find a possible explanation of what may have happened to all the other species of homo, that had co-existed for hundreds of thousands of years. It is not a matter of whether it was a world-wide flood resulting from the melting of the glaciers following a particular ice age, or a major shift in tectonic plates that caused low lying areas to sink below sea-level for a period of time but by so doing, eliminating any coastal hominins. Whatever the case may have been, the Old Testament may be explaining what was a major event that resulted in the selection of only a few remaining hominin lines that were able to continue onwards towards Homo sapiens, explaining it in the only way that the people would understand.

The actual effect of such a world-wide catastrophe can be seen in Figure 38, below, where all of the intertwined branches of the bush suddenly appear to come to an abrupt end with only *Homo sapiens* remaining and spreading out across the surface of the planet. Of course the abrupt end is in evolutionary time, meaning that it may have taken a span of one hundred and fifty thousand years for almost all of the other competitive branches to finally become extinct. But as to how or why these other successful branches should or could become extinct is not provided by the paleoanthropologists that should be working hard on answering this riddle. The lack of any answers after almost six decades of trying, might astound you because the impression that has been provided to the public through National Geographic and similar journals is that they have the answer. But the truth is, they can't even agree on what should be the actual question, because the more fossils they find, the more confusing the historical record becomes and the more mysterious the final ascent of modern man truly is. Examining the records and histories of these actual finds is the best way to expose you, as the reader, to just how deep the answers are enshrouded in mystery, because this information is not released to the general public but remains concealed in the lecture rooms of universities and laboratories.

Olduvai Gorge still proved to be a very productive site for Louis and Mary Leakey, who in 1960 found the fossils of an early hominin that was clearly not *Paranthropus boisei*. They considered these bones to be more likely of the genus Homo and named it *Homo habilis* or the 'handy-man', considering him to be well acquainted with tool use. Their declaration was met with resistance, some looking at the bones and saying it was just another *Australopithecus africanus*, while others even looked at it and pronounced it to be merely an early *Homo erectus*.

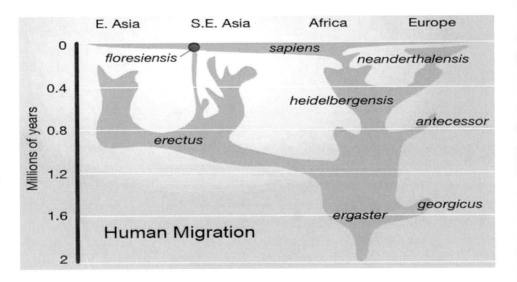

Figure 38

It wasn't until more bones from others looking like *Homo habilis* were discovered that it was recognized to truly represent its own species. With more and more discoveries, both at Olduvai Gorge and the Omo region, the number of remains being collected suggested that there were more than one species of early hominin being looked at. At a minimum there were at least two different species, perhaps more, but that raised concerns that too many variations would destroy the argument of a linear descent of man and look more like the genus was mutating totally out of control producing as many variations as perhaps we have breeds of dogs today. The name *Homo rudolfensis* was applied to a second and the goal was to try and fit all of these other fossil remains into at least one of these two species and ignore anything else that might suggest it being a different species. This was a conscious decision to conceal anything that contradicted their story line.

But as the paleoanthropologists wrestled with the concept of a variety of different Homo species that seemed highly plausible without turning their hunt for the single missing link into what would resemble more of a manhunt for multiple suspects on the loose after a prison break, other surprises were just waiting around the corner to spring into the spotlight. While discussing the dating of these African findings, the tests suggesting somewhere between 1.8 and 2 million years ago, the remains of a new form of hominin, *Homo ergaster* was also found in the Omo region of East Africa. This one could not be ignored and could not be fitted neatly into the two species resolution that had been adopted earlier. What distinguished this finding from all the other hominin that have been referred to earlier was the reduction in the relative and absolute size of the face, jaws and chewing teeth. Similar fossils had also been recovered from a site in Georgia called Dmanisi, which too was dated to about 1.8 million years ago. It was suggested that this new species could be a possible gap filler between *Homo habilis* and the African Homo erectus, which structurally would make sense except that its dating would make it as old as *Homo habilis* or *rudolfensis,* thus making it co-existent and not subsequent or a descendant.

Further complicating the issue were the findings from Indonesia, where there has never been any convincing evidence that any of the Australopithecines migrated outside of Africa but the findings of Homo erectus in Indonesia certainly would have required a predecessor moving in that direction. That was only one complication, the other being that the dating of the *Homo erectus* from Indonesia also suggested an age of approximately 1.8 million years ago. Furthermore, the digging sites of Orce and Sima del Elefante in Spain, were dated to 1.3 million years ago and those fossils looked to be something between *Homo habilis* and *Homo ergaster*, but once again the dates weren't reconciling with what were the perceived expected timeframes for human development in a linear progression. With very strong evidence now that *Homo erectus* existed in Asia for well over a million years, beginning about 1.8 million years ago and extending to only two hundred thousand years ago, that meant as a species, it overlapped everything from *Homo habilis* to *Homo sapien*, thereby definitely not fitting in well into any timeline for succession. The question was raised as to how was it possible that this primitive form of man not only co-existed with other more primitive forms of hominins, while at the same time also co-existed with far more advanced forms, while even spinning off its own offshoot, the *Homo floresiensis*, between one hundred thousand and sixty thousand years ago. None of these findings were fitting the expected chronology. None of it was making any sense.

The distinctive morphology of *Homo erectus* gave way to hominins with less remarkable features but still possessing a relatively wide mandibular body and cranium, as well as relatively thick long-bone shafts. The regional distinctiveness of the remains of the post *Homo erectus* fossils which have been discovered in Kabwe in Africa, or Petralona and Mauer in Europe, as well as Jinnuishan in China resulted in a lack of consensus among researchers regarding the most appropriate taxonomy classification for this material, opinions ranging from *Homo heidelbergensis,* to *Homo rhodesiensis*, as well as *Homo antecessor.* Meanwhile, others simply decided to ignore the variability and say that it was little more than typical variations that would be found in any species and therefore they are nothing more than later stage *Homo erectus*.

But as soon as you start attempting to change the rules to cover up the fact that you have become confused and unable to resolve the timeframe conundrum, then as a result you begin challenging other findings that you though were written in stone. Suddenly, *Homo neanderthalensis,* or Neanderthals, had many researchers questioning if perhaps this group of hominins was nothing more than an intraspecies variant of *Homo sapiens.* To do that meant ignoring the very distinctive morphology of this group, but it just went to prove that as long as scientists can make it fit their theory or narrative they will attempt anything. Neanderthal is found in sites spread across Europe, the Near East and western Asia, with remains dating from 300,00 years ago, or possibly even 450,000 years ago when including the Sima de Los Huesos fossils as Neanderthal, and this in itself destroys many of the proposed lineages of evolutionary development which suggests that Neanderthal must only appear on the timeline about 130,000 years ago. Of course, if Neanderthal could be eliminated from the fossil record as being nothing more than an anomaly, or an aberration of modern man, then it would no longer present this stumbling block in the timeline. The most vociferous for suggesting Neanderthal are just modern man with some unusual characteristics is Dr. Sergio Almécija who claims their heavy, sturdy long-bones and enlarged are merely the consequence of living in cold and rough terrain environments, while carrying large and heavy tools. As I said, they will attempt anything in order to try and preserve the narrative.

Fortunately, the dawn of DNA analysis has shown that Neanderthal were a separate species, and up to 8% of that Neanderthal genome can be found in some modern humans as a result of interbreeding. But whereas this would eliminate the issue of *Homo sapien* existing long before the timeline suggests, it doesn't explain how there could have been some early Neanderthals. All that Dr. Almécija has done is create a huge leap from even more primitive species of men to modern man without ever demonstrating how these major morphological changes could have possibly occurred.

Practically every effort to determine the ascent of the anatomically modern *Homo sapien*, results in massive confusion and little progress in determining when and how modern man burst on to the scene. The crux of this debate is how and why, we as anatomically-modern humans could possibly originate from a series of migrations out of Africa and not only displace our Neanderthal cousins but entirely replace those other populations of prehistoric men that had successfully populated many other regions of the world. The successive migrations out of Africa, of which there is no denial, only meant that they took their gene pools with them and unless they refused to interbreed with those other species they encountered, and found a means by which to actually eliminate in their entirety these other hominin species, then there is no satisfactory explanation as to how modern humans from Africa became the only species remaining and spread across the world.. The convergent hypothesis of evolution theory that is currently being proposed, that modern humans arose globally by a series of transformations by all of these different Homo species, thereby negated the need for significant interbreeding with these migrants from Africa in order to become *Homo sapien* borders on the absurd and ridiculous. To even think that by some natural means *Homo erectus, Homo rhodensiensis, Homo ergaster, Homo antecessor, Homo heidelbergensis* and *Homo neanderthalensis* all underwent a series of evolutionary transformations that were similar but not identical for no other purpose other than to look like modern man, even though they were all successful and well adapted to their environments, not only flies in the face of evolutionary theory, it doesn't even register as good science. The reality paints a very different picture and perhaps once again Table 15 is the solution where there was a deliberate destruction of the more primitive species, providing the space for *Homo sapien* to simply fill the gap and interbreeding with those few remaining members of those older species which no longer had the numbers to overwhelm the modern human genome.

But then the question becomes, how could nature even mount a natural disaster that only selectively eliminated those species that were no longer necessary for human development, while protecting the one species that is the pinnacle of that evolutionary process. The answer is it can't unless it was being intentionally controlled and wielded as a tool. In the same manner that a child discards all of its old toys because he or she has now been presented with a far more interesting and advanced new toy. We've all experienced that event in our own lives, where we've abandoned what once were our favorite toys to play with, simply because we received something better. It is not a statement to imply that God is a child but what he does share with mankind is the ability to recognize when something better has come along and all the experimental models along the way are no longer necessary. A world-wide flood that managed to cover Europe and Asia while sparing Africa due to melting glaciers from the last ice age is as good a theory as any.

For those that still have difficulty in viewing God as the ultimate scientist, I bring up one of those possible experiments as a topic of discussion over the next few paragraphs. Meganthropus is a name that has been applied to several large jaw and skull fragments that were found at the Sangiran site near Surakarta in Central Java, Indonesia. The original scientific name was *Meganthropus palaeojavanicus*, and though some argued that it had human characteristics, most viewed it as a prehistoric gorilla that had simply become extinct, without bothering to wonder how it was that the ancestor to gorillas could be found in Indonesia, yet there is no evidence of a migratory pattern either to or out of Africa for any gorilla related fossils. Similarly, there are no Meganthropus fossils found in Africa to even suggest gorillas had such a predecessor.

As of 2005, the taxonomy and phylogeny for the specimens were still uncertain, although by that time most paleoanthropologists consider them related to *Homo erectus* in some way. Furthermore, names such as *Homo palaeojavanicus* and *Australopithecus palaeojavanicus* have been used sometimes, creating even more classification uncertainty and confusion in the journals in which they are mentioned. But what should be the main focus and particular interest to these researchers is that whatever the classification, these creatures were giants, although there is still reluctance to admit that even though the findings suggest they are.

A large jaw fragment was first found in 1941 by von Koenigswald. Koenigswald was captured by the Japanese in World War II, but he managed to send a cast of the jaw to Franz Weidenreich. Weidenreich who described and named the specimen in 1945. Most of all he was struck by its size, as it was the largest hominid jaw ever uncovered. The jaw was from a creature having the same measurements as a gorilla, but had a different form, suggesting its hominin nature. Whereas in anthropoids. like the gorilla, the mandible has its greatest height at the symphysis, or the fusion point of the two halves of the jaw, in the case of this finding, the greatest height is seen at about the position of the first molar. Weidenreich considered it at first to be acromegalic gigantism, which the genetic form of gigantism in humans, but ruled that possibility out because it did not have typical features such as an exaggerated chin and small teeth of those with that genetic disease. Weidenreich estimated that it must have come from a hominid that was at least two thirds the size of Gigantopithecus, which was twice as large as a gorilla. That made Meganthropus's height somewhere around 2.4 meters or roughly 8 feet tall and as much as 275 kilograms or 600 lbs. in weight.

In his book Apes, Giants, and Man, Weidenreich states the following, "Therefore, it may not be too far from the truth if we suggest the Java giant [Meganthropus] was much bigger than any living gorilla and that the Chinese giant

[Gigantopithecus] was correspondingly bigger than the Java giant – that is, one-and-a-half times as large as the Java giant, and twice as large as a male gorilla.

As a one-off event, science felt it could ignore Meganthropus but in 1953 another jaw fragment was uncovered in Sangiran Indonesia by Marks, who confirmed it was about the same size and shape as the original finding. In 1979 another jaw fragment was discovered, having some characteristics in common with previous mandible finds. In 1993 another discovery and this one was dated to be between 1.4 million and 9 hundred thousand years ago. The ramus portion was badly damaged, but the mandible fragment appeared intact. This finding was only slightly smaller than the first Meganthropus discovery and very similar in shape. Sartono, Tyler, and Krantz agreed that their Meganthropus fossil was very likely to be the same species as the first finding. Another fossil was uncovered in Sangiran, and Tyler described this specimen as being a nearly complete cranium but it had been crushed. It was within the size limit of Meganthropus and outside the limits of *Homo erectus*. The specimen was unusual as it had a double temporal ridge or sagittal crest, which almost meets at the top of the skull, and the nuchal ridge was very thick. Again, whatever the species would turn out to be, it was a giant compared to men.

Tyer analyzed another skull fragment that has been found by Sartono in Sangiran back in 1982. Once again it was larger than anything in the normal range of *Homo erectus,* the cranium being deeper, wider and lower vaulted than anything seen before. The cranial capacity was a respectable 800 to1000 cc. Like his prior description it also had this unique double sagittal crest. Presenting his finding in 1993, most scientists accepted his reconstruction. No other *Homo erectus* specimen has the double sagittal ridge but at the same time they were unwilling to admit that it represented a giant hominin, insisting that they should take a conservative standpoint as published in 2005, that, "All earlier Homo populations that are sufficiently derived from African early Homo belong to Homo erectus, the Grenzbank/Sangiran group is allocated to a primitive group of this species." In other words, they accepted that it did not resemble any other *Homo erectus,* and it might even be a giant, but because it fell outside of their constructed lineage for mankind, then it had to be forced into the species grouping whether it belonged there or not. A race of giant hominins was not acceptable and therefore had to brushed aside even though findings of giant tools in Australia by researcher Rex Gilroy, which possibly place Meganthropus in Australia as well would suggest otherwise.

Meganthropus is an important story, not only because it represented a completely different line of hominins, that had no reason to exist as they certainly didn't appear to have any predecessors that would suggest a giant species of early man would come into existence but because of the lengths science will go to in order to make something which obviously existed, disappear, because it does not fit comfortably into their narrative. And yet, it does possibly fit into the biblical narrative which talks of a race of giants in Moab before the Anakim but now long gone according to Deuteronomy Chapter 14 as can be seen below in Table 15.

הָאֵמִים לְפָנִים, יָשְׁבוּ בָהּ--עַם גָּדוֹל וְרַב וָרָם, כָּעֲנָקִים. ׀	**10** The Emim dwelt therein aforetime, a people great, and many, and tall, as the Anakim;
רְפָאִים יֵחָשְׁבוּ אַף-הֵם, כָּעֲנָקִים ; וְהַמֹּאָבִים, יִקְרְאוּ לָהֶם אֵמִים. יא	**11** these also are accounted Rephaim, as the Anakim; but the Moabites call them Emim.

Table 15

We don't know much about the Emim, who were also called the Rephaim. Considering the Anakim were the typical people with the genetic condition of acromegaly, as noted with individuals in the family of Goliath, which elongated their bones so that they stood about 2.4 meters tall, the indication with the Emim is that they weren't merely a genetically afflicted family but an entire race of people. The bible gives us few clues to who they were or why they'd also be called רְפָאִים the Rephaim, which implies they were ghosts or wraiths. Other than indicating they were deceased and long extinct as a people there are no other clues But perhaps these two small sentences tell us that the ancients knew more about these Meganthropus than do our modern scientists. Perhaps they all weren't confined to Indonesia and were found in the Middle East as well. Far more primitive than the modern men they encountered, they easily could have been just one more species rendered extinct as a result of the savagery of man.

THE HUMAN FAMILY

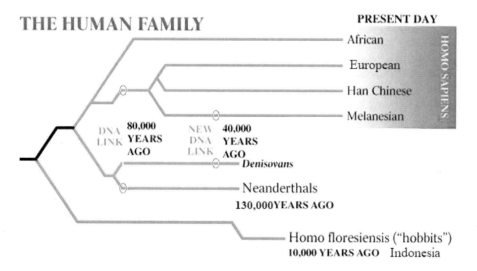

Figure 39

Before closing this chapter on the hominins, Figure 39 is a reminder that there were other modern species of men for which there was no apparent reason why they should have completely disappeared. Totally adapted to the varied environments in which they lived, their disappearance can only be attributed to a sudden mass extinction event of unknown origin. Which once again points us back to a most fortunate cause and effect relationship that needs explanation. The effect we know, the present day *Homo sapiens* dominate the Earth. The fact that we have Africans, Europeans and Asians as an aftermath effect is described succinctly in Chapter 9 of Genesis, with Noah's three sons populating the world, Ham in Africa, Japheth in Asia, and Shem in the Middle East and Europe. Was the story of Noah ever intended to be interpreted literally? As a Karaite, I doubt it. In Karaism we are taught that everything in the Old Testament is true but truth can have different meanings to different people and my truth is no less correct than someone else. I believe the story was intended to explain events that occurred long in the past, where ancient memories told them there had been more than one species of mankind. The same way they understood there were other creatures like the leviathans and the behemoths that once lived on this planet but existed no more. Even the story of Noah would have been seen as having fail-safes already in place that God could not extinguish every living creature on Earth, except for those in the ark. Anything that lived in the seas would have survived, which meant there always would have been mammals, fish, crustaceans, arthropods and mollusks, as well as some birds that can swim and float for extended periods of time. Mountains would have always stood higher than the levels of the waters could reach, which meant any animal that could climb or birds that could fly high would escape. A God that creates, only to admit that He regrets what was done, would be an admission of not being all powerful, all knowing and omnipotent and that hardly describes the God of Israel that Moses delivered to the people. So the truth is, that the story is just that, a story, which was intentionally designed to make you ask the question as to why, because we already knew the effect, which was an orderly aftermath with less variation of species and more organized pathways and patterns of development. Which meant the why or the cause was not God's recognition of everything having become evil, which one can hardly judge a creature other than man as being evil, but instead a recognition that laboratory Earth had spun out of control and was producing multiple lines of evolution for each species which would have caused eventual extinction due to lack of fertility of offspring from the mating of related but different species. Whatever the corrective measure may have been, a flood as in the story, or a sudden snap ice age, or a fiery ring of volcanoes all erupting simultaneously producing a toxic atmosphere, the fact is that it worked and the more science stumbles over itself trying to explain the disappearance, the more visible God's hand in this matter becomes through another **GodSpark.**

Section Five: The Science of God

Chapter 19: A New God

Science would like you to believe that they have replaced God. If ever he was alive, then he must certainly be dead now, because there is no place for Him in a scientific world. The scientists of today will point to the existence of dinosaurs, proclaiming that there is no accommodation for their existence anywhere in the Bible. They will quote Copernicus, Darwin and Nietzsche as proof that He probably never existed. The day science discovered that the Earth was not the center of the universe, they thought they had their proof that since our planet was the only focus of attention for God, that it must therefore prove that the omnipotent all-knowing and all-seeing being could not be real as we were nothing more than a single grain of sand on the beach of creation. For God to be this all powerful being, he could not be earthbound, ignoring the rest of creation. Of course, the statements of these scientists and philosopher were made long before the days we coined the phrase, multitasking, recognizing that all of us are capable of doing more than one thing at a time. Therefore, if we can multitask, then so can God. In our attempt to anthropomorphize God, we have placed His essence into a body with one set of eyes just like us, as if He was human. It is our failure as humans, or our ego, depending on how you wish to look at it, that assumes God is limited by human frailties. Of what need does God have for a body? Why just two eyes? Why not the ability to see everywhere throughout the universe simultaneously. Is that not what traffic cameras do for a city; provide visualization of thousands of places around a city simultaneously? The need for a single traffic cop standing on a corner, watching the traffic within his limited view are long gone. We learned to do away with human limitations, yet scientists would rather believe that God still has these limitations that we overcame with just a bit of technology.

But it is not just scientists that have attempted to dispute God's existence by wrapping Him solidly in a coat of human limitations. The religious structures are no less guilty of having done the same thing. In their efforts to humanize God, the religions of the world have painted Him with the same frailties that affect all humans. They have endowed God with a psyche and a set of emotions that render Him subject to all the strengths and weaknesses displayed by humans. He loves, hates, is jealous and vengeful and if you adhere to the Christian set of beliefs, He also engages in sexual reproduction. By doing so, religious bodies have muddied the waters so much that they practically handed the argument against God to the scientists. When challenged on some of these issues as to why God must display human characteristics, the clergy are trapped by their own assertion that they must

269

have faith, recognizing they have absolutely no factual based evidence to support any part of this claim. If anything, they required faith in accepting a God that is not and could not be measured by human standards. A God that does not uniformly fit onto any scale of measurement that we have in our possession. A God that does not conform to any psychological profile that medical science has available. As He told Moses on the mountain, "I am that which I am." He exists, but nothing in our world now or in the future will ever be able to accurately describe His being.

It is obvious to someone like myself that the conflict between science and religion arises only when someone doesn't know how to apply what is written in the Bible or in scientific journals to the world that surrounds us. In other words, those on the religious side of the question fail to view God as the ultimate scientist, and those lodged firmly in the science world cannot see the big picture laid out before them, their minds focused on a singularity to the exclusion of everything related in the periphery. For example, the Bible may say that with a strong exhalation through His nostrils, God made the winds of the storm blow that sank Jonah's ship. Once again the misguided attempt to anthropomorphize God, even though admittedly He is invisible, undefined, and unknown other to a very few select individuals to whom He revealed himself and even they admitted that they could not describe the Almighty. But science would take that same story and talk endlessly of how there was a low pressure zone created by the warm air moving over cold water and this in turn caused the winds from high pressure zones to flow towards the low pressure area, creating the storm, typically seasonal for that time of year. How wonderful that each side can have two diverse opinions on what capsized the boat without tackling the real question of why there are winds at all from a real-world or biological perspective. That same wind blows the seeds released by the grass, the flowers and the trees across large stretches of land, so that vegetative life does not remain confined to one particular area. It ensures that the rains are spread across the globe and therefore the life-giving waters not only cause those seeds to germinate but thrive as needed. Those same rains guarantee that animal life has a source of water even in some of the most uninhabitable and inhospitable regions of our planet. Essentially the wind is a transport mechanism that helps to spread and maintain life across the face of the Earth. It is the result of certain geophysical elements and rather than assume that the effects it may have on life are merely accidental, we should concede that from a religious perspective they were certainly intentional, as both sides should recognize that the ultimate scientist carried out his design and structure of a biosphere in which the winds were merely an essential component of His creation.

It is time for scientists to render unto God that which is God's and for religious leaders to be more knowledgeable regarding science and not rely on Googled information to render their opinions, and in so doing making it remarkably easy for the other side to dismiss any statements made. Religious experts must adopt scientific principles if they are going to learn to support a creationist theory. Just as scientists must develop a hypothesis for every theory and then support that hypothesis through the gathering of facts from research and experimentation, it is necessary for religious experts to take the same rigorous approach. As science will argue that something cannot form from nothing and similarly once there is something it will always devolve as it seeks out its lowest level of energy usage as laid out in the Law of Entropy, then the Big Bang is in direct conflict with what are regarded as sacred laws of science. As discussed in the chapter 'In The Beginning' the Big Bang required a tremendous amount of energy in order to occur. If science insists that it was the result of an inexplicable blip in the void, then either the void was not a void at all, and the Big Bang was merely a transformation of something that already existed into something new, which then contained our universe, or else it can only be called a supernatural event in which a tremendous amount of energy that did not pre-exist suddenly came into existence, defying the Thermodynamic Laws. Not only did it require a burst of energy, but a complete reversal of devolution where matter began to reorganize itself into more complex states, which in itself required the influx of energy that also had not existed before.

Furthermore, the organization of this matter was of an increasing magnitude of complexity which implies an intelligent design. To place this into context, let us think of the Big Bang in terms of a potter. The potter begins with nothing on his potters wheel until he mixes the clay with water. These two ingredients would have to come from out of nowhere and be brought together in order to make the material from which the potter would work. Perhaps the water and clay would find a way of combining in the right proportions on their own without the help of the potter but that is unlikely. Once mixed, there is a lump of unshaped, non-homogeneous material sitting on the wheel. It requires the hands of the potter and the energy he exerts to ensure it is mixed thoroughly and is uniform in consistency. But even so, it is nothing more than a well-mixed lump of material devoid of shape or purpose. The potter must start spinning the wheel, exerting a large amount of energy in order to begin shaping the lump into a useful object. But what will it be? A plate, a cup, a vase, perhaps even a pitcher, only the potter knows what the final objective might be and depending on the requirement, his hands will start shaping accordingly. So just like the item being spun from the clay, the universe required intelligent design in order to achieve the final goal and its intended purpose which was to see the development of life in a universe that was initially devoid of anything living. This is the conundrum that science faces when it comes to discussing the beginning of life in the universe. As Einstein said, "God does not play dice." Life in the universe could not have been random or accidental. It had to be intentional and not all the scientists in the world can prove otherwise because the entire episode of the Big Bang defies every law of physics that we know to exist. Something did come from nothing or else we have to admit something preexisted and drew upon itself to create the universal Big Bang. Either way, even establishing itself from the Void would require a sentience that had the desire to create.

The release of energy to create the Big Bang would have been of an immeasurable magnitude but science would like you to believe it came into existence spontaneously, even though long ago it was proven that spontaneous generation on any scale does not occur. Therefore the energy had to be contained within a pocket of this Void that for some reason decided to transmute itself into the Big Bang catalyst. And lastly, science cannot explain how intelligent design resulted from chaos, if chaos is an excepted end point of physical laws. There had to be a potter's hand somewhere in the creation of our universe, otherwise increasingly complex steps, requiring more and more energy will not take place on its own accord. To do so would defy our Law of Entropy.

Long ago, Aristotle made the statement that nothing comes from nothing. His way of dealing with our universe was to assume it was eternal, having neither beginning nor end. As long as science adhered to Aristotle's statement, they were able to fend off the teachings of religion that there, was a creation point. But even science eventually admitted there must always be a beginning, in the same way there would always be an ending to everything that exists in order to adhere to the physical laws of the universe. The day they admitted that the universe had a beginning was the day that they harmonized with religion, though neither side recognized that fact. Religion was two busy still trying to prove that universe began in the autumn of 4004 BCE based on the 17th Century calculations of Archbishop James Ussher. As long as religion insists that everything in the Old Testament must be taken literally, it will never understand God's true intention to provide keys to unlocking the mysteries of the universe but concealed them in stories that could be understood by the primitive minds of the people that first received His words. After all, how would you describe nuclear physics to an intelligence that just emerged from a cave and had just invented the wheel? Exactly in the manner we find at the beginning of the Book of Genesis. All things evolve in our universe, even our understanding of the

Bible, yet this evolution is neither in the manner that science believes, nor in the manner that religious leaders refute. It is necessity based, but the real question is who's necessity: That of the creature or the Creator? Perhaps it is a little bit of both.

Thus far, this book has expressed God in Universal terms, as a cosmic being that can directly affect the universe and event events on our planet at a major macro level. He adheres to the physical laws of the universe, because after all, He created these laws. This in itself tells us that God and physical universe are practically one and the same, as that part of Himself, the רוּחַ אֱלֹהִים or the Spirit of God as expressed in Genesis Chapter 1 in the opening sentences, is admixed with the matter and energy of everything around us. God is the living essence in everything and everyone as a result of the expenditure of His own creative forces, but for the many faithful, this is not the God that they want to believe in. And for that reason, concerning this view, this will probably be the hardest chapter to write because it will not satisfy what many of those people want to hear. They want a personal God, one who is focused on their lives and their issues, someone or some being that they can forge a relationship with. But at no point was it ever claimed that God works at a micro-level where He takes responsibility at an individual level for everyone on this planet. If we look at the entire scope of Biblical history, the number of humans that actually had a two-way conversation with God, if we include some of the prophets such as Nathan, that never had a book to record their deeds, would be about forty individuals. According to the Hebrew calendar, 5781 years of Biblical history, billions of people and the number that shared in such communication as a percentage is 2.7×10^{-7} , or in other words, practically no one. Of course there were those individuals with the help of God that did change the world, such as an Abraham, a Moses, a Joseph, a Jesus or a Mohammed, but that hardly would suggest that God should be expected to involve Himself with every person existing in this world. To know God was an expression of enlightenment by adhering to a code of morality and decency. It was never a suggestion that He would be your BIFF (Best Invisible Friend Forever). Sadly, that is what people have come to expect, which means they actually don't know God at all.

But does that mean that God doesn't play an active role in our lives? Certainly not! God is involved as you have read in the preceding chapters in practically every event that has brought us to this very point of time in which we live. Not as a puppeteer, pulling every string as some people would hope, but as an overseer, a constructionist, providing us with several paths to choose from, but ultimately we are in control of our lives even if it is common for people to select the wrong path It's not about God saving us from the decisions we have made, but about us having the courage to go right back to that fork in the road and select an alternative path, no matter how exhausted, or crushed, or discouraged we may be. It's not easy, and that is exactly what the story of Job is all about.

The inclusion of Job has always been a mystery to some, especially to religious leaders who have difficulty with the concept that God could inflict injury and suffering on a person for no other purpose than it was a game. This is not the God they want to know. They cannot drill down past the superficial layers of the story to see what it was really about. Simon the Just could and that was why he insisted that it become one of the canonized books of the Old Testament. The Book of Job is probably one of the deepest, most soul-searching, heart-wrenching and God revealing stories in the Bible, yet most people can't even be bothered to read it. Those that try to explain it as a morality play in which the lesson to be learned is no matter how bad things get, if you never lose faith in the Almighty, then you will eventually be rewarded are wrong! It's a revelation about the nature of God versus the nature of men. It is about how man was created in God's image but that image is not physical, it is not about the emotional aspects, it is about one thing only, and that is never giving up. It is about being knocked down, only to rise again, and doing it all over again and again but always getting back up. In the first Chapter God gives permission to Satan to take everything away from Job, his riches, his livestock, his crops and all of his children. And when he would not renounce God, in the second chapter Satan afflicts Job with sores all over his body, so that people will avoid and despise him. But still he does not renounce the Almighty and the answer of why he does not is found in his response in Chapter 9 to his friends, who are all suggesting that he should pray and plead for forgiveness for surely he had done something wrong to offend the Almighty. Job knew he had done nothing that would be considered wrong or evil, but he also understood that what he did or didn't do was irrelevant to God. He responds to his friends by explaining the true nature of God. which they cannot appreciate or understand.

ה הַמַּעְתִּיק הָרִים, וְלֹא יָדָעוּ־ אֲשֶׁר הֲפָכָם בְּאַפּוֹ.	**5** Who removeth the mountains, and they know it not, when He overturneth them in His anger.
ו הַמַּרְגִּיז אֶרֶץ, מִמְּקוֹמָהּ; וְעַמּוּדֶיהָ, יִתְפַּלָּצוּן.	**6** Who shaketh the earth out of her place, and the pillars thereof tremble.
ז הָאֹמֵר לַחֶרֶס, וְלֹא יִזְרָח; וּבְעַד כּוֹכָבִים יַחְתֹּם.	**7** Who commandeth the sun, and it riseth not; and sealeth up the stars.
ח נֹטֶה שָׁמַיִם לְבַדּוֹ; וְדוֹרֵךְ, עַל־בָּמֳתֵי יָם.	**8** Who alone stretcheth out the heavens, and treadeth upon the waves of the sea.
ט עֹשֶׂה־עָשׁ, כְּסִיל וְכִימָה; וְחַדְרֵי תֵמָן.	**9** Who maketh the Bear, Orion, and the Pleiades, and the chambers of the south.

10 Who doeth great things past finding out; yea, marvelous things without number.	עֹשֶׂה גְדֹלוֹת, עַד־אֵין ● חֵקֶר; וְנִפְלָאוֹת, עַד־אֵין מִסְפָּר.
11 Lo, He goeth by me, and I see Him not. He passeth on also, but I perceive Him not.	יא הֵן יַעֲבֹר עָלַי, וְלֹא אֶרְאֶה; וְיַחֲלֹף, וְלֹא־אָבִין לוֹ.

Table 16

Thus, Job explains is the God of the Hebrews. An entity that is an elephant compared to man who is no more than an ant. What knowledge does the elephant have of how many ants have been crushed beneath its feet. None, for the elephant is on a scale beyond measure to the ant, and like God, it passes by the ants never seeing them, and the ant sees nothing of the elephant until it finds itself beneath a descending foot. Job knew that his suffering was not directly by the hands of God and what ever had happened in his life would still be beyond the notice of God's attention. After all, God left it up to Satan's own devices without interfering.

32 For He is not a man, as I am, that I should answer Him, that we should come together in judgment.	כִּי־לֹא־אִישׁ כָּמוֹנִי אֶעֱנֶנּוּ; נָבוֹא יַחְדָּו, בַּמִּשְׁפָּט.
33 There is no arbiter betwixt us, that might lay his hand upon us both.	לג לֹא יֵשׁ־בֵּינֵינוּ מוֹכִיחַ־ יָשֵׁת יָדוֹ עַל־שְׁנֵינוּ.

Table 17

At this juncture, Job is revealing to his friends the nature of God as they try to juxtapose their concepts of a God with human features, that can be appealed to and negotiated with. Job quickly shuts down the misconceptions of their God, saying that He is nothing like us. There is nothing human or man-like about God. That it is foolish even to think of God in human terms. As he says, there is no arbiter or negotiator between man and the Creator of the universe. Once again it would be like the ant trying to negotiate with the elephant.

22 Shall any teach God knowledge? seeing it is He that judgeth those that are high.	כב הַלְאֵל יְלַמֶּד־דָּעַת; וְהוּא, רָמִים יִשְׁפּוֹט.

בְּעֶצֶם, יְמוֹת--זֶה **כג** שַׁלְאֲנַן וְשָׁלֵיו, כֻּלּוֹ; תַּמּוֹ.	**23** One dieth in his full strength, being wholly at ease and quiet;
וּמֹחַ; מָלְאוּ חָלָב, עֲטִינָיו **כד** עַצְמוֹתָיו יְשֻׁקֶּה.	**24** His pails are full of milk, and the marrow of his bones is moistened.
בְּנֶפֶשׁ, יְמוֹת--וְזֶה **כה** בַּטּוֹבָה, אָכַל-וְלֹא; מָרָה.	**25** And another dieth in bitterness of soul, and hath never tasted of good.
עָפָר -עַל, יַחַד **כו** תְּכַסֶּה עֲלֵיהֶם, וְרִמָּה; יִשְׁכָּבוּ.	**26** They lie down alike in the dust, and the worm covereth them.

Table 18

In Chapter 21 Job contemplates what is the reason why one man should do good all his life while another does evil, since in the end their fates are the same. He does not dispute the fact that there are evil and wicked people that outwardly appear to be prosperous and have enjoyed all the benefits that life can offer. Some would say that this would suggest God is an unfair judge, but Job asks how can anyone actually know what is fair and what is not fair if we do not even know the end game. Although he concedes to his friends that he would argue his case that he has done no wrong before God, if he was given the opportunity to do so, over the next few chapters he explains why man would never be afforded such an opportunity, his friends finally agreeing that man is nothing more than a maggot in God's eyes. But despite all the reasons why mankind should not even care about how they live their lives, since God is nothing more than a bystander, in Chapter 27 Job tells everyone, God's aloofness makes no difference to him, he would still live a just and upright life, not because he wants God's approval and blessing but because it is the right thing to do. That is the meaning of being created in God's image. For us to do the right thing whenever we are called upon. With his inner insight he pronounces the following in Chapter 28:

הֵן יִרְאַת --לָאָדָם, וַיֹּאמֶר **כח** וְסוּר; הִיא חָכְמָה, אֲדֹנָי מֵרָע בִּינָה.	**28** And unto man He said: 'Behold, the fear of the Lord, that is wisdom; and to depart from evil is understanding.'

Table 19

Job now reveals to his friends what is meant to be made in God's image. It is not about the worship of God but the practice of living in God's ways in order to obtain wisdom, while the avoidance of evil is designed to endow a man with compassion and understanding. It is this revelation to them that it would be wrong for man to believe in God simply because he believes by doing so that there will be a reward. In essence, it is not about the belief in God but the following of His words that matters with the goal of becoming a better man. You practice doing good things all your life for no other reason than the desire to do so. At the same time Job recognizes that we place little value on a good man, practically all that honored him did so because he had wealth and fame but as soon as he lost it, they cursed him and provided no aid. Finally Elihu, a young man full of youth and full of pride, the son of Barachel the Buzite challenges all that Job had said thus far in the closing chapters as is seen in this statement from Chapter 34:

לה אִיּוֹב, לֹא־בְדַעַת יְדַבֵּר ; וּדְבָרָיו, לֹא בְהַשְׂכֵּיל.	**35** 'Job speaketh without knowledge, and his words are without discernment.'
לו אָבִי־־יִבָּחֵן אִיּוֹב עַד־נֶצַח : עַל־תְּשֻׁבֹת, בְּאַנְשֵׁי־אָוֶן.	**36** Would that Job were tried unto the end, because of his answering like wicked men.
לז כִּי יֹסִיף עַל־חַטָּאתוֹ פֶשַׁע, בֵּינֵינוּ יִשְׂפּוֹק ; וְיֶרֶב אֲמָרָיו לָאֵל.	**37** For he addeth rebellion unto his sin, he clappeth his hands among us, and multiplieth his words against God.

Table 20

According to Elihu it must be Job's fault and he must be a wicked man. His refusal to admit his guilt and lead his friends astray is even further evidence of that wickedness. He accuses Job of being ignorant of the ways of God and that he speaks with words that are designed to make others sin. The substance of Elihu's traditional argument that God rewards the good and punishes the evil and anyone that doubts that must be a sinner is unfortunately the standard portrait painted by so many of our religious leaders today. Elihu accuses Job of being a vain man that cannot even appreciate all the good that God has done for mankind. He points to himself, exclaiming to all to look how good fortune has rewarded him because he has devoted himself to God and followed all the precepts and praised the Lord for all he had

been given, at which point in Chapter 38 God finally intercedes and decides he can listen to this no more:

א וַיַּעַן־יְהוָה אֶת־אִיּוֹב, מנהסערה (מִן הַסְּעָרָה)\; וַיֹּאמַר.	**1** Then the LORD answered Job out of the whirlwind, and said:
ב מִי זֶה, מַחְשִׁיךְ עֵצָה בְמִלִּין־ בְּלִי־דָעַת.	**2** Who is this that darkeneth counsel by words without knowledge?

Table 21

Most readers of this portion of the book don't actually recognize that God had just condemned what is the common thinking of practically every religious minded person today. All the millions upon millions of adherents to religion that think if they follow God's words, then they will be rewarded. That their adherence to living according to the commandments is due to expectation of reward rather than to the joy of self-fulfillment. God admonishes Job's three friends for insisting that he must have done something wrong in order to warrant such punishments and repeats much of what Job had already described, that His concerns are on a universal scale and rarely will the elephant have time to see the ant beneath its feet. As for Elihu, he is accused of being a fool, lacking the wisdom of age to understand that devotion to God is less important than devotion to truth, to understanding, to wisdom and to compassion. In other words, devotion to your fellow man.

Simon the Just knew exactly why he was canonizing the Book of Job, though others may have questioned his wisdom. Without a doubt he understood that the book had painted a particular picture of a God, as a being that was rather indifferent to his 'Chosen People' on an individual basis. Certainly there were times that a few of them actually communicated with God, like Job, and God extended his mercy and his benevolence upon them, though a price might have had to been paid, but those people had some special gift that most others did not possess. God had an awareness of them and in turn they could communicate with God on a level the rest of mankind will never partake. As previously mentioned, totaling all those in the Bible with this special gift may only amount to forty or so people. Considering that once a year, during Yom Kippur, Simon the Just would enter the Holy of Holies to plead on behalf of the nation for God's forgiveness, he knew exactly how rare any intercession by God into the people's lives was, limited to a single day, where it was said that if the High Priest exited the Holy of Holies alive at the end of the day then God had heard and approved of the request. But should the High Priest perish within the Holy of Holies, then God surely did not approve. It was a heavy price to pay, and I can assure you that Simon probably prayed that he did not directly encounter God on that day.

So how did we reach this point where religion has sold itself through promises of heavenly rewards and God's salvation for every little ill that befalls us? Clearly it was not within any of the original promises made by God. In fact there is no mention of a reward or even an afterlife in the Old Testament after death. God demanded observance, He expected faithfulness, and required righteousness on everyone's part, but other than the grand promises to Abraham to have his seed multiply across the globe, and the promise to Moses to take his people to a land of milk and honey, it is hard to point towards any other promises that guaranteed an easy life, a long life, a healthy life, or similar. These are the personal issues that matter to us but that does not necessarily mean they are on the priority list of activities for God. But Job had the correct answer in that God gave us wisdom and understanding. The two most precious gifts that if mankind could ever use properly would ensure that all mankind could live long, prosperous and happy lives. There is enough wealth and food in this world to ensure that every person on this planet does not have to suffer for lack of either resource. Unfortunately, we are unable to utilize those gifts properly because we are obsessed by other matters designed to benefit the few rather than the many.

I will provide the reader with a simple math equation to show you how we are not fulfilling God's intentions for us. Imagine if the 25 Trillion dollar annual expenditure of the United States, as it is expected to be in 2021, was divided among the adult population of its citizens, which is 255 million over the age of 18. Or the 80,508 individuals that had a net personal worth of more than 50 million dollars in 2019 in the US decided to give just 10% of their wealth one time to others as a tithe, that would be another 400 billion dollars. Or if the 10.23 million households that were millionaires in the United States in 2019 were willing to share their prosperity with those less fortunate of again only a minimum tithe of 100,000 dollars. That would be another trillion dollars available for the good of their fellow man. Of course there will be the usual arguments that the government needs to pay for normal state and civic operations and health management, etc. etc. Every excuse under the sun why it can't or shouldn't be done. But just imagine if for one year they did away with all those arguments and excuses, equally distributing those sums to the less fortunate adult population, but with the agreement that everyone had to continue to work, no exceptions in order to receive the payment and it was a one-time only offer. That way the economy still continues to function, the government still collects its taxes for the following year and every business gets a holiday of paying wages for one year because people are receiving this lump sum. Suddenly, every adult in America that year would have well over a hundred thousand dollars in their pocket. Of course there will be those that just fritter it away and have nothing as an end result because that is human nature. We can't avoid those people but at least we can try at the same time to show everyone how to invest that money, live within their means, and secure their future. Doing so means that everyone will come to the same realization that Job did. God did give us the greatest gifts possible, being wisdom and understanding; the knowledge that if we work collectively for the benefit of all, then we can all have better lives and better opportunities. Now I agree, that this is a naive perspective on my part, for me to ever think that people will act and behave in this manner, because sharing the wealth is not ingrained within our human psyche or genome. I raise it only to point out what is within our power, though it is unlikely to ever happen. On the other hand, it is naive of people to think God is only here to help them if they are unwilling to help themselves and others. So as Job said, how you choose to live you life is up to you, but no matter what may have befallen him, he chose to live his life as God intended him to.

There definitely is a God of the Universe, but any attempt to chain Him to this planet to be everyone's personal genie that grants your every wish is a failure to understand and appreciate exactly whom God is. We are all a part of this creation and as such that makes us all part of God, as I hope the reader has been able to appreciate from everything that has been written thus far. What is most amazing is that at certain time-points in our history, He has communicated with a few individuals. And I do believe that connection was possible because we are part of him as indicated which provided something to those people that made them special and unique. But when you read their stories carefully, you will see that even those individuals had to deal with hardship and suffering even though they had this direct line of communication. Read their biographies contained within the Old Testament and you find that all of them made sacrifices, some actually paying a heavy price that none of us would have dared to suffer. Most of the prophets probably regretted that they had any gift that permitted them to speak directly with God because it placed them immediately into conflict with their rulers, other religious leaders, and very often they had to run for their lives or hide in caves for years to escape persecution and even execution. The rewards and benefits were often outweighed by the severe price that had to be paid. Still, they did not shirk their responsibilities, which meant that they had no doubt that they were in communication with God and therefore His elected servants. In the next chapter, how such communication was even possible will be examined. Was it all in their heads or did they really hear the voice of God?

Chapter 20: Talking With God

Last year South African and Swedish scientists discovered that dung beetles can navigate using the Milky Way for orientation. They are the first animals proven to use our galaxy for navigation. The electric eel has three pairs of abdominal organs that occupy 80% of its body and are responsible for producing two types of electronic discharge, being both high voltage and low voltage. The high voltage can be as much as 860 volts for two milliseconds. The platypus possesses the ability to sense an electrical field generated by the muscular contractions of its prey. Salmon sense the Earth's magnetic field, which guides them home to their place of origin for spawning. Bees can sense the electric field within a flower and use it to find pollen. Bees also use the Earth's magnetic field for navigation. And they know to return to the hive as soon as a storm breaks because they can also sense the changing electromagnetic waves of the atmosphere. The brown oriental wasp possesses solar cells across its back that traps 99% of the light that hits them and converts it into electricity. Scientists still don't know what it does with all that electricity. Chickens can see the electromagnetic forces around the earth and orient themselves according to these bands. These are but a few of the many animal species that use electricity and electromagnetism in ways that man can no longer do, if we assume as a more primitive life form that we may have possessed some of these abilities in the past. Electricity, and therefore electromagnetic waves appear to be integral to many organisms, giving them abilities and capabilities that one might even call supernatural. Their functions all rely on there being a transmitter and a suitable receiver and since we know from Chapter 2 regarding the Cosmic Microwave Background (CMB) that there have been signals transmitted since the beginning of time throughout the universe there must be in nature a suitable receiver. The interpretation of some of these signals from the creation and the Creator, only requires that someone possess the correct receiving equipment.

Although there is no proof that can be conducted for this hypothesis until we have subjects that are willing to come forward and admit they have been in communication with God, in a manner no different from the ancient prophets, then the proposal to suggest that some individuals are gifted with the ability to receive and transmit at these specific wavelengths cannot be disproved either. Since 1924 when German physiologist and psychiatrist Hans Berger recorded the first human EEG brainwaves we have known that the human brain can produce measurable electromagnetic waves. It was Berger that invented the electroencephalogram, commonly referred to as the EEG. Today, the EEG has resulted in headset technology that permits what is referred to as BCI or Brain-Computer Interface. Through a direct neural interface (DNI), the electrical signals from the brain can be decoded and have been used to control both virtual and physical objects. The science is available as you read this. In 2017, Rodrigo Hübner Mendes, a formula one race car driver who became a quadriplegic after a serious accident, was able to return to the cockpit and pilot a race car only through the use of his brainwaves being interpreted by an EMOTIV EEG Headset. This being the case, then the transmitter side of this same hypothesis has been proven, as mankind can generate electrical signals mentally that can be received and interpreted as long as their is an available receiver. In this case, it was done through the use of a mechanical interface, but what if there are people that can emit strong enough signals that they can be received by someone or something that doesn't require any additional equipment? There should be no doubt in anyone's mind if the Creator could expend vast amounts of energy to create an entire universe, then producing electromagnetic waves of sufficient magnitude and strength across vast expanses of space would not present any difficulty, but they would be meaningless if there was not some other being capable of receiving and deciphering them. Clearly though, if we have the capability to transmit such signals as shown in the above example, then we must also possess a receiving apparatus, though it may either be rudimentary or else has become vestigial, like an appendix after so many generations of non-use. In either situation, the majority of us have no ability to utilize this function but that should not mean that there haven't been exceptions in the past where some were able to communicate directly with God in this manner.

There are billions of cells in the human brain, each producing a very small electrical signal, that form non-linear patterns referred to as brainwaves. The EEG machine only measures the electrical activity of the cerebral cortex, which is the outermost layer of the brain. Considering that it is reported that we use only 10% of our brain capacity, then what we see as highly active recordings only displays a small fraction of what our brain can produce. The sensors attached to the scalp are recording several thousand impulses of electrical activity generated in any second. These are then attached to a recording device that records the impulses as waves either on a digital screen or simple graph paper. The wave pattern is produced by the varying voltage. The receiver also expresses the electrical activity in different EEG frequencies, each frequency having its own distinct wave. These frequencies, are directly related to the speed of the electrical oscillations, and measured as cycles per second. When we hear the term Hertz (Hz) being used, that is a reference to wavelength oscillations on a scale where one Hertz is equal to one cycle per second. Based on their oscillations, brainwaves are categorized by their frequencies into four main types: Beta, Alpha, Theta and Delta.

Beta waves are most closely associated with being awake and in a conscious, alert and attentive state. These low-amplitude waves are associated with focused concentration, or when the mind is in a busy or anxious state. Beta waves are also associated with motor decisions as feedback on motions. The Beta waves have a Hertz measurement greater than 13 cycles per second. If the Beta wave is greater than 30 Hz then it is referred to as being a Gamma wave. Gamma waves can be as high as 60 Hz. Less than 15 Hz and the Beta wave is associated with quiet, focused, introverted concentration. From 15 to 20 Hz indicates increased energy and anxiety. From 20 to 30 indicates significant stress and high arousal. There is no agreement among academic researchers regarding what cognitive functions might be associated with gamma activity.

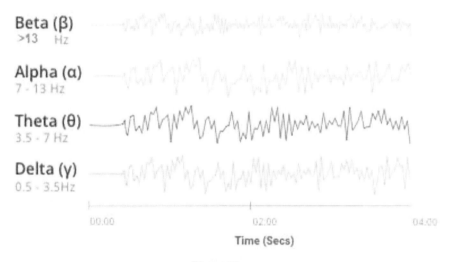

Figure 39

Alpha waves have a recorded frequency from 7 to 13 Hz and are often associated with a relaxed, calm and lucid state of mind. They are emitted by the occipital and posterior regions of the brain. When the subject closes their eyes and relaxes they will produce Alpha waves. These waves are rarely present during intense cognitive processes such as problem-solving. On average, alpha waves range in frequency from 9 to 11 Hz.

Theta waves have a frequency between 3.5 and 7 Hz and are often found in young adults over the temporal regions and during periods of hyperventilation. In older individuals, theta activity is rarely seen except during a state of drowsiness. Theta brainwaves also occur when the individual is sleeping or dreaming but not when in the deepest phase of sleep. It is believed that theta waves are important for processing information and the formation of memories. The theta wave is also associated with natural intuition and creativity.

Delta activity has a frequency of less than and equal to 3.5 HZ and is the predominant wave in infants. Delta waves can also be identified when older subjects enter into a deep stage of sleep. Delta waves have also been documented in patients between seizures, which often involves a brief but sudden lapse in cognitive awareness.

In 2019, neuroscientists from Columbia University released a report of having made a major advancement towards the goal of successfully translating brain waves into intelligible speech. The team's research, which was published in Scientific Reports, involved recording neurological patterns generated by test subjects listening to others speak. The brainwaves they produced while listening to someone speak were then fed into an artificial intelligence algorithm that synthesizes speech, which then converted them into words that were identical to the phrases that had been heard by the participants. This clearly establishes the brain produces waves that can be merely thoughts or stored as memories and are recorded in such a way that they are directly convertible to speech. Therefore if the brain should intercept and receive a similar wave from an outside source, it could be heard inside one's head as if someone was speaking to them. Suddenly all those people that claim to hear voices may not be insane, but merely have a finely tuned receiver within their brains. The head researcher, Mesgarani says that in the future, he and his colleagues will synthesize more complex phrases and follow this with decoding brain signals generated by test subjects who are thinking or imagining the act of speaking Eventually. Mesgarani adds that one day he foresees the technology being transformed into an implant capable of translating a wearer's thoughts directly into words.

It is evident that the technology is about to be developed that will permit one's thoughts to be translated directly into speech, a tremendous achievement for those that have lost the ability to communicate through speech. The question we need to ask is whether it was possible that people were born with the ability to do exactly that without the assistance of mechanical technology. In spite of this amazing scientific breakthrough which suggests that some people could receive electromagnetic waves that their brains then transform into proper speech, it is still the tendency of psychologists and psychiatrists to accuse anyone experiencing these non-corporeal voices as being mentally unstable. In fact, a group of research psychiatrists presented their findings into what they label as AVHs, auditory verbal hallucinations, at a conference in Durham, United Kingdom in September 2013. Hearing a voice as if someone has spoken, without an external stimulus, is what they have called an auditory verbal hallucination. Psychiatrists have estimated that hallucinations are a symptom experienced by approximately 75% of people diagnosed with schizophrenia, 20% to 50% of people with bipolar disorder, 40% in post-traumatic stress disorder, and 10% suffering from major depression. Auditory hallucinations can be generated also by conditions other than mental illness, such as temporal lobe seizures, dementia, and infections of the brain. Clearly, it is their opinion that should you hear a voice without an external stimulus then you must be mentally ill. Is it any wonder why anyone that could possibly hear the voice of God today would be reluctant to admit such a thing.

Estimates of the percentage of college students who have reported hearing hallucinatory voices when asked on a survey have ranged from 13% to 71%. Since it was unlikely that all these college students were suffering from mental illnesses, the researchers decided the variance must have been the result of failing to define auditory hallucinations properly, or a result of providing incorrect survey instructions, and possibly other methodological variations. In other words, since these students weren't admitted as patients, and some were probably university psychiatric students themselves, then it must have been the result of an incorrect survey because they couldn't possibly have over seventy percent of the students hearing voices naturally. So after reassessing their results, they came to the conclusion that perhaps the actual rate in the general population is between 5% and 28%, but the 25% of those saying they heard such voices were likely mentally unstable, which in turn would reduce the results to between 1% and 21% of people who report hearing voices as being generally psychologically healthy. Even so, this is still a big admission on their part that as much as one in five people could be normal and still hear voices in their head.

In order to try and explain how this could even be possible, they further broke down these numbers to suggest that the majority of these people only heard voices in times of loss or bereavement, with 30% reporting they heard the voice of their deceased loved ones. Oddly, they do not say what the other 70% were hearing if it was not a loved one. Those would be the ones of keen interest since they were considered to be mentally stable, yet talking to someone not as a result of great personal loss.

In regards to their mental patients, one study in South Africa reported that 51.8% of verbal hallucinations were attributed to God, while another study in Pakistan found that only 6% reported hearing voices they identified as being God.

The fact that these are people known to be mental patients should not be in any way a determination of what kind of people hear the voice of God. This negative connotation only results in individuals concealing what may be an actual ability for fear of being labeled and locked away by society. If scientists were to do actual research, then they should investigate the hearing of God's voice in healthy individuals as opposed to those with a known mental disorder. Mother Theresa admitted that she started serving the poor and conducting her life long mission to help the people in need only after hearing the voice of God telling her to do so. I don't think any of us would ever accuse Mother Theresa of having been mentally ill, but because of her fame and notoriety she was able to express her experience of auditory hallucination without fear of reprisal. But the fact that medical science still wants to refer to it as a hallucination is not only defamatory to what was a great woman, but an injustice to anyone that is instructed to dedicate their life on a similar mission. In Mother Theresa's case it was reality, and by no means a hallucination as far as she was concerned.

In the few reports of healthy individual that hear such voices, it needs to be noted that often the voice is giving them comfort or encouragement, These normal, sane and healthy people rarely report that the voices actually cause them distress or discomfort in their daily life. These researchers need to admit that hearing voices might well be more common among healthy, sane people than they have presented. Those in psychiatry and psychology need to shed the prejudice they have been instilled with by William James, one of the founding fathers of modern psychology, who established the first experimental psychology laboratory in America at Harvard, who said, "That vast literature of proofs of God's existence drawn from the order of nature, which a century ago seemed so overwhelmingly convincing, today does little more than gather dust in libraries, for the simple reason that our generation has ceased to believe in the kind of God it argued for." James concluded that God is real in the reality of the impacts on those open to the possibility. Considering whether or not to choose such openness, James decided that it is more beneficial to act as if there is a transcendent that gives an ultimate meaning to life. It was his way of saying they choose to believe and therefore such beliefs impact their lives, so in their minds He exists. But at the same time medical science says if you choose to believe in that which does not exist according to their perception, then you must be insane. It can only be normal if everyone does it or considers it to be so, and since that is not the case, then they must be abnormal. But by their own surveys of normal populations and college students, if over 70% in each claim to have heard these voices, then it could very well be that is the true norm, and those that deny the existence of such voices are the abnormal population.

Science needs to take a serious look at what they have classified as auditory verbal hallucinations. While one field of science is demonstrating that they can convert electromagnetic wave patterns in the cortex of one's brain into actual auditory speech that can be heard by anyone, the medical field is classifying the ability for someone to translate those same wave patterns in their own mind into speech as suffering from hallucinations and possibly psychotic. We know from the few examples that began this chapter that there are various animal species that can receive, translate and react to electromagnetic waves and they are perfectly normal animals. The same way science is beginning to understand why there has been such a decrease in the bee populations around the world. It has to do with the electromagnetic waves emitted by our mobile phones. They are on a similar wavelength as the bee's navigation system and it is confusing them. When a bee cannot find its way back to the hive, it dies. You haven't heard science speak much about that finding. Considering how much money is poured into the universities from Big Tech, they don't want any bad publicity about how Apple, Google, Facebook and Twitter are killing the bees. Unfortunately, that is the world we live in now and the one that the Book of Job was trying to tell us about. It is not up to God to save the bees when we have it within our capacity to do so.

But before I digress too far, if it is within other species capability to receive and decipher and transform electromagnetic waves into meaningful information, then it certainly may have been within primitive man's scope of senses at one time as well. That sensory skill may have fallen into disuse after so many centuries of technical advancement where we have actually displaced our need for certain attributes, but that does not mean it is still not contained within our genetic code. What psychiatrists and psychologies wish to call hallucinations, may just be a sensory perception that is reawakened in some individuals. By the medical label, all of the prophets of the Bible would be suffering from a psychosis. I think there readiness to make such a statement again emphasizes the need for better research and investigation. When one man, claiming to hear voices can affect an entire nation and be proven correct in the dichotomy of choices he offers, whether they choose to listen and obey or refuse, then it can only be assumed that the voice he heard was that of a higher power. Science has spent so much time trying to prove that none of these individual could have been or done the things they accomplished that they forget that the Old Testament is actual history as well as religious instruction, and the events these prophets predicted did occur. That's why they merited a book. Not everyone who claims to hear the voice of God is sane, but not every that does is insane either. The science proves that if God can transmit electromagnetic waves, then it would be possible that He could communicate with certain individuals based on the current evidence of the research presented.

Chapter 21: The Shekinah: Psionic Energy

One of the most interesting concepts in the Old Testament is the Shekinah. Essentially, the Shekinah is a visible manifestation of God in our world but it is not God, Himself. Although described as the presence of God it is only through an object or substance from our world that He can appear, such as a cloud or a pillar of smoke or a burning bush as described in Exodus 3:2. We are told that when Moses spoke to God in the cloud, it was to be considered the same as speaking to Him "face to face" as recorded in Exodus 33:11. We are tole that Moses asked to see God's face directly, but God refused, saying "you cannot see my face, for man shall not see me and live" nine sentences later. To Biblical scholars, they took this to mean that the direct sight of God was too much for the human mind to encompass and one would surely die. But was that really God's meaning when he told Moses that or is there more to the science that prevented God making direct contact and instead using substances or materials from our world to act as his avatar, so to speak. If we refer back to Chapter 6, assuming that God may be the proto-energy that I referred to, then the presence of any part of His energy, or proto-matter for that fact, could set off a catastrophic chain reaction if it comes into contact with its oppositely charged energy or matter in our world. In that chapter we assumed at the time of the Big Bang it would be dark matter and dark energy, but since those two exist in our world, then it actually could be any source of energy that was created after the Big Bang explosion, and as a result, Moses would surely die. So the cloud, or the bush made from the matter of our world serves as the indicator of His presence but is not to be confused with God.

The term Shekinah is not found in the Old Testament. It only became commonly known in the centuries before the Common Era. The sages and wisemen understood that it meant a presence without substance. It could fill the Temple as it did in 2 Chronicles 7:1 or it could be in a cloud as reported in Exodus 14:19. It could radiate like a fire that does not burn, or a cloud that sits heavily upon a building or structure but in each case, everyone knew it was not God, Himself, but an allusion to his presence and a sign of His relationship with the Children of Israel. A sign-post that He was not there in body but in spirit. As it is written in Exodus 13:21, "And the Lord went before them by day in a pillar of cloud to lead the way, and by night in a pillar of fire to give them light." Both the fire and the cloud symbolize divine leadership and protection but it is not to be interpreted as God actually marched alongside the Children of Israel. In the Book of Numbers, Chapter 9, we read how the cloud actually controlled the activities of the Israelite community, even more than just providing them with the reassurance that God was with them. The impression provided is that God could not maintain the direct connection with cloud or whatever manifestation he might create to represent himself for a prolonged period of time. It is as if one is driving a remote vehicle, reaching a point where the batteries in the controller finally are out of power and then the vehicle remains in the place where it stopped until the batteries can be recharged. There is no explanation for the delays, as can be read in Table 22 and this in itself is a mystery. The use of the word בְּהַאֲרִיךְ tarried in Sentences 19 and 22 is quite interesting because it suggests an indeterminate length of time.

טו וּבְיוֹם, הָקִים אֶת-הַמִּשְׁכָּן, כִּסָּה הֶעָנָן אֶת-הַמִּשְׁכָּן, לְאֹהֶל הָעֵדֻת; וּבָעֶרֶב יִהְיֶה עַל-הַמִּשְׁכָּן, כְּמַרְאֵה-אֵשׁ--עַד-בֹּקֶר.

15 And on the day that the tabernacle was reared up the cloud covered the tabernacle, even the tent of the testimony; and at even there was upon the tabernacle as it were the appearance of fire, until morning.

טז כֵּן יִהְיֶה תָמִיד, הֶעָנָן יְכַסֶּנּוּ; וּמַרְאֵה-אֵשׁ, לָיְלָה.

16 So it was always: the cloud covered it, and the appearance of fire by night.

יז וּלְפִי הֵעָלוֹת הֶעָנָן, מֵעַל הָאֹהֶל--וְאַחֲרֵי כֵן, יִסְעוּ בְּנֵי יִשְׂרָאֵל; וּבִמְקוֹם, אֲשֶׁר יִשְׁכָּן-שָׁם הֶעָנָן--שָׁם יַחֲנוּ, בְּנֵי יִשְׂרָאֵל.

17 And whenever the cloud was taken up from over the Tent, then after that the children of Israel journeyed; and in the place where the cloud abode, there the children of Israel encamped.

יח עַל-פִּי יְהוָה, יִסְעוּ בְּנֵי יִשְׂרָאֵל, וְעַל-פִּי יְהוָה, יַחֲנוּ: כָּל-יְמֵי, אֲשֶׁר יִשְׁכֹּן הֶעָנָן עַל-הַמִּשְׁכָּן--יַחֲנוּ.

18 At the commandment of the LORD the children of Israel journeyed, and at the commandment of the LORD they encamped: as long as the cloud abode upon the tabernacle they remained encamped.

יט וּבְהַאֲרִיךְ הֶעָנָן עַל-הַמִּשְׁכָּן, יָמִים רַבִּים--וְשָׁמְרוּ בְנֵי-יִשְׂרָאֵל אֶת-מִשְׁמֶרֶת יְהוָה, וְלֹא יִסָּעוּ.

19 And when the cloud tarried upon the tabernacle many days, then the children of Israel kept the charge of the LORD, and journeyed not.

כ וְיֵשׁ אֲשֶׁר יִהְיֶה הֶעָנָן, יָמִים מִסְפָּר--עַל-הַמִּשְׁכָּן;

20 And sometimes the cloud was a few days upon the tabernacle; according to the

עַל-פִּי יְהוָה יַחֲנוּ, וְעַל-פִּי
יְהוָה יִסָּעוּ.

commandment of the LORD they remained encamped, and according to the commandment of the LORD they journeyed.

כא וְיֵשׁ אֲשֶׁר-יִהְיֶה הֶעָנָן,
מֵעֶרֶב עַד-בֹּקֶר, וְנַעֲלָה הֶעָנָן
בַּבֹּקֶר, וְנָסָעוּ; אוֹ יוֹמָם
וָלַיְלָה, וְנַעֲלָה הֶעָנָן וְנָסָעוּ.

21 And sometimes the cloud was from evening until morning; and when the cloud was taken up in the morning, they journeyed; or if it continued by day and by night, when the cloud was taken up, they journeyed.

כב אוֹ-יֹמַיִם אוֹ-חֹדֶשׁ אוֹ-
יָמִים, בְּהַאֲרִיךְ הֶעָנָן עַל-
הַמִּשְׁכָּן לִשְׁכֹּן עָלָיו, יַחֲנוּ בְנֵי-
יִשְׂרָאֵל, וְלֹא יִסָּעוּ;
וּבְהֵעָלֹתוֹ, יִסָּעוּ.

22 Whether it were two days, or a month, or a year, that the cloud tarried upon the tabernacle, abiding thereon, the children of Israel remained encamped, and journeyed not; but when it was taken up, they journeyed.

Table 22

Obviously God had no need to rest, and it is apparent that it had nothing to do with the enforced rest of the Sabbath day or any other Festival. The cloud appears to have simply run out of power and needed to be recharged. This is expressed in the phrase of 'when it was taken up' as in disappeared and went back to heaven. Most often, it just had enough power to run through the night and then in the morning it was discharged and the people could move. Other times it would last longer, but as long as it was present, the Children of Israel would not move. It was only when it had been 'taken up'. The other aspect of the Shekinah that we are made aware of is that it can be formatted in any size and shape. From the cloud over the Tabernacle, to a pillar that led them through the desert, to a small undefinable appearance that hovered over the top lid known as the Mercy Seat of the Ark of the Covenant as we can read int Leviticus, Chapter 16.

וַיֹּאמֶר יְהוָה אֶל-מֹשֶׁה, דַּבֵּר
אֶל-אַהֲרֹן אָחִיךָ, וְאַל-יָבֹא בְכָל-
עֵת אֶל-הַקֹּדֶשׁ, מִבֵּית לַפָּרֹכֶת--
אֶל-פְּנֵי הַכַּפֹּרֶת אֲשֶׁר עַל-הָאָרֹן,
וְלֹא יָמוּת, כִּי בֶּעָנָן, אֵרָאֶה עַל-
הַכַּפֹּרֶת.

2 and the LORD said unto Moses: 'Speak unto Aaron thy brother, that he come not at all times into the holy place within the veil, before the ark-cover which is upon the ark; that he die not; for I appear in the cloud upon the ark-cover.

Table 23

From this it is evident that what has been translated as עָנָן cloud, is not a cloud at all. It would be understandable if the people saw something opaque floating above the tabernacle and at times having the appearance of fire as lightening flashes through it and calling it a cloud because it would be the closest object they could imagine that appeared similar in nature, floating in the sky. But to take that same cloud, condense it in size, move it inside the Holy of Holies and still consider it to be a cloud would be absurd even for people existing at that time. They knew it wasn't a cloud but they had nothing else they could even compare it to, so the description remained, inaccurate as it was. But it is important that we gain some understanding of the Shekinah if we are to appreciate the few interactions that God did undertake with individuals on Earth. The question we must ask is whether we have anything in our time that to the uneducated could be confused as being a cloud with bolts of lightening flashing through it, that can be varied in size and can exist in almost any location because it moves through the air. Perhaps not as sophisticated as the Shekinah but having a semblance to what the Children of Israel may have felt when they first saw it, that feeling of shock and awe

Figure 40

We can see in Figure 40 the picture of Nikola Tesla, sitting calmly as he reads his notes while bursts of electricity shoot across the room above his head as if they were part of a stationary cloud that came to rest in this building. Beautiful flying arcs of electricity that would have amazed everyone except for Tesla himself, who saw his invention as nothing more than a simple apparatus. Flying blue streamers of electrons flow off the coil and through the hot air searching for a conductive landing place. They heat the air and break it into a plasma of glowing ion filaments before dissipating into the air or surging into a nearby conductor. It is this last sentence which may be key to the principle behind the Shekinah. In a laboratory demonstration of the Tesla coil, there is a conductor provided so that the arcs of electricity are targeted and controlled, thus providing these arcing filaments with direction. Without that target conductor, the electrical filaments are scattered and simply dissipate into the air, as if one was watching the sky lit up by fireworks, each beautiful display of coloured flashes from the gunpowder just disappearing into the darkness of the night sky. In a similar situation, the plasma cloud of the Shekinah would remain stationary, hovering above the Tabernacle, or the Ark, until such time that it had exhausted its energy source.

Without becoming too technical, the principle behind the Tesla coil is electromagnetic induction, not too unlike the principles discussed in the previous chapter regarding the transference of speech into brainwaves and back. Simply stated, a changing magnetic field creates an electric potential that compels current to flow. The converse is also true that a flowing electric current will generate a magnetic field. Therefore, as we know that when electricity flows through the center of a wound up coil of wire, it will generate a magnetic field that will surround the coil, then it holds that the converse must also be true. When a magnetic field flows through the center of a coiled wire, then it causes the wire to generate a voltage, which then causes electrical current to flow. To build up enough charge to arc across the room, as in Tesla's experiment, a capacitor is required to hold or concentrate the electricity until it discharges it as the electrical arc through the air.

Although you will be told that the Tesla coil is generally a safe apparatus unless you touch the coil while the power is on, the general consensus was that the streamers of electrical discharge were safe, possibly causing a mild burn if they contacted one place on your body for too long. But what they don't usually caution you about is far more serious than a slight burn. Both our nervous system and heart function on electrical impulses. That means that prolonged exposure will likely affect both your nervous and circulatory systems, possibly causing death. Suddenly, the restriction of the High Priest entering the Holy of Holies only once per year on the Day of Atonement begins to have an ulterior motive behind the restriction. There is no reason to doubt that the Shekinah did not produce the same high voltage radio frequency emissions as the Tesla coil, assuming that it functioned on similar principles and therefore would need similar voltages to produce a sustained cloud over the Tabernacle and the Ark. And as discussed in the early chapters, the transformation of energy is part of the Thermodynamic Laws of the universe, so even if God should prove to be the proto-energy as discussed, the ability to convert part of His own energy into electromagnetic waves would not be an issue. But for the sustained release of this energy, if adhering to the same model as created by Tesla, then in some way the charge would have to be held, concentrated and then released as a spark in a continuous cycle that supports the electrical light show, as if there was a capacitor present. The key to that problem may have already been answered in the Book of Exodus, Chapter 25 as we can read in Table 24. For years, there have been those who have been advocating the alien conspiracy theories that the gods were actually visitors from other solar systems, targeting the Ark of the

Covenant as some sort of radio receiver and transmitter, even though it was missing all the essential parts to have even rendered that as a possibility.   But what they overlooked was the fact that it may not have been suitable as a transmitter of any sort, but it certainly was suitable if it was to be used as a storage capacitor for the purpose of creating a sustained arc lightning show as the Old Testament describes.

וְעָשׂוּ אֲרוֹן, עֲצֵי שִׁטִּים ׃ אַמָּתַיִם וָחֵצִי אָרְכּוֹ, וְאַמָּה וָחֵצִי רָחְבּוֹ, וְאַמָּה וָחֵצִי קֹמָתוֹ. **י**	**10** And they shall make an ark of acacia-wood: two cubits and a half shall be the length thereof, and a cubit and a half the breadth thereof, and a cubit and a half the height thereof.
וְצִפִּיתָ אֹתוֹ זָהָב טָהוֹר, מִבַּיִת וּמִחוּץ תְּצַפֶּנּוּ ; וְעָשִׂיתָ עָלָיו זֵר זָהָב, סָבִיב. **יא**	**11** And thou shalt overlay it with pure gold, within and without shalt thou overlay it, and shalt make upon it a crown of gold round about.

Table 24

To understand how it would be possible, it is necessary to look at some very old experiments conducted by Dutch physicist Pieter van Musschenbroek of the University of Leiden in 1746, and independently by the German inventor Ewald Georg von Kleist in 1745.   Van Musschenbroek was looking for a way to collect and store static electricity.   Using a glass vial, partly filled with water, the mouth of which was closed by a cork pierced with a wire that dipped into the water, he brought the end of the exposed wire into contact with a friction device that produced static electricity. When the contact was broken, a charge could be demonstrated by touching the wire with his hand and he received a shock. In its primitive form, Van Musschenbroek had created a capacitor. Later developments to what is now called a Leyden Jar, involved coating the inner and outer surfaces of the insulating jar with metal foil. The outer coating was grounded to the earth, and the inner coating was attached to a metal rod that projected through the mouth of the jar. This coated jar became the standard model for capacitors used presently in our modern equipment.

In the March 5th, 1933 edition of the Chicago Daily Tribune, Frederick Rogers, the Dean of the Department of Engineering at the Lewis Institute of Technology, conducted a careful study of the construction of the Ark of the Covenant as described in the Old Testament, and concluded that its design was a match for perfectly constructed simple electric condenser. The acacia wood inner wooden insulating box was about 40 inches long and just under 30 inches wide. Lined with gold foil metal both internally and externally, Rogers recognized this as being just another version of the Leyden Jar, except that the Ark of the Covenant was a much larger condenser. The cherubim placed on the top of the Ark and facing inwards, Prof. Rogers explained would have been the positive pole of the circuit, their likely having a bolt that secured them in place but which also provided a direct metal conductor to the inside of the box. If there was anything generating electricity outside of the box, it would also be directly fed inside the interior of the Ark where it would be stored. Enough energy stored that by accidentally touching the cherubim which were directly connected to the inner charge, it might cause instantaneous death as had been recorded when a priest accidentally touched the Ark to stop it from falling off a wagon.

But let me repeat, the Ark as a capacitor has nothing to do with aliens from outer space or being a radio of any kind. As it is being presented here, it is only serving as a capacitor to store electrical energy which then would be used to spark whatever else might be serving in the same fashion as a Tesla coil to produce arcing filaments of electrical discharges to light up the sky. Once the capacitor had discharged all its collected electricity, then the Children of Israel would continue on their journey to the Promised Land.

Psionic Energy

It is impossible to close this section of the book without any reference to psionic energy. Although, as stated previously, God tends to act on the universe at the macro level, which alienates him from many people who seek a god that is directly involved with every aspect of their life, but what they actually are seeking is a nursemaid and that has never been what God is about. We have all been given the tools to manage our lives. A few do it very well, most manage and live a full life, and then there are those that will not take any responsibility for their lives and when they turn completely upside down, they curse God and blame him for all that has gone wrong, until they reach a point where they don't believe in God any longer. It reminds me of a story that I have often told but I find never gets old because the attitudes of people never seem to change.

The story takes place in Eastern Europe in a little town laying in a valley along side the Danube River. One spring the rains begin and they continue for days until the river overflows its banks and water begins to flow into the town. There's so much water that eventually the streets are covered by a foot of water and as it begins to enter the houses, the people begin to pack their belongings and head to higher ground. One family is rolling along in its wagon when it passes the synagogue and notices that it can see the lights are still on. The father of the family pulls the wagon to a stop in front of the synagogue and goes inside where he finds the Rabbi praying at the podium.

"Rabbi," he shouts, "It is time to leave. Come with us. I have room in our wagon.

To which the Rabbi replies, "No I must stay here and pray to God that he stops these rains and saves our town. Do not worry, God will save me."

Seeing there was nothing to do, the man turns and leaves.

The next days the rains are still falling and the water is now as high as a man's chest. One family is floating by the synagogue in a little wooden rowboat when they see that there are candles still lit inside. Rowing to the front doors, the father of the family sees the Rabbi sitting in the loft and praying.

"Rabbi," he shouts, "Come with us, there is plenty of room in our boat. Leave with us now."

To which the Rabbi again replies, "No, I must stay here and pray that he spares all that we hold dear. But do not worry, God will save me."

Seeing there was nothing more to do, the man rowed his boat away from the doors and took his family to safety.

By the next day the waters had reached the eaves of the houses and everything was underwater. One family had escaped, paddling their way on a makeshift raft they had made out of barrels and wooden crates, floating along until they saw the Rabbi clinging to the chimney on the synagogue roof. Paddling over to him, the man shouted out, "Rabbi, let go of the chimney and climb on to our raft. We are all that are left in the city, it is time to go."

But the Rabbi refused to let go of the chimney, screaming at the man and his family to leave him alone. "Can't you see," he shouted at them, "God will save me! Who are you to interfere with God's work!"

Seeing that there was not any way they would convince the Rabbi otherwise, the family paddled away and left the Rabbi to his fate.

The following day the Rabbi found himself sitting in a damp and cool place that was unfamiliar. "Where am I?" he cried out and a voice answered, "This is the House of the Dead."

"Am I dead?" the Rabbi was confused.

"Yes, you drowned last night," the voice replied.

"I demand to see God!" the Rabbi screamed over and over again until the Angel of Death took him to see the Almighty.

Standing before God, the Rabbi wagged his finger in anger, "How could you let me drown. I prayed and I prayed that you come and save me, but you never came! What kind of God are you? I denounce you! A God who does not answer my prayers is no God of mine!"

Calmly, serenely, the Almighty replied, " Three miracles I made for you but you were too blind to see them. Too absorbed with what you wanted to actually see what you had been given. The first miracle concerned a man's horse that had been ill for days and was likely to die from fever. But it was that man's only horse and without it he would be unable to pull his wagon and take his family and belongings to safety. So I cured his horse and set him on the road that passed by the synagogue so that he would see your light. But you turned him away.

The second miracle was when I sent a wind that blew down the tree that snapped the rope that held a small boat tied up at the marina. The wind blue that boat along a path that took it to the man's house where he and his family were trapped on the second floor with no chance of escape. It sailed directly to his window and they all climbed out to safety. Then I had him row a course past your synagogue, where he saw your candles. But still you turned him away.

The third miracle was when I saw a man and his family trapped on their roof with nothing but a rope that he tied around all their waists so that they would not become separated. So I floated barrels and boards towards him and he was clever enough to use the rope to lash them all together and make a raft. And once they were all safely upon the raft I floated it towards your synagogue where they saw you clinging to the chimney. But once again, you turned them away.

In all your foolishness, you never realized that it was not them that you turned away but it was your God that you had turned your back upon. So obsessed were you to show everyone how your were special in God's eyes that you never knew how blind you truly were. Every day I perform miracles, but only a few will ever see them."

So in this last section, it is not my intent to suggest that God doesn't interact with us on a regular basis. His miracles surround us constantly but we fail to see them even though they're right before our eyes. In our need for personal interaction, we cannot see the big picture and our near-sightedness only fills us with discontent and disillusionment. We all possess the ability to make our lives better, but how many actually seize the opportunities when they're presented? Yes, there have been people that have managed to talk directly with God as recorded in the Old Testament, but not that many. In fact so few that we really should have no expectation that we should have that opportunity ourselves. And it is not surprising that the numbers have been so minimal because that which is called psionic energy and supposedly resides in all of us, is only mastered by a handful of people around the world. What is it? Psionic energy is the psychic ability to manipulate electromagnetic fields. It is exactly what has just been discussed concerning having one's own personal received and transmitter built into their brain and it is the operational mechanism of the Shekinah. Examining the facts, the concept of a Leyden Box fits rather well into the story of the Shekinah and the Exodus Story because we can appreciate that God has that ability to generate the initial energy, which is then transformed into electromagnetic energy and as an electrical charge in a capacitor that just happens to be always placed in the Tabernacle upon which the Shekinah rests.

If we agree that everything is made of energy according to the Law of Thermodynamics then transformation through the psionic process of God willing that a portion of his energy becomes electromagnetic and contained in a type of Leyden box is a perfectly normal process. As we saw in Chapter 20, thought itself is energy that can be expressed in wave form and even converted to sound energy. Emotion is energy as well, as evidenced by the changing wave patterns to Beta or Gamma when we become highly anxious.. But imagine what happens when you can combine thought with emotion; it must be a powerful form of energy. And if we can combine that thought energy with enough alternative sources of energy then probably everything is possible, as was evident by God's role throughout the Exodus story.

If we think of Psionic energy as basically being a thought-form of energy with chi energy added to it, and chi energy is essentially our life force, then it should be incredibly powerful. Though usually the stuff of comic books, telepathy and telekinesis would be naturally associated with this type of energy. There is no doubt that God possesses mastery over thought and life energy, and therefore the implantation of thoughts through electromagnetic waves into our brains is mere child's play for him. The difficult part is as the receiving party, whomever God selected to communicate with, must also possess similar psionic energy skills in order to interpret those messages. In other words, have the capability to be a receiver. That is the issue. Whereas we all may have the potential to harness Psionic energy, similar to those examples in the animal world that were presented, as history has shown us, very few have been successful and most of us I suspect have lost that ability if our species had it.

To date, medical research provides us with enough evidence to suggest that human energy fields exist and that they carry information for growth and repair. These fields are evident a two levels, the first being an electromagnetic field that interfaces with the physical body according to Burr and Becker, and the second, an etheric field or magneto-electric field according to Reid and Steiner. The implications are that distortion or disturbance in either of these fields, whether caused by electromagnetic, nutritional, or genetic factors may contribute to the basic causes of disease.

To summarize or distill the essence of this chapter for those that are still looking for a personal God, then there is still hope for some if they can properly harness their Psionic energies. Other than Moses, at the time of the Exodus, no one else was on a personal conversational level with the Almighty. What the others saw was the Shekinah. They could not talk to it, they probably didn't even understand it, but that didn't really matter. They were satisfied with the knowledge that God was still operating behind the scenes for their benefit and that is all they needed to know. And that is exactly that message this chapter is trying to convey. Even though most will not have a personal interaction with God, they just need to know that He is there, He is functioning on a macro level. God exists!

Conclusion

Long ago I was taught that if it looks like a duck, walks like a duck, and quacks like a duck, then it is a duck no matter what anyone else says. No ifs, ands, or buts! Unfortunately, we live in a world where there is a deliberate attempt to tell you it must be a mouse, or a cow, or anything other than a duck, and you are mistaken. They will present theory after theory trying to explain why it must be some other animal, and why you cannot state the obvious, because if you do, then they will accuse you of not following the science, or worse. They will give their theories fancy names such as uncertainty principle, quantum flux, string theory, ghost condensate, convergent realities, and even something called the sterile neutrino theory. Actually, they will sooner impose upon you any alternative reality that they can think of, rather than confess that what you really are looking at is a duck. And when those theories begin to fray and break down, they will create and invent new theories that explain how the old theories were correct but they weren't being looked at properly through the lens of equipment and technology that doesn't yet exist and perhaps may never exist, but then if it did exist, then their theories would be proven correct. Sadly, it would seem that they can pull the wool over almost everyone's eyes and perpetuate this shell game.

One top scientist that wished to remain anonymous because he feared the backlash, explained his reason for towing the line and not screaming out, "It's a bloody duck!" He described his reasons for absolute submission as follows, "One, it would be insane to believe in evolution when you can see the truth for yourself. Two, it would be insane to say you don't believe in evolution. All government work, research grants, papers, big college lectures – everything would stop. I'd be out of a job, or relegated to the outer fringes where I couldn't earn a decent living. But in the meantime, we have to live with the elephant in the living room... Creation design... it moves around, takes up ...space... smells like an elephant. And yet we have to swear it isn't there!"

Sadly, that is the way the world now operates. Denial of one's own principles in order to have job security is a must and I must confess, I probably wouldn't have written this book twenty years ago when I was lecturing at the university but now that I'm at the twilight of my career, bordering on retirement, I feel much safer in expressing my true thoughts without the fear of reprisal. The scientist that made the statement regarding the elephant in the room knew, like the rest of us, that it is far easier to say there is no God and everyone will leave us alone to continue our work uninterrupted, rather than say to them, "Prove to me there is no God." The request for proof would incite a storm of confrontation and reputation smearing, without ever answering our request for proof. Their position has always been for those that believe in God, that we should prove it to them, knowing it is impossible to provide proof for a cosmic being that has no independent traceable energy patterns registering on present day equipment, but is essentially part of everything that surrounds us merely by using our own senses. They know that as a concept, to prove there is a God would take a tremendous effort and the ability to cross sect all the sciences in order to pull information together, which usually isn't collated or compiled by anyone because of the different silos in which scientific research has isolated itself and how we have separated our fields of study. That is until now! This book in fact has done exactly that. I felt it was time to tear down those silos and look at the matter from the viewpoint of all the different scientific fields. In my effort, I have reached out to existing and developing research in biology, chemistry, physics, biochemistry, astrophysics, geography, paleontology, anthropology, climatology, nuclear physics, virology, psychiatry and practically every other scientific field that exists in order to pull together information that by itself proves very little but when seen in the context and as an adjunct or juxtaposed with scientific discoveries in other fields, creates a picture that was far greater than the sum of their individual parts. I hope that I have done that successfully and armed you, the reader with this combined information, so that when the question is posed to you, you can turn the tables and confront these deniers of God's existence with enough scientific proof, that the onus suddenly falls upon them to prove their hypothesis that there is no God. I admit that there has been a lot of information provided in this book, and I wanted to present the science and the concepts in a way that even the most unscientific reader would still understand what I have written. If I have been successful in doing so, then these deniers will be crushed under a massive burden created by the weight of the combined information.

The tables turn when it is no longer the case of proving there is a God, as the information in this book substantiates, and it becomes the null hypothesis that they must prove, if they are going to convince the world that there is no God. And that null hypothesis, which simply stated would read as , "There is no God because…." And that is where their arguments fall apart because of their own discoveries that say otherwise, and their insistence on theories to prove prior theories that we know to be non-provable. Let me show you how the null hypothesis works against them as I provide a few examples from this book of Science's list of failed arguments and then you will see just how weak and tenuous their position has become:

A. Null hypothesis being that there is no God because…

1. …the universe can be created from nothing.
But we know that to be false because of the laws of thermodynamics. Therefore if this null hypothesis statement is false, then the converse hypothesis that God exists must be true.

2. …evolution is a natural phenomena involving random series of events over a long time as a result of small mutations in all species.
But we know the Cambrian explosion is proof that the sudden appearance of new life forms can be practically spontaneous as evidenced by the lack of any fossil history to show this slow evolution. Therefore, if this null hypothesis statement is false, then the converse hypothesis that God exists must be true.

3. …convergent evolution can result through a series random events, even in species that are from completely different phyla, resulting in identical developments in species with no relationship.
But we know the octopus easily puts the nail in the coffin for random convergent evolution. Here is an animal from a completely different time period, a completely different environment, not even a vertebrate so not having any common ancestor to man, yet the eye of the octopus is as sophisticated and essentially identical in structure to that of the human eye. Therefore, if this null hypothesis statement is false, then the converse hypothesis that God exists must be true.

4. …intelligent design can exist without any intelligence behind its initiation. Either this is an oxymoron or simply moronic. For scientists to imply that you can have intelligent design without any intelligence or a designer makes no sense at all. In fact it is the most unintelligent statement science could ever make, yet they are rarely challenged on their admission that there must be a genetic structural pattern that was designed for visual organs hundreds of millions of years ago, as in the case of octopus vs. Man. Rather than evolving independently in different phyla, a mathematical impossibility, a pattern has

been used over and over again. Though they are loathe to say it, they are suggesting a universal genetically engineered pattern exists without daring to ask who was the engineer. Therefore, if this null hypothesis statement is false, then the converse hypothesis that God exists must be true.

5. …there is no problem in creating the building blocks of life such as amino acids in an artificial environment mimicking the early Earth environment. Not only have they taught this falsehood for over sixty years in the school system, even scientists laugh at how Miller and Fox published data where they didn't even try to hide how they added components that didn't even exist in the early Earth environment, and still couldn't achieve the original intent of the experiments. Therefore, if this null hypothesis statement is false, then the converse hypothesis that God exist must be true.

These are just five examples from the pages you have just read. There are hundreds more that can be generated from the contents of this book and I encourage the readers to do so. To read the book over and over again until you have armed yourself with so many of these null hypothesis statements that you are prepared to take on any challenge to your faith.

I recognize, there are those that want support for defending a literal translation of everything in the Bible. As a scientist, inspired by God, I see our role in His creation very differently from those that choose to believe a particular word rather than the intent. I don't believe support for a literal translation will ever be possible because I don't believe God ever intended for it to be read in that manner. The Bible should be a living, breathing, dynamic document that is relevant no matter in which time period it is read. On a literal level, it served a primitive, tribal people very well thousands of years ago, but the selection of words in the original Hebrew version with their double meanings and suggestive implications, indicates to me that the books of the Bible were intended to remain relevant no matter what era they are presented through updated interpretation.

God wouldn't tell us there was only Adam and Eve with two surviving sons, only to reveal several chapters later that Cain is wandering the cities of the Earth. Those people had to be the descendants of other people that never trod upon the Garden. He intended the stories to be much more than a simple narrative that could be disputed so easily. There are reasons he referred to the first man as Adam, a word that can mean 'red' and 'ground'. It was so that we would recognize one day we were descended from creatures that were no different from any other animals in the Garden. We slept on the ground, fed from the ground and once we died we were buried beneath the ground, having no aspirations to rise any higher than the animals we originally were.

And the woman was called חַוָּה which phonetically is pronounced Chavah, but we have instead called Eve, but her name when translated does not mean life as is suggested but could be interpreted as either an inspiration or an opinion. And that is what she did do, inspiring man to abandon his days as a foraging animal in the Garden in order to evolve into a thinking, creative, and cognitive being capable of so much more. It did not matter if there was a tree of knowledge, fountain of knowledge or even some magical potion that man could take that would increase his intelligence because it was never God's intent to keep us as some domestic beast in this corralled off area referred to as Eden. One does not put a bale of hay in front of his horse unless he intends for his horse to eat it, and if any believe God did so without this expectation, then once again, they do not really know God. There were two choices, a tree that would provide eternal life, but not life in the way that you think of it. Instead life as a creature of the forest, living one's days out simplistically, in the same way that our Chimpanzee cousins do, with no hint of ever evolving. Man, or rather I should say Australopithecus made the better decision and chose knowledge. As a species, we decided that we would rise above the other creatures that were earthbound in their thinking and their development. While every other creature looked to the ground beneath their feet, our ancestors looked up towards the stars. And even today, we are still looking to those stars as our next area to explore.

The story was never about God trying to stop us, because He gave us that choice. Was it a sin to become who we are now? There are those that would probably say it is, but I prefer to think of it as a test, as in the story of Job, a test to meet our true potential. God is the ultimate scientist and I believe of all that He has created, we are His supreme achievement. Now it is time that we try to live up to that label and prove it to Him.

Dr. Allen E. Goldenthal

Made in United States
North Haven, CT
07 March 2025